Mukat's People

THE CAHUILLA INDIANS OF SOUTHERN CALIFORNIA

Mukat's People

The Cahuilla Indians of Southern California

LOWELL JOHN BEAN

University of California Press
Berkeley, Los Angeles, London,
1972

University of California Press
Berkeley and Los Angeles, California
University of California Press, Ltd.
London, England
Copyright © 1972, by
The Regents of the University of California

ISBN: 0520-01912-1
Library of Congress Catalog Card Number: 78-145782
Printed in the United States of America

For Nepiwi

Contents

4

FAUNAL ENVIRONMENT   56

Introduction, 56 Large Game Animals, 56 Small Game Animals, 58
Birds, 60 Reptiles and Amphibians, 61 Insects and Worms, 61 Fish, 62
Carnivores, 63 Pets, 64 Technology of the Hunt, 64 Meat Processing
and Consumption, 66

5

SETTLEMENT PATTERN   68

Introduction, 68 Social Environment, 68 Sib Areas, 70 Village Locations, 73 Population, 75 Factors Contributing to Population Variation,
77 Personal Hygiene and the Control of Disease, 81 Summary, 81

6

SOCIAL STRUCTURE AND ORGANIZATION   83

Introduction, 83 Cahuilla Groups, 83 Cultural Nationality and Moiety,
85 The Sib and the Lineage, 86 The *Maiswat,* 88 Adaptive Functions of
Cahuilla Principles of Organization, 89 Marriage and Alliance, 90
Marriage and Kinship, 91 Kinship Terminology, 93 Lineal and Col-
lateral Relations, 94 Affinal Relatives, 96 Joking Relationships, 97
Diminutives, 98 Some Operating Principles in Cahuilla Kinship, 99
Ascribed Status, 102 Achieved Status, 104

　　The *Net,* 104　　*The Paxaaʔ* 105　　The *Haunik* and His Ritual Assistants, 106　ɲeɲewiš (Dancers), 107　The *Puvalam* (Shamans), 108
The Association of *puvalam,* 113　The *Paʔvuʔul,* 115　The *Tetiwiš,*
116　The *Neɲaɲaniš,* 116　The *Tiɲaviš,* 116

Summary, 117

7

OTHER INSTITUTIONS   120

Introduction, 120 Law, 120 Economic Relations, 122 Concepts of
Property and Ownership, 125 Warfare, 129 Games, 132 Summary, 133

8

RITUAL   135

Introduction, 135 The *Nukil* and Other Rituals for the Dead, 135
Eagle Ritual, 138 Rites of Passage, 141 First-Fruit Rites, 143 *Weyčiyail*
Ritual, 144 Rain Ritual, 145 Curing Rituals and Medicine, 146 Rituals
of Subsistence, 146 Bird Dance, 149 *Wexily* Songs, 150 Other Rituals,
151 Ritual Congregations, 151 Functional Aspects of Taboos and
Fasting, 153 Nutritional Aspects of Ritual, 154 Summary, 158

9

WORLD VIEW: EXISTENTIAL AND
NORMATIVE POSTULATES   160

Introduction, 160 ʔivaʔa (Power), 161 Assumption of Instability and

10

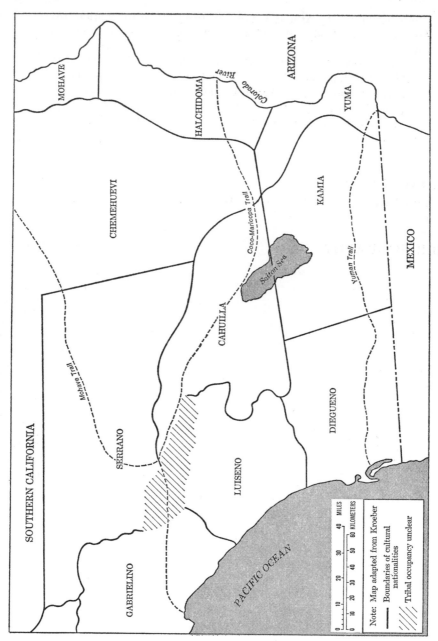

THE CAHUILLA AND THEIR NEIGHBORS

I

Introduction

A viewpoint widely held in scientific circles is that religious and folk attitudes impede or prevent people from effectively adapting to their environment. This attitude was expressed at a scientific conference sponsored by the Environmental Services Administration. Twenty-four scientists from various disciplines were brought together to study the relationship between human populations and their environments. The "common notion" expressed at this conference was "that people's folkloric and religious attitudes prevent them from following adaptive strategies in using their environment effectively" (Vayda, 1969:71). Two exceptions to this viewpoint were expressed; one by a geographer (Robert Kates) and another by an anthropologist (John Bennett). In the conference report Bennett, a specialist in Anglo-American Great Plains farming cultures, argued that the folk attitudes of plains farmers were adaptive to environmentally induced stress (Garnsney and Hibbs, 1967:114–120).

From the conference report the question arises whether anthropologists and geographers have theoretical orientations which encourage them to see folkloric and religious phenomena differently from other scientists also concerned with relationships between human populations and their environments. Some anthropologists and geographers do.

In recent years the method of cultural ecology has added considerable knowledge to our understanding of the relationships between environmental conditions, technology, and social organization. The concentration of some scholars upon the interdependent aspects of these factors has led to a vigorous reexamination of some ethnographic data collected in the past. The method is now basic to the discipline of anthropology, and significant literature exists. Cultural ecologists are now often challenged for placing too much emphasis on the adaptive aspects of technology, settlement pattern, and social organization, while excluding the potential adaptiveness of less easily measurable aspects of culture such as ritual, values, and world view.

Thus, whereas anthropologists see various aspects of culture as adaptive mechanisms from a theoretical position, a review of recent anthropological literature indicates a conflict within anthropology, similar to that expressed in the Environmental Services Administration conference. This conflict concerning the function of folk beliefs and religious attitudes is seen in two theoretical orientations. Lowie (1920; 1938), Linton (1936), Homans (1941), Simoons (1961), and Goode (1951) suggest that ritual and religious institutions are often dysfunctional, irrational, or nonadaptive in cultural systems. Alternately, ritual and religious institutions may be seen as playing an economically practical role in cultural viability essential to the dynamics of a culture [Carneiro (1968); Harris (1966; 1968); Miller (1964); Rappaport (1967); Suttles (1968); Vayda (1968)].

Harris (1968:366) pointed out that the first perspective is exemplified by Lowie who wrote:

It should be once more emphasized that even where practical considerations play a dominant role, capricious irrationality checks the full and rationalist exploitation of domestic beasts, i.e., failure to milk mares, taboos against pork, not milking cows by Chinese (1938:306).

One main objection to the economic interpretations of culture that have hitherto been offered is that they fail to come to grips with those problems that obtrude themselves spontaneously on any unprejudiced observer of the data. The theorists of this school ignore even so obvious a fact as the irrational ingredients of economic activity, a fact so convincingly corroborated by later inquiry. To take a single example, East Africans are enthusiastic stock-breeders; but is their animal husbandry to be gauged by our standards? Far from it. A Shilluk keeps hundreds of cattle, yet slaughters them so rarely that he is obliged to maintain his hunting techniques for an adequate supply of meat. His small cows yield but little milk, his oxen normally serve no purpose at all. But these Negroes, who eschew a beef diet, expend enormous effort on massaging the humps of their beasts and twisting their horns into grotesque shapes (1920:242).

In a similar vein Simoons (1961:3) suggests that irrational ideologies frequently compel men to overlook foods of high nutritive value abundant locally and to utilize other foods of lesser value that may be in short supply. He says:

The foodways determine which of the available food resources a group eats and which it rejects; through cultural preference and prejudice they may present major barriers to using available food resources and raising the standards of nutrition. It is not rare for the foodways to lead men to overlook foods that are abundant locally and are of high nutritive value, and to utilize other, scarcer foods of less value. Beef, chicken flesh and eggs, dogmeat, and horse and camel flesh comprise such important potential sources of animal protein that their more general use might contribute substantially to reducing the widespread and serious protein deficiency that prevails in large parts of the Old World.

Simoons is skeptical of attempts at rational explanations of these findings:

In discussing the origins of their own group flesh avoidances, people often claim that they were determined solely by reason. The supposed origin of the avoidance of pork as a health measure is a good example. Despite the attractiveness of such "rational" explanations one must be wary of accepting them too readily; not only are they usually presented with little or no supporting evidence but they conform suspiciously well to the Western bias in favor of the rational (1961:111).

Ralph Linton, in his classic work *The Study of Man*, supports Simoons, seeing a tendency for cultures to develop unnecessary and injurious ideologies. He points out that these ideologies may put

societies at a disadvantage in competition with outsiders. However, a few cases have been recorded of elaboration carried to the point of actual injury when there was no outside interference. Although this means little under ordinary circumstances, there are times when it is highly injurious. It is said that if land game fails a tribe will often starve when there are plenty of seals in sight. This taboo even extends to bringing the flesh or skins of land and sea animals into contact and is thus a constant source of inconvenience (1936:90).

Consistent with these perspectives is that of Goode (1951) who maintains that religious restrictions often prevent production at the highest level of efficiency. For example, funerary practices are often a burden on a distribution system because they might take the people away from work, and certain periods of the year may be given over to ritual rather than economic activities.

In keeping with the ideas expressed above, but recognizing a psychological function in ritual, Homans has written:

Ritual actions do not produce a practical result on the external world—that is one of the reasons we call them ritual. But to make the statement is not to say that ritual has no function. Its function is not related to the world external to the society but to the internal constitution of the society. It gives the members of the society confidence, it dispels their anxieties, it disciplines their social organization (1941:172).

As Harris (1968) has so aply pointed out, the above statements are less directly associated with, but not unrelated to, the theoretical assumptions of scholars who utilize psychological and sociological frames to explain the practical roles of ritual and religion, than with techno-economic explanations. Some scholars (Wallace, 1966) feel that ritual and philosophical phenomena are cultural devices which alleviate anxiety otherwise leading to social disorganization. Sociologically prone anthropologists suggest that these institutions maintain sociological equilibrium (Gluckman, 1953:1–26), or conversely, articulate mechanisms for introducing innovation or change (Lewis, 1971:27). Consequently, there is a very respectable literature which either ignores the ecological adaptiveness of ritual and belief or assumes that ritual activities and beliefs may be significantly dysfunctional to the efficient operation of any given ecosystem.

The opposite viewpoint is well expressed by Carneiro and Miller. Carneiro argues that:

All aspects of culture may contribute to the ecological adjustment of a society. . . . Basically, societies adapt to their environment by three means: technological, organizational, and ideational. . . . Granted that social organization is adaptive, can the same be said, for example, of rituals and ceremonies? Some anthropologists have held them to lie outside of the realm of the rational and the functional, and therefore to be nonadaptive. Yet it is possible to examine rituals and ceremonies in the broader context of adaptation, and the results of such analyses have been to throw new light on them. . . . The ideational aspects of culture also serve to adapt society to the prevailing conditions of existence . . . a sociocultural system works best when it makes people want to do what they have to do (1968:552–554).

Miller goes a step further and suggests that religion cannot be separated from the study of culture, and, by implication, religious institutions are intimately related to techno-environmental conditions. He says:

Each formally organized religious system in a culture accepted as a whole is assumed to be a potential supervisor of the command pattern of a culture. Each religion then, as an organized symbolic, structural, functional system proposing to order the world and to extend its order (realized in organization) into economic, political, and social aspects of the culture, seeks to become the culture, to absorb the culture into itself, to provide the command pattern. The degree to which it succeeds is demonstrable in the lived orders in respect to patterning of interpersonal relations, timing of activities, reference of the locus of command to its defined locus, acceptance of its patterning of relations between men and the rest of the universe, its concept of the universe, etc. (1964:96).

Although Miller and Carneiro have argued toward the recognition of ritual and belief as significant components in understanding man's adaptation to his environment, Harris, Vayda, Rappaport, and Suttles have most clearly argued for the implementation of techno-economic models to explain the adaptive functions of ritual and belief.

Harris is perhaps the most outspoken proponent in anthropology today of social organization and ideology as adaptive responses to techno-economic conditions. He has leveled a broad-scale attack on various anthropological theorists in his work *The Rise of Anthropological Theory* (1968), and he has examined (1966) the concept of *ahimsa*, or "nonviolence," which has been cited as an example of how men will diminish their material welfare to obtain spiritual satisfaction in obedience to nonrational or frankly irrational beliefs. Harris says:

I believe the irrational, noneconomic and exotic aspects of the Indian cattle complex, are greatly overemphasized at the expense of rational, economic, and mundane interpretations. . . . The relationship between Indian cattle and human populations is demonstrably symbiotic. Cattle and people derive their caloric ration from separate spheres of the ecosystem; cattle are India's prime scavengers; their dung is essential for fuel under the prevailing techno-environmental conditions of agriculture. Dairying is carried out to maximum limits compatible with traction and good planting requirements, while Hindu taboos against slaughter and consumption of beef by low castes and Moslems. There is no evidence that these taboos under present day techno-environmental conditions adversely affect the welfare of the rural populations. Indeed, insofar as there is a severe shortage of cattle in India, such beliefs may be regarded as an adaptation by which the exploitation of cattle, especially during famine, is kept within safe limits. . . . The probability that India's sacred cattle is a positive-functional part of a naturally selected ecosystem is at least as good as that it is a negative-functional expression of irrational ideology (1966:51–52).

Others have examined ritual and religion in particular societies reaching conclusions similar to those of Harris. Rappaport maintains that the ritual cycle of the Tsembaga has a regulatory function. He says:

Ritual cycles of the Tsembaga, and of other local territorial groups of Maring speakers living in the New Guinea interior, play an important part in regulating the relationships of these groups with both the nonhuman components of their immediate environments and the human components of their less immediate environments, that is, with other similar territorial groups. To be more specific, this regulation helps to maintain the biotic communities existing within their territories, redistributes land among people and people over land, and limits the frequency of fighting. In the absence of authoritative political statuses or offices, the ritual cycle likewise provides a means for mobilizing allies when warfare may be undertaken. It also provides a mechanism for redistributing local pig surpluses in the form of pork throughout a large regional population while helping to assure the local population of a supply of pork when its members are most in need of high quality protein (1964:17–18).

Other studies further support the conclusions of these students and indicate the cross-cultural validity of the model (or conclusions). Vayda (1966) has indicated that trade feasts among the Pomo Indians of California aided in the redistribution of wealth and allowed for "banking procedures" for insurance against crop failures in local areas. Suttles (1960; 1962; 1968) suggests that among the northwest coast Indians of North America the potlatch systems were elaborate means of stimulating and preserving economic viability rather than responses to highly productive environments or mechanisms for status enhancement.

In conclusion, these scholars argue that religious activities and beliefs are often significant variables in the operation of any given ecosystem.

SOME ASSUMPTIONS AND
HYPOTHESES TO BE TESTED

As in our original problem, that an apparent dichotomy exists in scientific circles concerning the role of religion and belief systems, a similar dichotomy exists among anthropological theorists. Two assumptions seem to prevail: ritual and world view are more ecologically nonadaptive than adaptive; or ritual and world view are more ecologically adaptive than they are nonadaptive.

To examine the relevancy of the opposing theoretical views I

will develop hypotheses concerning a particular culture, the Cahuilla Indians of Southern California, which will be used as a test
case. I will present two sets of hypotheses which logically follow
from each of the assumptions. From the first assumption I suggest
that the economic needs of society are impeded by ritual actions
which are not only wasteful of productive goods but decrease the
production of goods; they take people away from productive
activities because of ritual obligations: and from the second I
suggest that the economic needs of society are impeded by normative and existential postulates (for definition see page 160) which
indicate that valuable resources are outside the realm of the economic order; these postulates are disruptive to the production of
goods by encouraging people to behave in such a way that they
are taken away from productive activity. From this latter viewpoint two other hypotheses follow: the economic needs of society
are facilitated by ritual action which conserves and increases the
production of goods and fosters productive activity by directing
personnel toward producing activities; and the economic needs of
society are facilitated by normative and existential postulates
which foster the use of valuable economic resources and increase
the productive process by directing behavior which involves people in productive activities.

The validity of the hypotheses will be tested by asking specific
questions related to the hypotheses. The questions are:

Were goods wasted because of ritual action?

Did ritual action take people away from productive activities or
did it direct people to produce more goods?

Were valuable resources placed outside the realm of economic
order by existential postulates?

Did normative postulates disrupt the production of goods by
rewarding behavior which took people away from productive activity?

Or did it reward behavior which fostered the production of
goods?

Additional questions are:

Did ritual and world view encourage the full and rational use
of the Cahuilla environment?

Did ritual and world view aid in adjusting man–land ratios?

Did ritual and world view support a social structure and organization which was adaptive to an environmental base?

Did ritual and world view support institutions that were adaptive, such as law, property concepts, warfare, and games?

Did ritual and world view have regulatory functions?

Did ritual and world view stimulate or facilitate the distribution of economic goods from one part of the system to another?

Did ritual and world view limit the frequency and extent of conflict over valuable resources?

METHODOLOGY

Methodological problems arise in attempting to discover whether there are rational or practical effects of religious activities in hunting and gathering societies. These problems have been reviewed by several scholars (Vayda, 1968: *passim*). Their approach is a major departure from the methodological approaches of cultural ecologists such as Steward (1955) who excludes several aspects of culture in his analysis. They claim that a systems approach is necessary for the study of cultural-environmental relations. This approach does not isolate prematurely any element from the analysis of how a society adapts to its environment. Rather, it examines a culture as part of a larger system, an ecosystem, and various institutions within the culture are assumed to be part of a social system. All the social system's constituent parts are examined for their possible direct and indirect contributions to the viability of the society.

In this study a systems approach will be used in data analysis. The Cahuilla will be viewed as an ecosystem member, including the associated plants and animals together with the physical features of their environment, each in an intricate and systemic relationship with one another. Within the ecosystem the Cahuilla are seen as members of a community, an aggregation of ecologically related individuals belonging to two or more different species sharing a common habitat (Dice, 1955:2). Interrelationships are thus emphasized between the Cahuilla, their neighbors, other groups of organisms (the flora and fauna), and soil, water, climate, and topography. Homeostatic processes were in operation because the habitat was in a constant state of change; each part of the ecosystem was interdependently affecting the other, thus the habitat and biota were influenced, changed, and manipulated by the Cahuilla. The Cahuilla, in turn, were influenced by changes in the habitat and biota.

From this point I explore the adaptiveness or nonadaptiveness of Cahuilla institutions for the Cahuilla. Adaptive here means an adjustment to changes which a society makes because of pressures occurring from other parts of the ecosystem. In order to adapt to the constant changes in physical and cultural conditions within an ecosystem, the community must have regulatory mechanisms (servomechanisms) which prevent fluctuations from reaching an unviable (or intolerable) extreme (Dice, 1955:2). For regulatory mechanisms to serve the system they must be automatic in their responses; uniformly dependable in their application, and not easily subject to change by whims of persons who have authority and power; smooth and effective in operation by increasing or decreasing their control in proportion to the need for it, and economically consuming as little as possible of the resources of the ecosystem (Dice, 1955:109). These processes which return a system to a normal state or create a tolerable state are often very subtle. For example, the regulatory mechanisms may be triggered by psychological stress which does not appear to be directly related to the cause of the stress, as Rappaport and Vayda have demonstrated with regard to the function of pig feasts in Melanesia (Rappaport, 1964:17–40; Vayda, 1961:69–77).

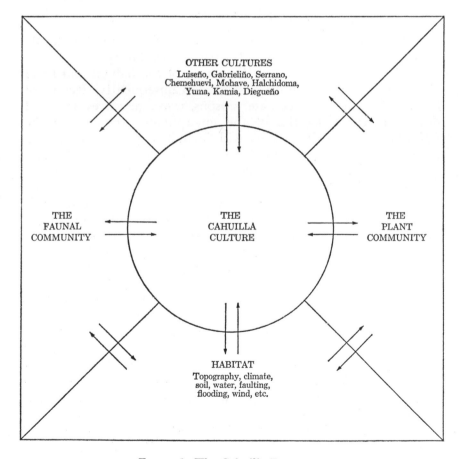

FIGURE 1. The Cahuilla Ecosystem.

To discover if these processes operate in Cahuilla culture, it is necessary to see how the group is organized, and how the parts (the individuals and institutions) interact. Institutions are specific areas of activity about which behavior is focused, and can be described in terms of the personnel, activities, material goods, and ideological assumptions concerning their presence (Bohannan, 1963:375).

I wish to discover if each part of the system operates to serve adaptive functions to the whole (or other parts). By demonstrating how the parts of the system integrated successfully for the Cahuilla, the question whether specific adaptive functions of ritual and religion operate in an ecological context will be answered; and how the system's parts did—or did not—integrate advantageously for the Cahuilla.

PROCEDURE

The hypotheses will be examined by viewing several Cahuilla institutions to determine if adaptive or regulatory mechanisms were operative. I will discuss the nature of the habitat and biota within which the Cahuilla subsisted. Consequently, factors of topography, life zones, climate, seasons, water resources, fire, and other physical properties of the environment relevant to the Cahuilla are presented. This will include a listing of the important plant and fauna and discussions of how, when, and where these were utilized for subsistence purposes. The discussions will be concerned with the features of those that affected Cahuilla life style. When the environmental circumstances have been established, various categories of the Cahuilla culture will be presented. The first will be settlement pattern. In this chapter the manner in which the Cahuilla placed themselves in space and time will be described because this was of paramount importance to their adaptation to the environment. Population control and density are also related to environmental factors, and therefore will be examined in relation to the environmental circumstances. A review of social structure and organizational activities will follow. The nature of groups—the moiety, sib, lineage, and family—will receive special attention. The kinship system and other status and role relationships will be outlined and their contribution to the viability of the culture demonstrated. Several institutions such as law, economic relations, concepts of property and ownership, warfare, and games will be delineated. Each of these will be examined to determine how they contributed to Cahuilla subsistence. The next two chapters will deal with central concerns to this work: ritual and world view. The more significant rituals in Cahuilla life will be discussed. In each instance, particular attention will be given to adaptive functions and nonadaptive features, when rituals were given, who was involved in them, and any associated economic features.

World view will be analyzed in terms of existential and normative postulates. The effects of these postulates upon the Cahuilla's conceptualization and use of environment will be examined, because they are significant to the hypotheses being tested.

The hypotheses will, then, be reviewed in light of the questions posed in the first chapter. From this review, other questions of a theoretical nature will be raised.

WHY THE CAHUILLA HAVE BEEN SELECTED AS A TEST CASE

Most studies of California aboriginal cultures are fragmentary, dealing only with specialized aspects of the cultures, and are generally descriptive rather than analytical. Therefore, it is fitting that a California Indian culture should be selected for analysis in view of recent theoretical concepts such as cultural ecology, systems analysis, and cultural integration.

In recent years several students (Beals and Hester, 1956; Baumhoff, 1963) have called attention to the ecological variations used by native Californians, and have suggested that meaningful correlations between culture and environment can be established. They have suggested that in-depth studies of particular cultures in California would help to clarify the relationships between environment and behavior. Only one published study, *Luiseño Social Organization* (White, 1963), has attempted to outline these relationships. Another notable attempt, although unpublished to date, is Kunkel (1962), who analyzed the ecological variations in the Pomo and Yokuts areas to correlate social-structural poses with environment. The combination of ecological and cultural complexity in California makes it one of the richest ethnographic laboratories in the world for such studies. In addition, native California is intriguing because many of these cultures continually provide exceptions to generalizations about hunting and gathering peoples. For example, contributors to the symposium published under the title *Man the Hunter* (1968), Lee and Devore, tended to exclude California cultures from consideration because of the seeming atypical nature of cultural development among California

Indians. Several scholars have been impressed with the sociocultural complexity of native California peoples in contrast to other societies in similar technological situations. Goldschmidt, in his book *Man's Way* (1959:146–147), remarked upon this situation as did Willey and Phillips (1958) in *Method and Theory in American Archaeology*.

The Cahuilla Indians of Southern California are among those cultures of California which have not been adequately described in the ethnographic literature. Only one account (Strong, 1929) attempted to explain the social structure of the society with regard to cause-and-effect relationships, or in terms of the relationship of the culture to its environmental base. Strong worked among the Cahuillas in the late 1920s; no one has since attempted to reconstruct the aboriginal culture, or analyze it from a functional standpoint. The Cahuilla provide a fresh body of data to be seen for the first time within the context of contemporary anthropological method and theory.

The Cahuilla offer another interesting challenge: they lived in a multienvironmental and multicultural milieu which had certain similarities to that of the Indians found throughout the Southwest (Beals, 1956:256–260). The environmental base was varied, ranging from low deserts to high mountains, and the cultures surrounding them ranged from desert-oriented people like the Chemehuevi to the very rich and powerful Gabrielino on the Pacific Coast, to the Colorado River agriculturalists (the Halchidoma and Yuma). The cultural backgrounds of their neighbors were also varied. Yuman-speaking peoples were to the east and southeast, Shoshonean speakers were on the west and to the north. The Cahuilla, then, provide a natural laboratory for research problems because their environmental and cultural diversity, together with a well-articulated social system, caused them to stand out as a culture which had time to develop institutional solutions to many problems.

The wealth of data which has been collected over seventy years by keen observers is also a significant advantage. Most of this data has been published—the works of Barrows (1900), Kroeber (1908), Gifford (1918), Hooper (1920), Strong (1929), and Drucker (1937) are especially noteworthy.

Scattered articles and papers have been published on the Cahuilla since these works, and several scholars have drawn them into their research in dissertations (Thomas, 1964; Hicks, 1961; Sutton, 1964), but no single major work has been attempted since Strong's contribution was published in 1929, although two overviews of the history of the Cahuilla have recently been published (James, 1960; Oswalt, 1966). A book containing the recollections of Patencio (1943), a Cahuilla scholar of the highest order, is also important for understanding the Cahuilla. The strong persistence of tradition among the Cahuilla adds still another parameter. This has been preserved in the rich oral literature which has yielded a great deal of new information for this study.

How, then, does this study differ from previous work by anthropologists?

Barrow's *The Ethnobotany of the Cahuilla Indians of Southern California* (1900) was the first published anthropological study of the Cahuilla. Barrows did more than study Indian uses of plants. He was interested in many aspects of Cahuilla life and culture. In this work he placed the Cahuilla for the first time into an ethnographic perspective by examining their relation to other Southwestern cultures and by describing their history, settlement pattern, technology, subsistence pattern, and religion. His principal concern was to demonstrate how the technology of this culture was adaptive to what appeared to be a harsh and unyielding environment, and what effect that process had upon the psychology of the people.

Shortly after the turn of the century, Kroeber made a brief trip among the Cahuilla collecting artifacts and interviewing Cahuilla. He subsequently published his findings as a monograph (Kroeber, 1908). His focus was on material culture, although some information was presented on other subjects such as comparative linguistics and social organization. The first major work of a social anthropological nature concerning the Cahuilla was done by Gifford, who collected data on kinship terminology, social structure, and oral literature. Without his pioneering efforts further work would have been extremely difficult. It was Gifford who first appreciated the extensive distribution of moiety, lineage, and clan principles in aboriginal California social organization (Gifford, 1918). Shortly after Gifford worked among the Cahuilla, Hooper (1920) published a valuable set of ethnographic notes which describe material culture, social organization, ritual, religious beliefs, and oral literature. This work added significantly to the ethnographic perspective provided by the earlier observers.

The major work on the Cahuilla and the one most important for understanding aboriginal culture and Cahuilla history was published by Strong: *Aboriginal Society in Southern California* (1929). Strong spent six months in Southern California, during which he devoted considerable time to the Cahuilla. He collected a massive body of data on social structure, ritual, settlement patterns, and oral literature, and integrated it with data collected by others. It remains an outstanding achievement in comparative and historical California ethnography. Its major theoretical orientation is the explanation of social structure and the ritual complex of the Southern California Shoshoneans as part of a historical continuum of the Southwestern cultural influence. The wealth of detail provided by Strong can be most appreciated by attempting to replicate his findings. It is cautiously written, carefully detailed, and well organized. No meaningful study could be accomplished at this time without the information he presented.

Very little work has been done since Strong published his findings. However, Drucker's *Culture Element Distributions: Southern California* has contributed many ethnographic details. It provides an excellent body of data on most aspects of Cahuilla culture collected from several older Cahuillas who had not been interviewed by Strong.

The present work stands apart from these studies in several ways. It is concerned solely with the reconstruction of the ethnographic past in as complete a fashion as possible without concern for either origins or change, and it treats the Cahuilla culture as one, unified whole, in one place and at one time. Although other studies were concerned with particular aspects of the aboriginal culture, none attempted as comprehensive an overview utilizing the structural and functional analysis while emphasizing an ecological integration and a systems analysis as the methodological base.

For example, although there is a considerable literature regarding the specifics of Cahuilla ritual and myth, there has been no attempt until now to explain the economic functions of the rituals or the ways in which oral traditions defined or affirmed the behavioral action related to subsistence.

VIEWING CULTURE AT A DISTANCE

Selection of the Cahuilla as a case study raises certain methodological problems. They are now 184 years removed from the time European culture first intruded upon them. Can a culture be described with any certainty after 184 years of exposure to foreign cultures and consequent changes in technological and economic life have taken place? Opinions vary among anthropologists. Some claim that so much change occurs within a single generation that any attempted culture reconstruction is seriously frustrated. Other anthropologists take the view that cultures can be reconstructed even though they have undergone significant changes. This is so, it is argued, because cultures persist in the mind long after the actual circumstances of the culture disappear (Lee and Devore, 1968a:5–6). I am convinced that cultural reconstruction is a legitimate and productive endeavor; and I carry four operative assumptions for viewing culture at a distance which encourage me to go ahead with confidence.

My first assumption is that a model of a culture can persist through time in the minds of the people, and that it is accurate in a broad sense. This is so because an ideal model exists at an implicit level in the minds of the members of a culture, owing to the subtle manner in which enculturation occurs in any society. Many aspects of a cultural model, then, will be retained for a long period of time, often after the functional context of that model no longer exists. Examples are from American ethnic groups. Cultural models of behavior have sometimes persisted for several generations after immigrants have come into a new culture. This is significant because in these instances immigrating cultures were consciously attempting to assimilate themselves into a new cultural system and rejecting that from which they came. In contrast, many cultures, such as the Cahuilla, never consciously or deliberately assimilated themselves into another system. On the contrary, they have consciously preserved their own model of cultural reality, preferring it to the Hispanic or Anglo-American systems which have been available to them. When this condition occurs we should anticipate positive results to cultural reconstruction.

Second, cultures which have a tradition of oral history are skilled in maintaining extensive and minutely detailed information about themselves. Techniques for preserving history in such cultures are sufficiently inculcated in its members so that information is passed from generation to generation in detailed fashion. Amos (1968) has convincingly argued for the efficacy of oral tradition in reconstructing history.

Third, when a language is retained, a major part of the culture is maintained because the many basic cultural conceptualizations reside in the language. At the time I first visited the Cahuilla, in 1958, approximately 25 percent of the population spoke Cahuilla, and many more understood the language although they did not speak it. This linguistic persistence served as a historic-cultural reservoir of immense consequence to the preservation of the Cahuilla culture. The traditional oral literature of the culture was preserved, and was still being told to younger people at that date.

Fourth, when a culture remains in the same locality for long periods of time remembrances of the past are very persistent because of the close association of belief and history to specific geographic phenomena. This has been demonstrated by Gayton (1946: *passim*) in her studies among the Yokuts. The Cahuilla have never had to leave the territorial base within which their culture existed, contributing importantly to the retention of information.

These factors have contributed to the persistence of a large and accurate reservoir of traditional knowledge. This cultural memory bank appears very remarkable to persons from a literate tradition who customarily rely on the written record for precedent and historical events, but it is taken for granted in nonliterate cultures. Later in this discussion specific circumstances of this will be applied to the Cahuilla example. Evidence readily available from other cultural systems indicates the validity of such material. For example, recordings from Biblical literature and Greek mythology have proved to be accurate as demonstrated by archaeological findings in Israel and Greece, as have studies done in Australia by Norman Tindal (personal communication), and by Amos in Africa (1968).

A study of the Cahuilla culture of the past I assume is therefore possible. The persistence of oral tradition, however, is not the only source for ethnographic reconstruction. Historical accounts of the Cahuilla begin very near the time of contact, and ethnographic descriptions of the Cahuilla are scattered throughout many accounts from that time until David Prescott Barrows began observing the Cahuilla in the 1890s. Formal ethnographic study started with Barrows, who first visited the Cahuilla in 1893, and ethnographers have continued to collect data until now. Archaeological data, while not extensive, have helped to validate the data base. Therefore, there is a continuity of information beginning in Cahuilla oral literature and perpetuated in the living memory of the elders which is supported by historical and anthropological findings. There is, significantly, an internal consistency throughout this literature, supporting the assumption that ethnographic reconstruction is accurate and valid.

These various sources confirm one another regarding the patterns of Cahuilla culture, so this reconstruction, I maintain, is valid for examining contemporary anthropological theory.

A brief review of the history of the Cahuilla will place this into perspective.

The first recorded Cahuilla contact with European culture was in 1776 when Anza passed through the Los Coyotes Canyon, the home of the *wiastam* Cahuilla (Bolton, 1930). There is little record of contact after that time until 1809, 161 years ago, when baptisms of Cahuillas began to be recorded by the San Gabriel Mission. About a decade later, several Asistencias were established near the Cahuilla territory: San Bernardino, Pala, and Santa Ysabel. The Asistencia of San Bernardino (near Redlands) was established in 1819, and a few Cahuillas lived there, where they learned European agricultural and cattle-raising techniques (Beattie, 1939). As late as 1823, the Cahuilla area was not well known to the Spanish-Mexican population. Two expeditions into the area (1823 and 1826) were made by Jose Romero (Bean and Mason, 1962), who described the northern Cahuilla area for the first time. Some Cahuillas could speak Spanish at that time, and apparently the Mission San Gabriel was occasionally running cattle through the San Gorgonio Pass as far east as Palm Springs. The Cahuillas further in the desert and in the mountains do not seem to have been involved in the Spanish-Mexican culture at that time. Thus, only a few Cahuillas were influenced by this foreign culture. There were some sporadic expeditions into the area in the 1830s and in the 1840s (Cleland, 1929: *passim*). In the 1840s some Cahuillas from Cahuilla Valley, under the leadership of Juan Antonio (a Cahuilla), served as guardians of a Mexican rancho whose cattle were being stolen in raids by other tribes. Thus, a new leadership pattern commenced. In later years, Cabezon and Antonio Garra assumed leadership positions which were comparable to that of Juan Antonio. These leaders commanded the allegiance of some Cahuillas from several groups. They functioned as intermediaries between the Cahuilla and European cultures, but they protected and maintained the traditional Cahuilla system; they were not innovators attempting to impose radical change upon their people. Nor was their leadership of sufficient strength so that they could command overall obedience to decisions which they made. By 1851 Cahuilla traditional political organization was still intact. This is evidenced by the treaty of Temecula in 1851, signed by various traditional leaders of the Cahuilla groups. As late as 1860 the historical records do not indicate any readily observable changes in Cahuilla institutions discussed here, although changes in settlement pattern had occurred, and the population density had probably been decreased owing to epidemics. The smallpox epidemic of 1863 was the most significant event in recent Cahuilla history. Large numbers of the population died, and there was considerable shifting of village locations. The re-action of Cahuillas up to this time had been to retreat from the circumstances imposed by European culture rather than to seek assimilation. Reservations were established in the 1870s. They, too, functioned to preserve the Cahuilla in relative isolation from Anglo-American culture. The Cahuilla participated with Anglo-American culture only as it was necessary for survival, and pre-served their traditional ways in the privacy of their newly estab-lished homes.

From the time when Barrows began his study until Strong be-gan his in the late 1920s, much of the traditional culture was still intact and well remembered, although it was one hundred and fifty years after contact. Only seventy years had passed since the first important contact with the Cahuilla in 1823, and it was less than forty years after the smallpox epidemics when Barrows was there. Thus, ritual and world view were very much as they had been prior to European contact, though they were somewhat separated from their original context.

Strong was certain that his data regarding settlement pattern was accurate for circa 1875 because his informants were adults at that time. The accuracy of this data and other aspects of tradi-tional Cahuilla life were confirmed time and time again by the information which I collected from persons over eighty years of age (1959–1962) who learned about their history from their grandparents and great-grandparents. The memories of these peo-ple date, in some instances, as far back as the 1850s. For example, locations of abandoned village sites were remembered by these Cahuilla historians. Some of the villages which Strong could not locate were located for me in 1960 by several old men. These sites had been abandoned before 1875. This data is supported by sur-veyors' maps drawn in the 1850s which locate some of these sites at that time. Furthermore, the specific reasons why the villages had been moved were remembered.

What is remembered is often idealized, yet what is remembered is very consistent with historic, ethnographic, and archaeological reports made in later years. The time span involved does not allow a view of the many variations within the Cahuilla model of reality. However, this is not a major disadvantage because it is allegedly a model of the culture that is retained for long periods of time. The model of a culture, knowing what is appropriate, directs behavior most of the time in any given culture. The task, then, is to see how the model of cultural action relates to the physical and cultural pressures placed upon the Cahuilla. The question is whether the model of the Cahuilla was functional to the ecosystem of which the Cahuilla were a part.

DATA COLLECTION

The data used in this study have been acquired by interviewing Cahuillas who have knowledge of the past, and by reviewing published anthropological and historical literature. Archival resources of the Bancroft Library, University of California, Berkeley; the Huntington Library, San Marino; Los Angeles County Museum of History and Science; Malki Museum, Morongo Reservation, Banning; Serra Museum, San Diego; and the Southwest Museum in Los Angeles have provided invaluable unpublished sources.

Site surveys and travel throughout the Cahuilla area with Cahuillas and specialists in other fields on foot and by automobile also have been significant aids in understanding the nature of the topography and the biotic communities as well as settlement pattern.

The summers of 1959, 1960, and 1961 were spent in residence at the Morongo Indian Reservation, and discussions with Cahuillas about their culture have continued since that time.

In addition, people of other tribes were interviewed: Luiseños Macario Calac, Gertrude Chorrie, and Jim Martinez; Cupenos Julia Calac, Merced Gabriel, and Rosinda Nolasquez; and Serranos Sarah Martin and Louis Marcus. These friends provided invaluable data for comparison.

Field methods ranged from nondirected conversations to highly structured interviews organized around previously prepared research schedules. These research schedules were particularly useful for obtaining information about subsistence factors and plant and animal uses. But the unstructured interviews were the most productive in the acquisition of new data and insights concerning philosophy and world view. Personal observation was critical for analyzing geographic factors, plant distribution variations, and behavioral patterns.

Each item of data has been checked with as many Cahuilla as possible. Considerable conflict sometimes arose, and it was necessary to select some interpretations rather than others on the basis of logical consistency and general reliability of the speaker.

In addition to the sources already cited, this work has been further amplified and deepened by the reminiscences of Patencio (1943), the collections taken by Curtis (1926) from William Pablo, and others, all which were substantiated and discussed with nu-

merous Cahuilla in order to formulate a composite view of Cahuilla culture.

Above all, it has been my good fortune to have had the opportunity to learn from several remarkable Cahuilla teachers who
were concerned with my understanding of their culture. They
have sat with me for hours and contributed to my learning at
each step, patiently waiting for the novice to struggle—as I still
do—to understand their complex cultural system.

A synthesis of this learning, then, is the subject of this study.

ACKNOWLEDGMENTS

Many of the Cahuilla people whose work was vital to this study
are now deceased. Their contribution cannot be overly praised
and they are gratefully acknowledged: Harry Hopkins, Joe Lomas,
Lupe Lugo, Salvador Lopez, Chono Toro, Calistro Tortes, Dona
Tortes, Juan Siva, Salvador Valenzuela, and Victoria Wierick.

I am also grateful to my many Cahuilla friends who continue
to help in my efforts to understand their culture, past and present.
They are: Marie Alto, Rupert Costo, Walter Holmes, William
Holmes, Gladys Hopkins Holmes, Robert Levi, Alice Lopez,
Cinciona Lubo, Lupe Lugo, Spencer Lyons, Matthew Pablo,
Jane Pablo Penn, Mariano Saubel, Alvino Siva, and Florian Tor-
tes. Katherine Siva Saubel has worked diligently and expertly, con-
tributing significantly to every phase of my work.

Several of these friends have added immeasurably to the collection of data by interviewing other Cahuillas in my behalf in order
to substantiate their knowledge or to get answers to questions
which they themselves did not have available at the time. Many
other Cahuillas, too numerous to mention here, have been of
assistance by their continued good will and interest in my work.
Many who have assisted in other research interests are not mentioned here because their contribution has been in other ways
which will receive attention in the future.

This work would not have been possible without the guidance
and encouragement of the many scholars who assisted, supported,
and evaluated the work in its stages of development. Professor
Ralph Beals has supported my work since its inception and provided much editorial labor to it. His support is gratefully acknowledged. Professor William Bright and Hans Jacob Seiler have
graciously provided linguistic materials and editorial advice. Professor Richard Logan accompanied me on a number of field
trips and his understanding of the area's geography and botany

was of immense help, as were suggestions by Karl Wandry. Professor Wendell Oswalt has guided me through all stages of my research. His editorial suggestions are greatly appreciated. Professors Walter Goldschmidt, Clement Meighan, Henry Nicholson, and Clarence Smith have also at various times assisted my work.

Others have helped by providing generously with information, time, and interest: Mrs. Edna Badger of Banning has contributed invaluable information concerning the local geography and floral and faunal conditions; William Nott of San Francisco and Robert Gill of Berkeley have aided in my analysis of Cahuilla kinship. Francis and Patricia Johnson of Banning have assisted me in learning about Cahuilla settlement pattern; Harry W. Lawton of the University of California, Riverside, has contributed insightful suggestions concerning Cahuilla oral literature; Elmer Penn of Morongo Indian Reservation has helped in my work from its beginning as advisor and friend. His encouragement and aid have been most generous. Professor Richard Thomas was very kind in introducing me to his Cahuilla friends when I first began my work. Jeannette Henry of the American Indian Historical Society in San Francisco has given of her time, knowledge, and encouragement during the progress of this work. Grateful acknowledgment is also offered to Stan Heeb and many others for editorial and substantive suggestions; Charles Allen, for several years of field-work assistance; and Mrs. Daphne Stern and Charles Smith for manuscript preparation and editorial advice.

STYLE

In the text of this study the past tense will be used to place the aboriginal Cahuilla culture in historical perspective. However, many of the activities presented are still a viable part of the culture today. Thus, by using the past tense to describe any activity, it must not be presumed that the activity no longer occurs. Moreover, the use of the present and past tenses would have disrupted the conceptualization that the Cahuilla have of their world as existing for eternity, with the past, present, and future being merely temporal—but interchangeable—aspects of that continuum.

The orthography utilized is that recommended by Professor William Bright, although occasionally, when terms are being quoted from other sources, the orthography used in the sources cited will be given.

Cahuilla names and terms have been used wherever possible to avoid confusion regarding these concepts and their use. Kroeber's *Handbook of the Indians of California* (1925) has been used as the source of tribal names.

When taxonomic terms are used in the discussion of flora and fauna, the Latin name is only given for the first reference. The common name is given thereafter.

In view of the comprehensive listing in the Contents pages, an index seemed to be dispensable.

2

The Cahuilla Physical Environment

INTRODUCTION

The ecosystem of which the Cahuilla were a part is difficult to understand because of its great diversity. Moreover, there is little published literature explaining the habitat and biota of the area. Studies of specific areas and subjects have been published such as Sauer's (1929) examination of the physical features of the Valle de San José and Russell's (1932) accounts of the geography of the San Gorgonio Pass. Some geographic reviews of the area have been published by Aschmann (1959*b;* 1966), and several small manuals and articles have been written describing climate, flora, and fauna.

Aspects of the Cahuilla ecosystem have been selected for examination because of their direct association with the culture. These are: topography, life zones and associations, temperature, wind, water resources, drainage patterns, faulting, drought, and fire. Specific problems or opportunities provided by these variables will be outlined, and some of the strategies by which the Cahuilla adapted to them will be discussed.

TOPOGRAPHY

The area is topographically variable. There are a series of mountain ranges interspersed by passes, canyons, valleys, and the desert floor which create a series of distinctive and separate microniches, the entire area being about 2400 square miles (roughly 44 by 53 miles).

It is difficult to indicate exact boundaries for the territory at this point in Cahuilla history. In general, the areas claimed as boundary indicators today are the summits of the San Bernardino and Chocolate mountain ranges to the north; the area approximate to Borrego Springs to the south; a portion of the Colorado Desert west of the Orocopia Mountains; and the Colorado River to the east; and the San Jacinto Plain near Riverside; and the eastern slopes of the Palomar Mountains to the west.

The most dramatic topographic features are the large and high mountain ranges. Elevations are extremely varied, ranging from peaks of San Jacinto Mountains and San Gorgonio Mountains (10,000–11,000 feet high) to 273 feet below sea level at the Salton Sink. Such extremes in altitudes may occur over a linear distance of less than ten miles in some areas. The whole area developed during the Late Tertiary and Quarternary as a result of folding, faulting, and volcanic action as it lies over a number of fault lines, two of which are the San Andreas and the San Jacinto (Sauer, 1929). This accounts for the irregular and varied topography.

Within and surrounding these mountain ranges are a series of valleys and passes. The broad, flat, high San Gorgonio Pass separates the San Bernardino Mountains from Mount San Jacinto and the Santa Rosa ranges; the Coachella Valley to the east of the Santa Rosa Mountains separates the Santa Rosa Mountains from the Little San Bernardino Mountains to the east. To the west lie a series of valleys and passes, one of which is the Valle de San Jose, a mountain valley with an elevation ranging from 3300 to 4300 feet bordering the Palomar Mountains.

A series of foothills blend the varying topographies with the lower desert regions. Numerous mountain valleys connect with canyons and passes and allow access from the desert to the high mountain areas. From the lower areas of the desert and the pass there are slightly elevated alluvial fans leading into canyons averaging four to sixteen miles in length, and often several miles in width at the mouth. The canyons lead steeply into mountain valleys which are flanked by high mountain scarps. Thus, separate and distinct environmental areas are formed—pie-shaped, broad and sloping at the bottom, narrow but flaring at the top. Characteristic canyons are: Los Coyotes and Rockhouse which connect the Borrego Desert and Cahuilla Valley of the Santa Rosa range; the Martinez and Deep which connect Coachella Valley with the pinyon flats area of the Santa Rosa Mountains; Palm and Andreas which connect the Upper Colorado Desert with the pinyon flats area; Whitewater and the other canyons of the San Gorgonio Pass which connect with the high mountain ranges of the Santa Rosas and the San Bernardinos.

LIFE ZONES AND ASSOCIATIONS

Hall and Grinnell's life-zone indicators (1919:37–44) have been used as a guide in describing four major types of ecological areas available to virtually all the Cahuilla. These are viewed as distinct habitats which are distributed vertically throughout the area. Considerable variations exist in the precise patterns of biota, and the descriptions should be regarded as ideal rather than exact for any particular locality. In reality, plants typical of one zone may occur in another because of one or more of the following factors: cold, warm, or hot air currents may change the plant pattern in an area; streams carrying cold water may cause higher level plants to be at a lower level than is usually expected; evaporation from moist soils and lingering snow banks may depress the temperature in some areas and change the botanical patterns; and rocky slopes and outcroppings tend to be warmer than surrounding areas, thus causing differences in plant formation (Hall and Grinnell, 1919:37–67). These factors frustrate any attempt to construct a neat, consistent overview of Cahuilla biotic resources. For the sake of demonstration, however, the zonal types are offered which convey an ideal and, for the most part, a real picture of what a Cahuilla had before him in the way of biotic resources.

The life zones are: Lower Sonoran, Upper Sonoran, Transition, and Canadian-Hudsonian or Boreal. A characteristic selection of plants, mammals, birds, reptiles, and insects will be presented for each of these zones. Emphasis will be placed on those known to have been important to the social life, belief system, and economy of the Cahuilla.

LOWER SONORAN

Grinnell and Swartz (1908:3) states that the desert region of the Lower Sonoran life zone is that zone which lies below the juniper-pinyon belt, but warns that this indicator must be viewed with caution as there are "tongues of this zone [which] extend into the foothills on either slope, and islands of it [that] occupy hot pockets at somewhat higher elevations" owing to variations in soil, water, wind, and other climatic conditions that are critical for the growth of plants and animals. These same sets of circumstances stand for all the other zone.

Some characteristic plants used by the Cahuilla are: arrowweed (*Pluchea sericea* Nutt.) Cov.; barrel cactus (*Echinocactus acanthodes* Lem.); bladder pod (*Isomeris arborea* Nutt.); cactus (*Echinocactus* Link & Otto); California fan palm (*Washingtonia filifera*

[Lindl.] Wendl.); cat's-claw (*Acacia Greggii* Gray); century plant
(*Agave deserti* Engelm.); chamise (*Adenostoma fasciculatum* H.
& A.); creosote bush (*Larrea tridentata* Sessé & Mociño); desert
ironwood (*Olneya tesota* Gray); desert tea (*Ephedra nevadensis*
Wats.); desert willow (*Chilopsis linearis* Cav.) Sweet; goatnut
(*Simmondsia chinensis* C. K. Schneid); mesquite (*Prosopis glandu-
losa* Torr. var. *Torreyana* [L. Benson] M. C. Jtn.); milkweed
(*Asclepias* sp.); Mohave yucca (*Yucca schidigera* Roezl ex Ortgies);
nolina (*Nolina Parryi* Wats.); ocotillo (*Fuquieria splendens* En-
gelm.); cholla (*Opuntia* Mill.); palo verde (*Cercidium floridum*
Benth.); saltbush (*Atriplex* spp.); sand verbena (*Abronia villosa*
Wats.); screwbean (*Prosopis pubescens* Benth.).

There are several contrastive habitats in this zone due to environmental conditions, and each of the habitats contains particular complexes of plants and animals. For example, the sand-dune
and creosote habitat is dry and contains very little vegetation;
whereas the sand-dune mesquite habitat is often luxuriant; the
creosote palo-verde and cholla palo-verde habitats are found on
the flood plain, sandy washes and small arroyos. It has been estimated that about 60 percent of the land within the Cahuilla area
lies in this zone.

Barrows explains the value of this habitat well in the following
passage:

To the unsophisticated it would seem that the dry and rocky slopes
of the desert's sides, with their curious and repellent plant forms,
could yield nothing possible for food, but in reality the severe competition and struggle with aridity have operated to invest desert plants
with remarkable nutritive elements. The very hoarding of strength
and moisture that goes on in many plants is a promise of hidden
nutrition (1900:54).

In addition to plant food resources, the Lower Sonoran provided more edible varieties of animals than any other zone and
was, therefore, significant to the Cahuilla hunter. The most characteristic of these were: badger (*Taxidea taxus*); chipmunk (*Eutamias* spp.); cottontail (*Sylvilagus audubonni*); seven species of
mice (*Peromyscus* spp. and *Perognathus* spp.); mule deer (*Odocoileus hemionus*); raccoon (*Procyon lotor*); three species of rats
(*Neotoma* spp.); three species of kangaroo rats (*Dipodomys* spp.);
bighorn sheep (*Ovis canadensis*); three species of squirrel (*Citellus*
spp.); and the gray squirrel (*Sciurus grisens*).

Each habitat was particularly attractive to certain fauna. For
example, the sand-dune mesquite habitat was a favorite locale of

the jack rabbit and several species of rodents because they were able to thrive on the abundant seed pods and green leaves as well as enjoy its protective cover. The thick growth of prickly cacti, on the other hand, made the cholla palo-verde habitat less attractive to the jack rabbit, but it was the favorite area of pack rats because of the succulent vegetation and the natural shelter available there. Detailed information concerning these faunal-floral relationships has been presented by Ryan (1968) in which he indicates that there was a wide variety of faunal life available in time and space. For example, he suggests that in Deep Canyon the agave-ocotillo habitat, at the upper end of the Lower Sonoran zone (1500–3500 feet), supported as many species of mammals as any other habitat area as well as many species of mammals characteristic of fauna found in the Upper Sonoran and Transition zones.

UPPER SONORAN

The Upper Sonoran life zone covers an area approximately one to two thousand feet to the five-thousand-foot level. This is known locally as the chaparral and juniper-pinyon zone and includes very important food-producing trees such as the pinyon and the oak. Yet this area (as do all the others) "interdigitates below with the Lower Sonoran and above with the Transition, while islands of it exist in both" (Grinnell and Swartz, 1908:3).

A number of important plants of the Lower Sonoran are to be found here also: cacti, agave, mesquite, nolina, and ocotillo. In addition, the following are characteristic: buckthorn (*Rhamnus* sp.); Christmas berry (*Heteromeles arbutifolia* M. Roem.); cotton-wood (*Populus Fremontii* Wats.); desert apricot (*Prunus Fremontii* Wats.); juniper (*Juniperus californica* Carr.); mahonia (*Berberis* L.); manzanita (*Arcotstaphylos* Adans.); oak (*Quercus* spp.); pep-pergrass (*Lepidium Fremontii* Wats.); pinyon (*Pinus monophylla* Torr. & Frem.); bladder sage (*Salazaria mexicana* Torr.); sage (*Salvia* L.); sugar bush (*Rhus ovata* Wats.); tansy mustard (*Des-curainia pinnata* [Wat.] Britton); yucca (*Yucca Whipplei* Torr.).

Approximately 60 percent of the plants used for food among the Cahuilla occurred in this life zone, a geographic area comprising about 30 percent of the total land available to the Cahuilla. The most important of these were the oak and pinyon trees that sup-plied the staple crops for the long months between harvests.

The value of this zone was increased by the availability of the abundant fauna including mule deer, antelope, and mountain sheep as well as numerous rabbits and other rodents. Several rodents were found in this area that were not characteristic for the Lower Sonoran, such as the pinyon mouse (*Peromyscus truei*), the parasitic mouse (*Peromyscus californicus*), and the dusky-footed wood rat (*Neotoma fuscipes*).

TRANSITION ZONE

The Transition zone is found at the five to seven thousand foot elevations and sometimes higher. It is characterized by cool summers and cold, snowy winters creating temperatures of 55 to 60° F. The precipitation at these altitudes is twenty to thirty inches a year, although more excessive amounts have been recorded (which again points up the contrast of climate, because the rain falls in the mountains whereas a few miles away only scant showers come to the thirsty desert) (Ryan, 1968:13).

Coniferous forests are interspersed with oak groves, and cottonwoods grow along the streams. On the south slopes facing the desert, a chaparral vegetation occurs.

For the Cahuilla the important food plants were the oak, of which *Quercus Kelloggi* was the most notable, elderberry (*Sambucus mexicana* Presl.), service-berry (*Amelanchier pallida* Greene), wild cherry (*Prunus ilicifolia* [Nutt.] Walk.), and manzanita (*Arctostaphylos Adans*). Grasses and annuals that cover much of the lower zones are also present. Of the plant species used, approximately 15 percent were to be found on what was 7 percent of the land.

The importance of the area was enhanced by oak groves and the deer herds, both providing a substantial portion of food. Other animals which were hunted were the gray squirrel, ground squirrel, chipmunk, deer mouse and pinyon mouse, and the pack rat. The presence of bear (*Ursus americanas*) and mountain lion (*Felis concolor*) are mentioned because they were dangerous to the hunter and were competitors for food resources.

CANADIAN-HUDSONIAN ZONE

The Canadian-Hudsonian is at the highest elevations. It has the heaviest precipitation, lowest temperatures, and has very little food resources. Approximately 5 percent of the Cahuilla area is represented by this zone. It was occasionally utilized by hunters in the summer because large game such as mountain sheep and mule deer were sometimes found there, as were some smaller animals such as rabbits, rodents, lizards, and snakes.

SEASONS

Extreme seasonal variations occur in temperature, precipitation, and winds causing dramatic differences in the relative abundance of flora and fauna. The differences between winter and summer temperatures are especially notable, the summers being very hot in the desert areas (sometimes reaching as high as 125° F) and cool in the alpine zone; winters are cold in the desert, where subfreezing conditions sometimes persist for weeks at a time, to the ultracold temperatures at the 10,000 to 11,000 foot level, where the snow lies deep. The canyon areas where most of the settlements were located are usually cooler in the hot periods and warmed in winter owing to wild-flow patterns.

The prevailing winds in the Cahuilla region are from the west, usually cool ocean breezes. In late summer, hot, uncomfortable winds known locally as Santa Anas enter the Cahuilla territory from the southeast. During the day, breezes begin from the heating of the desert floor which causes air to rise resulting in a slow movement of heated air up valleys or sides of mountains. In the evenings, mountain breezes result from the relatively rapid cooling of air on the mountain side. The colder air is heavier and flows downhill. Where this downward moving air is collected in small valleys or canyons, the velocity may be increased resulting in a strong breeze.

The warm and hot winds contribute to the semi-arid nature of the whole region; the dry winds affected food potential and increased the incendiary potential of the plant cover.

Winds of various high velocities were common. They had their greatest momentum in the open passes and deserts where hurricane velocity is common. Sometimes these were accompanied by great sandstorms which were corrosive and blinding. Whirlwinds were frequently seen, especially in summer and autumn, but they were usually small and relatively nondestructive to the countryside. Wind patterns were significant to Cahuilla existence. The social and cultural reactions to these will be discussed later.

WATER RESOURCES AND PROBLEMS

Numerous sources show that fluctuating amounts of rain and snow significantly affected the ecosystem of the Cahuilla. During some years abundant water was distributed in lakes, rivers, streams, flash floods, springs, cienegas, seeps, wells, standing pools, and tinajas; conversely, in other years serious drought conditions prevailed. These variations were accompanied by considerable stress upon the potential productivity of the environment, especially in periods of drought.

There also appear to have been definite cycles of wet and dry periods with droughts occurring now and then. Shepard (1965:9–10) has postulated an overall cycle of 427 years by examining the rings of a tree starting with the 1400s as a point of reckoning. He found that intervening periods of dry cycles ranging from twenty to twenty-six years peaked in the seventieth year of each century (such as 1570, 1670, and 1770 A.D. respectively). Alternately, the wet cycles ranged in time from two to twenty-six years (for example, 1505 to 1533) with peaks showing on an approximate hundred-year basis (1520, 1620, and 1720) which correlated with especially cold years every thirty-five years (for example, 1512, 1548, and 1582–1583). The seriousness of these extremes of climate are shown, in part, in the diaries of the Anza expedition which passed through the Cahuilla area in 1776, during an especially cold year. The Cahuilla were described as being in a very unhealthy and emaciated condition (Bolton, 1930:67–68).

These extremes in climate inhibited the growth of plants and caused decreases in the faunal population. For example, in 1858 and 1865, some Cahuilla villagers were on the verge of starvation because of drought conditions (Evans, 1889). In addition to the annual and seasonal fluctuations in precipitation, there was variation from one area to another. In the summer, for instance, a thunderstorm could cause a flash flood in one canyon, denuding a whole section of land, and thereby destroying much of the potential food supply of a village in that locale for a number of years. Simultaneously, in neighboring canyons just several miles away a different amount of rain would fall and "crops" for those villages were not disturbed. Thus, climatic variations affected one microniche favorably while destroying the food potential in another just a short distance away.

The variation in life zones was also considerable—rain fell heavily in the mountains and tapered off on the edges of the desert. At Indio the average annual rainfall is three and a half inches (Ryan, 1968:13), although less than one inch of rain has been recorded there.

Snow can reach a depth of several feet in the Boreal zones of the high mountain peaks and last for several months. During a winter storm, snow may also fall in the Upper Sonoran and even the Lower Sonoran life zones of the San Gorgonio Pass and Coachella Valley. The primary advantage of snowfall for the Cahuilla was that it provided a delayed run-off of water so that streams, rivers, and springs were fed water in the drier parts of the year from the supply stored in snowbanks in the mountains above. The snow also forced game to leave the higher areas, making them accessible to the Cahuilla in the winter when few fresh plant foods were available.

When rainfall is excessive and torrential, radical changes in the land are immediately visible; devastation left by flash flooding occurred when rain continued for several weeks. Mud slides, landslides, and drastic changes in drainage patterns occurred. The persistent storm conditions were sometimes accompanied by unusually cold temperatures, so the normal growth of plants which were not destroyed by flooding might be delayed. Personal injury and death were other consequences of these floods, and stored foods and goods were frequently washed away. An elderly man reported that a village in Martinez Canyon was destroyed several times. Cahuillas recall villages being destroyed in other canyons (Whitewater, Chino, Tahquitz and Los Coyotes).

Although flash floods caused great damage to the people, they also contributed to the subsistence of the Cahuilla. Flooding periodically enriched and expanded the soil base of the alluvial fans on which many important food plants thrived.

Persistent rainfall of less intensity, according to informants, interrupted much of the village routine. Attempts to dry foods were frustrated, special protective measures were necessary to prevent acorns and other stored foods from mildewing, and hunting and gathering activities were sometimes postponed.

SURFACE WATER

Although permanent springs were common, their distribution on the surface was irregular because of the conditions mentioned above. Occasionally, lakes of unpredicted duration appeared, and rivers, streams, springs, sloughs, and marshy areas were subject to considerable range in water potential throughout a year. Little is known of the precise locations and durations of many of these bodies of water because modern water control measures have radically changed the prehistoric situation. However, some areas, such as Hemet Valley, a few mountain meadows, and portions of the lower desert, are known to have contained small to large bodies of water, which attracted wildlife and enhanced the growth of plants.

The desert lakes, which extended up to sixty miles in length, were formed because of melting snows, torrential rains, and overflows from the Colorado River. From 1840 to 1910 this occurred some fifteen times. These lakes destroyed much of the biota of the desert. However, they contained fish, attracted waterfowl (ducks and geese), and changed vegetation patterns which provided foods for the Cahuilla (Nordland, 1968:15–18). The Salton Sink and the Borrego Desert areas frequently contained shallow bodies of surface water because of the underlying hardpan which slowed the infiltration of the water into the subsoil. This, together with the run-off from the surrounding mountains and intermittent break-through of water from the Colorado River, caused extensive flooding.

Standing water and tinajas, or "coyote wells," were also quite common, and it was not unusual after a rain to find these natural reservoirs containing several gallons of water. They ranged from those found in the open to small ones well hidden under a thicket of bushes. The locations of such reservoirs were memorized by hunters, collectors, and travelers.

Natural artesian wells were common in the Salton trough and Borrego Desert. They occurred where hardpan underlaid surface materials which, in effect, sealed off the area so that water did not infiltrate the subsoil. In such situations the water pressure built up and, where suitable surface materials lay above, the water rose to the surface. Consequently, water was easy to acquire. In other instances, where the water table was ten to thirty feet below the surface, deep walk-in wells were dug in the sand. In addition, the Cahuilla created small lakelets by banking the sand around such a well. This technique is thought to be a major factor in the selection of a village in the desert. The method has been described in detail by Lawton and Bean (1968:18–24, 29) and, in part, accounts for the suggestion that aboriginal agriculture may have been practised among some of the desert Cahuilla. With or without agriculture, however, the wells were significant for survival in the desert and were usually surrounded by large clumps of mesquite and other useful plants whose taproots were able to reach the water table below.

EARTHQUAKES

A survey of earthquake and faulting activity of the Southern California area was made by Robert Heizer in which records for earthquakes are cited. His data suggest that serious faulting occurred every other year. In 1800 and again in 1812 earthquakes were of sufficient intensity at the Mission San Juan Capistrano to cause great cracks in the adobe walls (Heizer, 1941:219–224).

Such earthquakes had considerable effect on the psyche and environment of the Cahuilla. For example, landslides followed an earthquake, tons of debris, huge boulders, and dirt were dislodged. If a flash flood came, additional damage to the area ensued. The locations of springs or other water sources often were changed because of faulting deep within the earth; even the direction and flow of streams and rivers were changed. Occasionally the water table rose or fell after faulting. In recent years informants have reported that more than one-third more water has been needed for irrigation in the Coachella Valley because faulting has altered the geological form of the soil under the surface. In other instances water has been suddenly impounded in new areas giving rise to changes in ecology such as the development of palm oases and new plant associations.

The nature of these changes is recalled dramatically in the memoirs of a Cahuilla, Francisco Patencio:

. . . one time—I was very small, I could not remember yet—there came such earthquakes as had not been known to any of the people. Whole mountains split—some rose up where there had been none before. Other peaks went down, and never came up again. It was a terrible time. The mountains that the people knew well were strange places that they had never seen before.

Then it was that Tahquitz Creek went dry, and only ran water in the winter time, and other streams that ran good water all year around have only been winter streams since. And so the Indians could not raise crops on that mesquite land any more. The climate seemed to change. The Andreas Canyon Creek that only ran in the winter became an all year stream, as it has been since. Before the earthquakes, the only water to be had there in the summer months was from a small spring which ran always in the creek beneath the caves. There were many springs on the mountain sides and on the level land. When the rains came less, they dried out and went away. No one knows where they used to be any more (1945:58).

The effect of faulting in terms of loss of human life or personal injury is difficult to determine. Large structures may have occasionally been damaged, but it was probably a rare occurrence that an individual would be harmed. However, many springs were located at intervals along the fault lines, and these springs

were favorite village sites. Thus, the people were subject to severe
ground movement during the faulting which may account for
the frequent references to earthquakes in Cahuilla oral literature.

Fires were a significant factor in the Cahuilla environment. They
were caused by lightning during thunderstorms, spontaneous
combustion when the humidity was at a very low level, or deliberately or accidentally set by human action. Fire brought functional and dysfunctional results which had great psychological
and physiological impact on the Cahuilla.

When a fire began on a hot, dry, and windy day, the heat it
generated caused an enormous firestorm of such violence, velocity, and extent that vast numbers of game animals were often
trapped and burned to death as they attempted to flee. Moreover,
some animals trapped in the general area were so desiccated by
the searing heat that even without direct contact with the fire
they died on the spot. In such instances thousands of acres of
tinder-dry vegetation were destroyed as well as much of the biota
that existed in the path of the fire. If in the following winter
torrential rains came which coursed down the denuded mountain
slopes and canyons, the configuration of the entire area was
altered. Such phenomena were often seen as visitations of the
supernatural by the Cahuilla.

On the positive side, the ashes remaining on the ground following a fire enriched the soil because of the minerals which
were released. As soon as the rains came to such an area a very
rich growth of seed plants such as chia sprouted, which provided an important food for the people as well as attracting
great numbers of game animals who found both food and protective covering for themselves.

Some Cahuillas have suggested that small fires were deliberately
set to chase game from thick brushy areas into the open where the
hunters captured them with nets and clubbed them to death.
More details will be given in the section on hunting technology.

Fire was also used to protect food resources from predators. In
some years immense grasshopper and locust hordes appeared
which completely stripped an area of its vegetation. The Cahuilla
attempted to control these predations by setting fire to the
area to destroy the hordes, thus providing them with an abundant
source of roasted insects of which they were very fond.

SUMMARY

The habitat within which the Cahuilla operated can be summarized as follows:

1) Local and discrete environmental areas were separated by topographic features. Within each of these a variable range of biotic resources existed which were also subjected to variations in climatic conditions affecting the entire area.

2) Water resources varied significantly from one area to another and from season to season as well as from year to year. The peculiarities of the patterns of rainfall and drainage caused a number of problems concerning human settlement patterns and food potential.

3) Temperature variations have always been extreme and have had their effect on plant and animal resources, which in turn have affected the Cahuilla.

4) Wind variations were extreme, sometimes taking a severe toll on the biotic elements by damaging the food resources.

5) Faulting activity was intense in the Cahuilla area. It caused changes in the topographic features: water drainage, the level of the water table, and the location of springs and streams, which have had other consequences for the Cahuilla biotic community and Cahuilla settlement pattern.

6) Fires were caused by natural phenomena and the action of man. They often disrupted and changed the environment—in both positive and negative ways—and contributed to the consequences of flash flooding.

The Cahuilla environment was more stable and productive than other areas such as the Colorado River area and the Mohave Desert. However, there were environmental factors which contributed to economic stress so that the environment was seen as an unstable, erratic, and unpredictable place in which to live.

3

Plant Environment

INTRODUCTION

Diversity of habitats in the Cahuilla territory produced a floral domain of immense variety, consisting of several thousand species, of which the Cahuilla remember using several hundred for food, manufacture, or medicine. These food plants provided the Cahuilla with a significant portion of their nutritional base. However, in order to extract the potential from these plants, ingenious methods and precise knowledge of plant ecology were necessary. I will describe and review the use of the flora. The most important plant foods will be discussed separately. With each, the common, botanical, and Cahuilla means will be given and the plants will be discussed together with their distribution, time of production, method of collection and preparation, and storage potential. Occasionally, where the knowledge is available, the nutritional data will be given. Ecological situations affecting the plant community also will be reviewed as well as some implications of these foods for social and cultural life. Other plant uses will be provided where they more appropriately belong, in later discussions of property, settlement patterns, social organization, and world view.

PLANT STAPLES

ACORNS

The most extensive food-producing tree for the Cahuilla was the oak. Six varieties were used: black oak (*Quercus Kelloggii* Newb., *quinyily*); coast live oak (*Q. agrifolia* Neé, *wiʔasily*);

canyon oak (*Q. chrysolepis* Liebm., *wiʔat*); scrub oak (*Q. dumosa* Nutt., *pawiš*); and two unidentified varieties which the Cahuilla called *ʔiʔmusily* and *tavasily*. These may be *Q. Engelmannii* Green or *Q. Wislizenii*.

The black oak, coast live oak, and canyon oak were the most productive and palatable of the species. Most commonly found in the Transition and Upper Sonoran zones, they were numerous except on the south-facing slopes. Some trees produced one good crop of acorns in three years; others more than one good crop in two years. Baumhoff (1963:163), for example, estimated that the canyon oak produced up to five hundred pounds per year and probably averaged a hundred and fifty to two hundred pounds per tree; whereas the black oak produced two to three hundred pounds per year per tree. Although rainfall and climatic fluctuation affected the quantity of acorns produced, the Cahuilla were supplied with a large annual food resource which matured during a two-to-three-week period in October or November.

Acorn groves were monitored to time the collection so that rainfall, or animals, birds, and other natural predators would not reduce the harvest. At the right time, the total available labor force of men, women, and children acted together to make a rapid and efficient collection. Processing equipment (mortars and pestles) was heavy and cumbersome to transport over long distances, so these items were kept at the acorn sites. Thus, greater quantities of acorn meal could be transported back to the villages in the burden baskets. Another significant adaptation was the division of labor in the harvest procedure. People worked in family units to exploit the acorns. The men climbed the trees to shake the acorns free, and the women and children collected them. Time permitting, the women also processed some of the acorns to reduce the weight and bulk before they returned to the village. An important concurrent economic activity of the men was the hunting of large and small acorn-foraging game, particularly abundant nearby at this time.

The characteristic growth pattern of oak groves is small groups of trees interspersed by other vegetation, varying in extent from area to area depending upon topographic and water conditions. This growth pattern is mirrored in property rights, political administration, ownership, and ritual, as will be discussed later.

Along with the obvious advantages, the use of acorns for food had some disadvantages. The presence of tannin required the performance of an arduous and time-consuming leaching process in order to make the meal edible. Other disadvantages were the susceptibility to spoilage from mildew if the rains came at the wrong time, and the infestation by insect larva which could suddenly reduce most of a year's harvest to a pile of shells filled with nothing but a webby powder.

Barring these difficulties, the good crops provided a highly nutritious source of food that could be preserved for several years. Properly shelled, crushed, and leached, the meal was the major staple of Cahuillo diet, and was eaten in combination with various other foods and condiments to give a variety of taste pleasures as well as bulk. Baumhoff has said that

California's acorns as a whole are inferior to barley and wheat in protein and carbohydrates but superior in fat and somewhat inferior in terms of total food content. The high fat content, however, makes the acorn superior to most grains in caloric value, 2265 calories per pound . . . compared to 1497 for wheat. . . . Coast live oak (*Q. agrifolia*) is the only species with a markedly high protein content. The black oak (*Q. Kelloggii*) and the coast live oak (*Q. agrifolia*) have high fat content, so they doubtless have high caloric value as well. . . . Generally speaking, the acorn compares favorably with other grains in nutritive values (1963:163).

The oak provided two advantages other than food: an excellent source of firewood, burning slowly and giving out high heat; and from the oak galls the Cahuilla made a medicine used in treating eye infection and open wounds.

MESQUITE AND SCREWBEAN

The second most extensive food-producing trees for the Cahuilla were the mesquites. Two varieties were used: honey mesquite (*Prosopis glandulosa* var. *torreyanna, ?ily*) and screwbean (*P. pubescens* Benth., *qwinyal*).

These plants were abundant in those portions of the alluvial fans and canyons where their roots reached the water table below; this was especially so on the edges of the Colorado Desert and the northern part of the Borrego Desert. They were less abundant in the westerly areas such as the San Jacinto Plain and the western end of the San Gorgonio Pass. Some areas had almost no mesquite or screwbean; in others, they were found occasionally in the cismontane regions.

These valuable plants produced edible blossoms in June and seed pods in July and August. The trees yielded large quantities of food on a dependable basis year after year: "One acre of land well covered with these trees may produce one hundred bushels of beans per year" (Bean and Saubel, 1963:60). And yet, as with the variation in the amount of food produced by the oak groves, the location of the plants and varying climatic conditions seriously affected the time and quantity of the crop. For example, severe winds or a late freeze often destroyed the blossoms, a torrential rain sometimes mildewed the pods, or parasitic growths (for example, desert mistletoe) extracted such vitality from the host plant that the pod yield was greatly reduced.

Easy food acquisition was a significant advantage of these trees. When the trees blossomed or the beans ripened, every available man, woman, and child visited the mesquite thickets. Children crawled among the branches to knock down the pods, men pulled blossoms and knocked ripened pods from the trees, and women and children collected them. In some instances, the clumps were close to the village; in others, the movement of the people meant camping at considerable distances from the village. As with the harvesting of acorns, the men hunted game nearby that also competed for this food resource.

The blossoms were roasted in a stone-lined pit and then squeezed into balls, or sun-dried and placed in water to produce a refreshing beverage. The pods were eaten fresh, or they were mashed in wooden or stone mortars and mixed with water to make a drink. The beans were dried and eaten directly without any preparation, or ground into a flour which was stored in the form of cakes to be consumed as drinks and porridges, or eaten dry. The Cahuilla liked the taste of these blossoms and pods, the honey mesquite being considered the sweeter and more palatable of the two. The dried beans were stored in granaries and emergency supplies stashed in dry caves in the mountains.

From a nutritional standpoint "the honey mesquite compares favorably with barley in which approximately eight percent is crude protein, and fifty-four percent carbohydrate and a little over two percent fat" (Bean and Saubel, 1963:61).

The mesquite also provided valuable construction materials and shelter for the people as well as a habitat attractive to important game animals, especially rabbits.

PINYON

Pinyon trees also furnished the Cahuilla with a significant, nutritious, but erratic food source, the trees yielding heavy crops in some years and only scant ones in others. The species that were used were *Pinus monophylla* Torr. & Frem.; *tevat* and *P. quadrifolia* Parl. ex Sudw.; *tevatwik*.

Large forests were found throughout the Upper Sonoran pin-

yon-juniper habitats. These forests were usually at a considerable
distance from village sites. Because the collecting and processing
of these nuts was very demanding, a considerable labor force was
required for several weeks during August when the cones were
ready for collection. They had to be knocked from the trees
prior to natural exfoliation, because deer, squirrels, other animals
and birds would rapidly eat all the available supply. While the
women and children collected the cones from under the trees,
the men hunted the deer and rodents that abounded in this rich
habitat.

The cones were baked in stone-lined pits, prematurely hasten-
ing exfoliation. At the same time the intense heat of the coals
burned off the abundant pitch on the green cones. The nut meats
were then separated easily from the charred cones. This baking
process converted the nuts into a more digestible product and
aided in their preservation. They were stored in ollas and baskets
until they were ready to be used. The shells were cracked by roll-
ing the nuts gently on a metate with a mano. The meat was removed, ready for eating.

The well-known qualities of the pinyon include: high fat content (60.7 percent), relatively high in carbohydrates (26.2 percent),
fairly high in protein (6.5 percent), ash (2.8 percent). Zigmund
estimated that there are some 3170 calories per pound (1941:273).

The pinyon tree also supplied pitch for adhesive purposes,
needles (used in basket making), and wood (for fires).

CACTI

There were many varieties of edible cactus in the Cahuilla
area. Those remembered as food sources included two species of
Echinocactus and nine species of *Opuntia* Mill.: barrel cactus (*E.
acanthodes* Lem., *kupaš*); nigger heads (*E. polycephalus* Engelm.
& Bigel., *uʔuyiš*); beavertail (*O. basilaris* Engelm. & Bigel., manal);
tuna (*O. magacantha* Salm-Dyck., *navet*); jumping cholla (*O.
Bigelovii* Engelm., *čukal*); pancake pear (*O. chlorotica* Engelm.
& Bigel.); silver cholla (*O. echinocarpa* Engelm. & Bigel.); prickly
pear (*O. occidentalis* Engelm. & Bigel.); pencil cactus (*O. ramosis-
sima* Engelm., *wiyal*); valley cholla (*O. Parryi* Engelm.); buckthorn cholla (*O. acanthocarpa* Engelm. & Bigel., *mutal*); and an
unidentified *Opuntia* called *qexeʔvily*.

The cacti ranged from the Lower Sonoran to the Transition
zone and were available in all the territorial units of the Cahuilla.
They were among the most important plants gathered in early
spring just after the rains. They were most abundant on the allu-

vial fans in the desert and in the Upper Sonoran zones. Cacti were available several months of the year depending upon the local climatic conditions, and produced food in great quantities.

The leaves, stalks, fruit, and seeds of cacti were used for food. They were collected by women and children. The buds or fruits were extracted by two sharp sticks pressed together to avoid the spines, then shaken in net bags to remove the prickles or peeled. Soft, tender leaves were diced, boiled, or dried. Seeds were extracted, ground into a powder for soup or mush, or parched.

The barrel cactus produced the largest quantity of edible fruit. It grew in large colonies or forests on dry, rocky hillsides and on alluvial fans. Each plant produced several pounds of edible buds in the spring months over a period of several weeks. Thus, a single plant could be exploited several times in one season. The barrel cactus was also valuable as an emergency water resource. In areas where the cacti grew in abundance they were owned by specific lineages. An example of this: related lineages which had segmented from one another returned to a particular area they had owned in the past.

AGAVE OR MESCAL

The agave (*Agave deserti* Engelm., ?amul), a particularly striking and nutritious plant, grew in the lower foothills and on the sides of the mountains facing the desert. It was also occasionally found in the San Gorgonio Pass, but rarely in the western Cahuilla area.

In these areas it grew in abundance, available for harvest every year beginning in the spring, and also in midwinter. The plant provided several foods, the most important was the flower bud, usually referred to as the mescal head. These heads were rich and juicy, each weighing fifteen to twenty pounds. The Cahuilla extracted the heads with a long, beveled lever. The leaves or stalks were cut at the same time although they were thought to be less tasty than the heads. The blossoms of mature plants were collected and parboiled. The seeds were extracted from the flowers and ground into flour. Because various parts of the plants were useful, the collecting season stretched through many months of the year.

Preparing the heads and leaves required a considerable amount of labor and time. Groups of men and their sons traveled to the agave areas, camped for several days, excavated baking pits, and proceeded to harvest and prepare the food. The baking process required one to two days, and it transformed an otherwise inedible plant into a rich and preservable food resource. After the heads and leaves were baked they were dried, cut into smaller portions, and sometimes preserved for years.

Although harvesting the agave was an arduous task, it was a very festive time accompanied by hunting of small game and mountain sheep. It is recalled vividly as a time when the men played games, told stories, sang songs, and generally enjoyed themselves while waiting for the agave heads to bake.

The agave also provided the Cahuilla with a sturdy fiber used in manufacturing shoes, nets, and other items. The agave leaf spine was used as a needle for sewing and puncturing purposes (tattooing, puncturing ear lobes and nasal septums).

YUCCA AND NOLINA

Yucca and nolina species grew abundantly throughout the Cahuilla area. In order of importance they were: yucca (*Y. Whipplei* Torr., *panuʔul*); Mohave yucca (*Y. schidigera* Roegl. ex Ortgies., *hunuvat*); nolina (*N. Parryi* Wats., *kukuʔul*).

These plants provided an abundant and nutritious food source for several months of the year as well as fiber. Thousands of yucca plants grew on the hillsides of the Upper Sonoran zone. They were less abundant on the desert flanks of the mountains and in the Lower Sonoran zone. Occasionally, they were found in the Transition zone. The Mohave yucca was most common in the Lower Sonoran and the Upper Sonoran zones facing the desert. Nolina was found primarily in the Upper Sonoran and occasionally in the Transition zone. Yucca and nolina provided two food resources for the Cahuilla: the blossoms and stalks.

The blossoms were collected and parboiled, and the stalks baked in stone-lined pits in order to convert the pithy material into a rich molasseslike food. Depending upon elevation and seasonal variations, they were ready for collection from April until September. These plant foods were collected by the women and children, but sometimes men returned from hunting trips with loads of the blossoms and stalks. The plants were usually fairly close to the village sites.

The Cahuilla sun-dried the blossoms and dried the stalks after they were baked. Both were stored in ollas or baskets for later use.

These plants were very responsive to temperature and rainfall: the quantity, taste, and time when they were available were dependent upon these factors. In general, however, they were an abundant and dependable food resource. Because of the scattered growth pattern of the plant, they were available to anyone within the territorial group after the first-fruit ritual was conducted, which will be described later, and were not subject to the specific ownership associations as were oak and mesquite trees.

Mohave yucca produced an edible pod as well as a blossom. It grew in the lower desert areas in abundance, matured in April and was available through August; but again the time, taste, and quantity varied depending on climate, elevation, and other factors.

The pods were baked to make them edible. The seeds within the pods were extracted, processed into a flour, and the blossoms were made edible after parboiling to release the normally bitter taste. As with the *Yucca Whipplei* and nolina, the parboiling leached out the bitter taste which was present in the flower and facilitated preservation of the blossom by checking enzyme action.

SEED PODS

In addition to mesquite and screwbean some other plants produced edible seed pods which the Cahuilla added to their diet. Among those recalled were: cat's-claw (*Acacia Greggii* Gray, *sičinily*); locoweed (*Astralagus* L. sp., *qašlam*); palo verde (*Cercidium floridum* Benth., *ankičem*); desert willow (*Chilopsis linearis* [Cav.] Sweet., *qaankiš*); and ironwood (*Olneya Tesota* Gray).

These plants ranged from the Lower Sonoran to the Transition zones, usually growing near springs or other wet places. The pods were available for gathering from about May to September. They were collected fresh or dried from the tree, shrub, or ground, and usually pulverized into a flour and made into cakes. Though less tasty than other plants they were valuable to the diet because of their high protein content. They were usually sought when other foods were scarce.

PRUNUS SPECIES

Several species of *Prunus* L. provided significant amounts of food. These were desert apricot (*Prunus eriogyna* Wats., *čawakal*); choke cherry (*P. virginiana* Liver. var. *demissa* [Nutt.] Sarg., *ʔatul*); and holly leaf cherry (*P. ilicifolia* Nutt., *čamiš*).

All these plants produced an edible fruit with a flesh coat and a large pit, which was ground into flour. They were commonly found in scattered groves in well-watered canyons and foothills from the Lower Sonoran to Transition zones. Depending upon local and climatic conditions the fruits were collected in late summer until early fall just before the acorn-gathering season. Because they were a favorite food of birds and browsing animals, it was necessary to gather them as they ripened. Most of the trees

were relatively close to the villages and the fruits were collected
in baskets by women and children, sun-dried, and stored in ollas
or baskets for later use.

OTHER FRUITS AND BERRIES

Numerous fruits and berries of the Cahuilla area added taste,
variety, and nutrition to the Cahuilla diet. The following plants
are remembered as being used whenever available: manzanita
(*Arctostaphylos* Adans. sp., *kelil*); service-berry (*Amelanchier*
Medic. sp.); wild strawberry (*Fragaria vesca* var. *californica* Cham.
& Schlecht., *piklyam*); juniper (*Juniperus californica* Carr., *yuy-
ily*); California holly (*Heteromeles arbutifolia* M. Roem., *aswut*);
boxthorn (*Lycium* L. sp.); mistletoe (*Phoradendron* Nutt. sp.,
čayal); redberry (*Rhamnus crocea* Nutt.); sumac (*Rhus* L. sp.);
blackberry or raspberry (*Rubus* L. sp., *piklyam*); elderberry (*Sambucus* L. sp., *hunqwat*); and currant or gooseberry (*Ribes* L. sp.).

These plants grew in most of the life zones, but they were most
common in the chaparral habitats in the Lower and Upper Sonoran. The Transition zone contained fewer fruits and berries,
but it was in this zone that the succulent elderberries, juniper,
currants, gooseberries, and manzanita berries grew.

Fresh fruits and berries were available to the Cahuilla from
March until November. They were also sun-dried and stored for
future use in soups or mushes. Some of the seeds were also edible
after being leached. They were usually picked by women and
children, but when the crops were unusually large, all able-bodied
persons aided in the collection process to prevent the crop from
being eaten by browsing animals and birds. The largest producers
among these plants were the juniper, currants, elderberries, and
manzanita. Some others, although not producing great quantities,
were considered delicacies and were sought eagerly by the Cahuilla collector.

FAN PALM

Fan palm (*Washingtonia filifera* [Lindl.] Wendl., *maul*) is one of
the most distinctive plants in western North America. It occurs in
abundance throughout the Cahuilla area, especially within the
foothills at the edge of the Colorado and Borrego deserts where
water conditions foster a biotic community of diversity and rich-
ness. Palm, Andreas, and Thousand Palm canyons are typical
locales. The trees grow in groves ranging from two or three to
several hundred; the larger groves are favorite village and camp
sites. The fan palm produces a small, tasty fruit with a very large

stone. The fruit hangs in large clusters, each tree producing perhaps several hundred pounds in a year. The dates, acquired by
detaching the stalk with long, pronged sticks, were eaten fresh or
dried and then stored in ollas for future use.

Insects and parasites inhibited the productivity of trees. To
counter the infestations, the trees were periodically set afire to
kill the predators. This action is thought to have also increased
the productivity of the trees (Lawton and Bean, 1968:6). The
groves usually occur along fault lines, therefore changes in water
patterns occasionally altered the distribution pattern of this
valuable tree.

The sturdy leaves of the tree were used in house and building
construction and for making various tools and utensils such as
ladles and spoons. The fibers were used for wearing apparel
and other purposes.

The biotic community associated with the fan palm made it
an attractive residence area. Numerous plants such as mesquite
and screwbean, and game animals, particularly rabbits and other
rodents, were found near there.

TUBERS AND ROOTS

An important source of starch in the Cahuilla diet came from
tubers and roots. Those recalled as particularly important were:
tule potato (*Sagittaria latifolia* Willd.); wild onion (*Allium* L.
sp., *tepiš*); Mariposa lily (*Calochortus* Pursh. sp.); desert lily (*Hes-
perocallis undulata* Gray.); tule (*Scirpus* L. sp., *paʔul*); cattail
(*Typha latifolia* L.; *kuʔut*).

These plants occurred in most of the life zones, but were especially abundant in the Lower Sonoran zone near or in marshy
areas. Some were available all year round, such as tule potato;
others were available from April until September. Collected by
women using digging sticks to pry the plants from the soil, the
edible parts were eaten fresh, or baked and dried for future use.
The tule potato was abundant at the edges of cienegas in the
Lower and Upper Sonoran areas. The cattail also provided edible
pollen which was collected and mixed into soups and mushes.

GREENS AND SUCCULENTS

The stalks and leaves of many plants were important to the
Cahuilla diet because of the vitamins and minerals they contained and the variations in taste they provided. They are: wild
celery (*Apiastrum angustifolium* Nutt., *paqʔily*); two species of
the milkweed family (*Asclepiadaceae* called *kiyal* and *wičal*); wild

buckwheat (*Eriogonum* Michx. sp., *hulaqal*), tarweed (*Hemizonia fasciculata*); pepper grass (*Lepidium* L. sp.); three species of sage (*Salvia* L. sp., *qasʔily, S. carduacea* Benth., *palnat, S. columbariae* Benth., *pasal*); dandelion (*Taraxacum californicum* M. & J.); pigweed (*Amaranthus Palmeri* Wats.); tansy mustard (*Descurainia pinnata* [Walt.] Britton, *ʔasily*); sea blite or seepweed (*Suaeda* Forsk. sp., *nayal*); and clover (*Trifolium* L. sp.).

These succulent greens were found in all the life zones, but they were most abundant on the edges of springs, streams, or lakes. Villages were always situated near a permanent source of water, therefore several species were available the year round.

They were collected by women and children and were used as pot herbs and regarded as delicacies. These plants were also very sensitive to ecological conditions, especially changes in water supply. They were abundant in burned-over areas, and were important to the diet in the early spring when other stored foods were running low.

OTHER SEEDS

Seed-producing plants added varieties of taste as well as significant food values to the diet. Found in all life zones, but most commonly in the Lower and Upper Sonoran, they were available from early spring until the dead of winter, depending upon elevation and climate, with late summer being the most prolific period.

The most important seed plants were: golden yarrow (*Eriophyllum confertiflorum* Gray); pigweed (*Amaranthus Palmeri* Wats.); Great Basin sagebrush or wormwood (*Artemisia tridentata* Nutt., *wikwat*); milkweed (*Asclepiadaceae, kiyal*); quail bush (*Atriplex lentiformis* [Torr.] Wats., *qasily*); goldfields (*Lasthenia* [Baeria], *aklakul*); downy chest (*Bromus* L. sp.); palo verde (*Cercidium floridum* Benth., *ankičem* or *ʔuʔuwet*); pin cushion (*Chaenactis glabriuscula* DC.); goosefoot (*Chenopodium Fremontii* Wats., *kiʔawet*); wild squash (*Cucurbita foetidissima* HBK., *nexiš*); Mormon or miner's tea (*Ephedra nevadensis* Wats., *tutut*); wild buckwheat (*Eriogonum fasciculatum* A. Nels., *hulaqal*); sunflower (*Helianthus annuus* L. ssp. *lenticularis* [Dougl.] Ckll., *paʔakal*); tarweed (*Hemizonia fasciculata* [DC.] T. & G.); tidy tips (*Layia glandulosa* [Hook.] H. & A.); *Lasthenia glabrata* Lindl., *aklakul;* peppergrass (*Lepidium Fremontii* Gray); boxthorn (*Lycium Andersonii* Gray); desert dandelion (*Malacothrix californica* DC.); devil's claw or unicorn plant (*Proboscidea* Keller in Schmid.); bur clover (*Medicago hispida* Gaertn. [*M. polymorpha* var. *nigra L.*]); blazing star (*Mentzelia gracilenta* T. & G.); panic grass (*Panicum* L. sp., *saŋat*); glasswort (*Salicornia subterminalis* Parish, *huat*); sage seeds (*Salvia* L. sp. especially *S. Columbariae* Benth., chia; *quasʔily*); bullrush tule (*Scirpus* L. sp.; *paʔal, paŋat,* and *kuʔut*); goatnut (*Simmondsia chinensis* [Link], *qawaxal*); tansy mustard (*Descurainia pinnata* [Walt.] *ʔasily*); sea blite or seepweed (*Suaeda* Forsk. sp., *ŋayal*).

Seed gathering was a painstaking and time-consuming operation conducted by women, sometimes aided by children. It required an entire day to collect two quarts of seed. Nonetheless, this was a valuable occupation, because the seeds were very high in protein, oil, and starch, and, after parching, were easily digested.

Chia, for example, was well liked for its nutty taste and high nutritional value. Balls (1965:25) says that "One teaspoonful of chia seed was sufficient to keep an individual going for twenty-four hours on a forced march." In addition, chia had another value: a few teaspoonfuls added to warm, alkaline water from desert water holes is said to neutralize the unpalatable qualities of the water, converting it into a refreshing and nourishing drink (Balls, 1965:25).

Other seeds high in protein were sunflowers, ocotillo, and wild squash. Others, such as juniper, chia, sunflowers, and goosefoot, were very high in starch and oil (Earle and Jones, 1962:221–250).

Seeds were usually parched in trays with small lumps of hot coals. By gently shaking and tossing the contents about, the seeds were toasted. The heat transformed the seed into a more digestible and delicious product that could be stored for unlimited time in ollas or baskets. The seeds were then ground and made into cakes or mixed with other foods as a condiment.

As with other plants, seed plants were very sensitive to differences in environmental conditions such as temperature and rainfall, and natural hazards like fire. The production of grass seeds was very much enhanced by firing techniques, some of which were deliberate.

PLANT BEVERAGES

Many plants, used for making beverages and teas, have already been mentioned. Other important beverage plants were manzanita, ephedra, wild rose and sugar bush. Desert tea (ephedra) was commonly found in the Upper and Lower Sonoran zones and was used as a daily beverage as well as a medicinal drink. It was used frequently as a cathartic and to aid in the relief of indigestion. Another favorite tea was made of the wild rose which contains a very rich source of vitamin C. Other teas were made by brewing ocotillo blossoms and sage seeds.

MUSHROOMS

Over a dozen species of edible mushrooms (*yulal* or *sakapiš*) were found in Southern California (Orr, 1968). They were available throughout the year but especially during wet and warm rainy periods. Mushrooms were most abundant in the Upper Sonoran zones, in oak woodland and chaparral grassland habitats, and were collected in great abundance in the spring and winter, usually by women, but men also gathered them. Mushrooms were sliced into bits and boiled. They were highly nutritious, high in protein, and were a tasty addition to the diet. These were high on the list of delicacies, and were sought eagerly.

AGRICULTURE

Lawton and Bean (1968) have suggested that a marginal agriculture existed among certain Cahuilla groups. Corn, beans, squash, and melons of the types utilized by the neighboring Colorado River tribes were probably the plants raised. Although this would have provided some advantages to a desert-oriented group, it does not seem to have had particular significance for Cahuilla cultural patterns. Some evidence suggests that certain sites were selected because of their potential for agriculture, and that some incipient division of labor specializations were developed because of it.

OTHER PLANT USES

Although the primary concern in this study has been to indicate the nature of the food plant community, some other aspects significant to Cahuilla adaptation are relevant to the discussion. Plants, such as arrowweed, fan palm, and tule, provided the Cahuilla with building materials. Willow, mesquite, and cedar provided heavier construction materials while other plants provided necessary fuels. Some were valuable because they produced an intense heat, burned a long time, and yielded very little ash (for example, oak and mesquite). Other plants were used for cooking or roasting because they imparted flavor to the food.

Medical uses of plants was a major factor in Cahuilla adaptation. Over two hundred of these have been recorded, and their curative efficacy is well documented in pharmacological literature

(Vogel 1970). These plants made it possible for the Cahuilla to cure diseases, decrease infections, and stimulate physical activities through the use of such plants as tobacco and datura (*Datura* sp.).

The subsistence-directed technology was dependent upon the plant community. Rabbit sticks and digging sticks were made from hard woods, and flexible woods were used for making bows and cradles, in building construction, and as basketry materials. Fibrous materials were used for manufacturing capital equipment such as carrying nets, nets for capturing game, articles of clothing, traps and snares, and threads and twines for sewing hides and weaving rabbit-skin blankets.

Plant materials were used also to make household implements such as brushes and eating utensils. Other plants were used for making a soapy lather; still others for concocting poisons used in hunting. Gum resins were often chewed to alleviate hunger when nothing else was available.

NUTRITION AND PLANTS

Vegetable diets are sometimes assumed to be especially low in protein materials. While this seems generally to be the case, the Cahuilla were fortunate because in arid climates plants produce high degrees of protein. Aschmann has suggested from his study of Baja California cultures that:

Throughout the year plant foods alone afforded the gross elements of a fairly balanced diet. Although most plant foods primarily provided carbohydrates, the seeds of leguminous trees and such plants as amaranth have a good protein content. Plant proteins would be available only for about half of the year, but with a little animal protein the human system can accommodate itself to such a seasonal imbalance in diet. The evident attention given the protein-rich plant foods, despite their ripening at about the same time as other more accessible items such as pitahaya fruits and their being considerably harder to gather, supports the thesis that foods of vegetable rather than animal origin constituted the basis of the aboriginal diet (1959a:93).

Other students have made similar statements about nutrition among American Indians. Zigmund (1941:269–271) suggests an adequate supply of nutrients essential for maintaining health was available from the plant communities of the Great Basin and Southern California Indian cultures. He also discovered that a high degree of roughage in the form of cellulose and meticellulose was available in the diet of these groups. Mineral content, Zig-

mund found, may have been higher than in contemporary American diets. A large number of the plants Zigmund studied are of
the same species as those used by the Cahuilla, therefore his remarks seem pertinent. Similarly Yanovsky and Kingsbury (1938),
in studying food plants of North American Indians, found that
they were unable to indicate if there was a significant difference
between the food intake of aboriginal North Americans and
those of modern man. But they found interesting food constituents
including inulin, "a tasteless, white, semicrystalline polysaccha-
ride, closely resembling starch, and found dissolved in the sap
of the roots and rhizomes of many composite and other plants
such as Inula and Helianthus, etc." (*Webster's New International
Dictionary*, 1942:1304). Inulin is usually not a part of the
modern American diet although it was very much present in the
plant foods eaten by Indians.

Among contemporary Cahuilla it is thought that the changes
from aboriginal diet to modern processed foods has been a cause
of sickness and physical debility. The loss of certain foods such as
chia and pinyon has been particularly mourned in this context.

ECOLOGICAL FACTORS

As has been shown above, unseasonable or excessive variations in
heat, cold, and moisture, as well as fire, wind, and parasites each
played a singular or collective role in the quality, quantity, and
the maturity time of food plants. For example, during the spring
of 1968 the weather remained so cold and inclement near the
Morongo Reservation that the maturation of some plants was delayed a full three months. Another example was in 1957 when a
premature heat spell caused an early blossoming of yucca (in February), followed by a freeze in March which destroyed the blossoms. Similarly, late frosts were damaging as they froze the
blossoms and caused a reduced crop not only for that year but
sometimes the next year as well.

Variations in moisture were equally significant. Under normal
conditions rainfall came at a time to foster the growth of the seed
plants. However, premature rainfall, or the lack of it, changed the
maturation schedule of plants. A local observer has described the
situation as follows:

The wild seeds start in the fall after the first rain. Under normal
conditions they will grow madly during the warm days and wait
during the cold ones but . . . should there be no more rain for a

month, many plants will die and those which are left will try to make seed as soon as possible. I have seen the chia three inches high making seed. Of course, this means a shortage of small seeds. The bigger plants and trees fare better but there is still the crop loss and smaller fruiting . . . unless there is a great deal of rain later. This helps the trees but delays the harvest. If the acorns ripen too late and it rains on them, they may mildew and spoil a crop (Edna Badger, personal communication).

Thus, variations in moisture patterns had a serious effect on the quantity, quality, and harvest time of plant foods.

By the same token, flash floods sometimes washed away the plants altogether; or flooding was so extensive that the standing water caused the plants to die.

In addition to climatic changes, competition by herbivorous members of the ecosystem also provided a threat to the normal harvest: grasshoppers, locusts, wasps, caterpillars, rabbits, mice, squirrels, birds, and browsing deer. However, the Cahuilla kept a sharp watch on the maturing plants so that they would be at the right place at the right time in sufficient numbers to gather crops as soon as they were mature. Thus, predations were usually kept to a minimum.

There is little data available indicating how plant diseases affected Cahuilla crops in the aboriginal period, but parasites such as the desert mistletoe (*Phorodendron* Nutt. sp., *čayal*) have at times affected the growth and vitality of mesquite. For example, Evans published a report (1889) which suggests that in 1820 or 1830 a serious food shortage existed among the Cahuilla because these parasitic plants destroyed many mesquite trees in the desert area. Fire and winds affected the environmental potential.

These factors produced an element of unpredictability in the otherwise relatively stable environment. Suddenly, and sometimes disastrously, a small or large area was affected, and, depending upon the severity of the destruction, the Cahuilla were subjected to change. They never knew from season to season, or even from day to day, whether the plant food in their area was going to be available in sufficient quantity or quality for their basic needs. That it was sufficient over the long range in no way relieved the tension caused by immediate needs. How these conditions and their concomitant tensions for the sociocultural system were alleviated by sociocultural mechanisms will be demonstrated in subsequent chapters.

THE TECHNOLOGY OF PLANT FOOD
PROCESSING: A SUMMARY

Techniques for transforming otherwise inedible vegetal materials into palatable, nutritious, and edible products were necessary for the Cahuilla. The most common processing method was grinding. For example, a hard seed is difficult to cook because of the kernel density, but when ground into a powder the starchy substance cooks easily, and becomes digestible. Grinding acorns and dried berries was done in stone mortars with stone or wooden pestles; stone manos were rolled on stone metates to mash softer foods like pinyon nuts; and wooden pestles pounded in wooden mortars were effective for pulverizing soft but fibrous foods like honey mesquite. Flourlike materials were sifted in baskets to segregate the larger particles from the flour, and the larger particles were then reground.

Parching preceded grinding. This process was generally used to alter the chemical nature of the seeds and change their taste. Parching was performed in a basket or pottery tray to which small nodules of hot coals were placed along with the seeds. The tray was then gently shaken and tossed so the coals would toast the seeds, but not burn them. When the proper degree of parching had been accomplished, the seeds in that batch were removed and set aside ready for grinding.

Grinding was a central and daily concern of the housekeeping art of the Cahuilla woman, although men occasionally performed grinding tasks. If a woman performed these tasks efficiently, she was judged a "proper" woman—her ground materials were very fine in quality and free of foreign substances; her acorn meal sweet, bland, and smooth.

Leaching acorn meal was essential because of the bitter taste of the tannin. This arduous and time-consuming process made it possible for the acorn to be used as one of the basic staples of everyday diet. Various other seeds or pits such as those in wild plums also required this process.

Some vegetable foods such as yucca, agave, and tule potatoes were cut into sections and baked in stone-lined ovens or pits to make them edible and palatable. Many foods such as fruits, blossoms, and buds were preserved by sun-drying. This process was enhanced because of the arid climate of the Cahuilla area. However, the dangers of this process were considerable when huge quantities of acorns were spread outdoors. They had to be gathered in great haste if there was an unexpected rain. Drying foods for future use permitted efficient use of food sources. Berries and fruits were dried and reduced in size, allowing the powdered materials to be stored in the form of cakes. As a result, a very large energy source could be contained in a small package. Mesquite flour, for example, was patted into cakes about a foot in diameter and several inches thick before drying in the sun. One of these cakes provided food for a number of people at some later date when the cake was placed in water and boiled into a mush.

Various foods were cooked in baskets with liquid to which intensely hot rocks were added for instantaneous boiling. Dried and fresh seeds, fruits, blossoms, and meats were boiled, usually in pottery containers, thereby enhancing their edibility and digestibility. For many plant foods, a parboiling process was necessary for releasing acidic materials in the food. For example, yucca blossoms, unless parboiled, had a very bitter taste. Boiling also purified nonacidic food that might otherwise prove to be lethal owing to botulism bacteria, and converted dried foods (seeds, fruits, and berries) into edible condiments once more.

Cooking also converts starches into a more digestible form (Jensen, 1953:163). Another significant consequence of boiling, steaming, baking, and roasting is that the nutritional quality of foods is not impaired under ideal conditions; in some instances, the processes improve the foods because uncooked starches have to be especially well masticated for efficient digestion. Jensen (1953: 163) found that thiamin B in carbohydrate-rich materials, such as cereals and vegetables, is stabilized when cooked with meat.

Many foods like berries, fruits, and dates were eaten fresh because they required no processing. Others, like some cacti, required no more than peeling.

All in all, Cahuilla technology was efficient in converting plant materials into a well-balanced diet, one that was both nutritious and varied.

FOOD STORAGE AND CACHING: A SUMMARY

As has been mentioned above, the climate of the Cahuilla area was exceedingly arid, a natural condition advantageous for the storage of food. And, as has been described, foods were dried and then stored for future use in large basket granaries and ollas. Preservation was facilitated by placing perishable foods in storage vessels and hermeticaly sealing with pine pitch, or in beeswax.

The large granaries were built near each household and each *kišʔamnaʔwet* (ceremonial house) and were used for storing enormous quantities of food. A single acorn granary, for instance, might hold several bushels of acorns; a single olla might hold several quarts of seeds, and a handful might produce a meal for several persons. Some clay storage vessels stood as high as four feet and two feet in diameter.

The storing of meat products was much less complicated because of the small quantities involved. Generally, most meat products were immediately consumed, although the large game animals were often stripped, and jerky was made from them by the men. The jerky was kept in a separate shelter near the house of the family, to be used when a dried-meat supplement was needed. It is difficult to assess to what extent this stored meat was in use: daily, or only sporadically.

Generally speaking, the storage activities of each household were sufficiently public so that all were aware of the amount of food being stored. A major amount of this stored food was easily in view of any visitor, and, as will be seen, hoarding or stinginess was a serious breach of normative postulates. Sanction for such activity was usually rapid, sharp, and public. However, other caching activities were admissible.

In addition to the storage of food in the granaries located about the village, families or individuals characteristically kept caches of food secretly hidden from everyone—sometimes in distant and remote places, sometimes buried in ollas under the ground, or placed in small caves. The openings to these small caves were carefully covered with brush to keep their presence unknown to others. Ritual protection was also employed whereby the owner made "spirit sticks" from which he dangled feathers or other magical items so that poachers who discovered the cave would be harmed if they stole the contents of the cache.

A safety mechanism was built into the caching system, however, to compensate for the negative aspects which might be attached to this. General etiquette dictated that a hungry traveler who was able to discover a food cache might partake of the foods. He was, of course, expected to reciprocate by returning goods to that cache at a later date, or in some way to compensate the owner. For this reason small food caches were placed along the trails. Today, Cahuillas frequently recall that while traveling, an olla of seeds was often found, providing them with nourishment for their journey.

It is interesting to speculate the extent to which these caches were secret or were deliberately placed in spots that would be found easily. As will be seen, etiquette dictated a set of reciprocity rules which could not be avoided, so the caching of secret supplies of food and other goods could have provided some release from the frustrations or obligations so prominent in sharing. The secret caching, then, could have acted as a safety mechanism for individual families or persons in times of great food stress.

Not to be overlooked are what might be called "natural caches." The food stores of rodents, squirrels, and birds were raided by Cahuilla in times of dire emergency or when on a journey. Using these supplies of food was a source of considerable amusement for the Cahuilla—as if a trick was being played upon the creature. It was always considered wise and prudent, however, not to remove all the food from the cache.

4

Faunal Environment

INTRODUCTION

Consistent with the diversity of plant communities in the Cahuilla area is a diversity in mammals, birds, amphibians, insects,
reptiles, and fish. Over two hundred terms for Cahuilla fauna
have been collected, suggesting a precise conceptualization of this
aspect of the biotic domain. Many of these species provided food
or raw materials. As with plant communities, a precise knowledge
of faunal ecology and ingenious methods for exploiting it were
necessary.

Large and small game animals will be discussed first, followed
by important birds, reptiles, insects, and fish. Also included will
be comments on carnivores, wild animals, and pets, which were
not normally eaten, but which figured in myths and supernatural
beliefs. The common, Latin, and Cahuilla names will be provided
for each of these when available as well as the distribution,
method of acquisition, preparation, and storage potential.

A review will be given of the technology of the hunt, the ethological knowledge necessary for efficient acquisition, and ecological factors affecting the density and distribution of the fauna.
Where appropriate, sociological data, ritual, and beliefs associated
with the hunting process will be mentioned. However, most aspects of these sociocultural factors will be given in greater detail
in other contexts.

LARGE GAME ANIMALS

Considerable cultural focus centered on large game animals because they were integrally involved in economic, social, and reli-

gious affairs. They were all called *suqatem* (literally "deer"), and were controlled and protected by a single spiritual being, *Pemtexweva.* The principal animals were: mule deer (*Odocoileus hemionus, suqat*); mountain sheep (*Ovus canadensis, paʔat*); and pronghorn, better known by the misnomer antelope (*Antilocarpa americana, tenily*). This game was particularly valued because of the quantity of food provided and the taste. They ranged through most of the life zones, shifting from one to another because of climatic and biotic factors. Because of these distributional patterns, they were available to the Cahuilla hunters throughout the year, and were particularly close to villages in the winter when fresh plant foods were scarce.

Mule deer were usually found in fall, summer, and spring in open forested areas and meadows, and in the winter when they frequented the chaparral-covered slopes and rocky canyons. The mountain meadows provided grasses and shrubs, but when snow blanketed these areas they moved to lower elevations—to the chaparral and canyons—where they could find grasses, green plants, and fruits, as well as protective cover.

Mountain sheep were found in the high desert scrub country and on the rocky canyon scarps, especially in the pinyon-juniper life zone. In colder seasons they moved into the Lower Sonoran areas to feed on the various desert plants.

The Cahuilla hunters found antelope in the lower passes (for example, San Gorgonio), and on the open flood plains, grasslands, and desert areas immediately surrounding the mountain foothills where they lived.

Hunting these large animals was often a dangerous and difficult activity requiring great stamina and skill. It was exclusively the occupation of adult, able-bodied men, who also tended to be specialists in the lore of dealing with supernatural power and adherence to ritual. Hunters spent long hours patiently stalking their prey, chasing it, or hiding in blinds to remain undetected until they were able to maneuver the animals into striking range of their arrows or clubs. It was also necessary to adapt hunting techniques to the specific quarry and to take advantage of its natural curiosity. For the animals, survival necessitated adaptive sensitivity such as keen smell, sharp eyes, acute hearing, and being fleet of foot.

Deer were most frequently hunted by a single man, although two or more sometimes cooperated. They often wore deer headdresses and simulated the actions of the deer to get close to the animal.

Mountain sheep were the most difficult and dangerous to hunt because they lived much of the time on the high, precipitous scarps. When possible, the hunters hid in well-camouflaged blinds at the water hole and shot the animals with their bows and arrows when they came to drink.

The swift-footed antelope ranged in the open plains and grasslands. They were able to run at seventy miles an hour for short distances. Thus, the favored hunting method was a relay chase. When a herd was spotted, up to several dozen men placed themselves in a long line along the canyon floor. They alternately chased and frightened the game into running along a predetermined route in order to box them into a side canyon or to tire them sufficiently so that they could be killed by clubs or shot with arrows. Hunting blinds were often used in conjunction with this method. One of the purposes of running the animals was to exhaust them so they would retire to a dense thicket where they could drink from a spring. Drinking excessive amounts of water temporarily disabled them, and they could be easily killed. The clever hunter used to his advantage the natural curiosity of the animal which contributed to his capture and the antelope's tendency to run in an arclike pattern running alternately away from and toward the hunters.

When slaughtered, animals were partially butchered on the site and carried back to the village. When a single hunter acquired more game than he could carry, he either cached the meat until he could return for it, or signified need for help by means of a smoke signal.

SMALL GAME ANIMALS

The principal small game animals were rodents: rabbits, rats, mice, squirrels, and chipmunks. They were found in all life zones, but were most abundant in species-specific habitats in the Lower and Upper Sonoran zones. Some were available all year round, but others were only seasonally available because of adaptational behavior patterns such as hibernation and estivation.

Methods of acquiring these animals were very different from those used for large animals and varied according to the peculiar characteristics of each type. These animals probably provided the bulk of the meat protein in the Cahuilla diet because of their great numbers and the ease of capture. In addition to food, some of these animals provided valuable skins for making blankets and clothing, and occasionally bone for making tools. For the most part, the bones of these animals were crushed and eaten in soups or mushes.

Three species of rabbit inhabited the area: the blacktailed jack rabbit (*Lepis californicus, suꞋis*); the brush rabbit (*Sylvilagus bachmani*); and the desert cottontail (*S. audubonii, tavut*). They provided the largest amount of animal food, and were the most easily acquired supply of meat.

These rabbits were found in most of the life zones but were especially abundant in the sand-dune mesquite and pinyon-juniper areas during the late summer and fall where they found many green plants for food. Their presence was significant to Cahuilla subsistence during the winter months when very few fresh plant resources were available. Furthermore, this was a time when large groups of people came together for ritual and social purposes, as will be seen in the section devoted to ritual.

Rabbits were taken in a number of ways. They were shot with the bow and arrow, stunned or killed with throwing sticks, captured in nets, snares and traps, or acquired by firing brush in which they lived. They were hunted by individuals as well as by large groups of people. This was almost a daily activity throughout the year for some men and boys. Old men tended to specialize in this activity because the task was not too physically demanding. Using the several techniques a single hunter might capture a dozen or more during the early morning hours.

As will be recounted later in greater detail, when large quantities of game were required or when rabbits were especially prolific, large-scale hunts were organized and directed by leaders. In such instances men, women, and children cooperated in spreading big nets in a large arc into which the rabbits and other small game were chased. Sometimes controlled fires were used to capture small game.

The rabbits were skinned by men and cooked by women. The fur was distributed to the women for making blankets and clothing.

Nearly three dozen prolifically reproducing rodent species were distributed throughout the area, in most life zones during all seasons of the year. Consequently, they provided a steady, dependable supply of food. The most important was the wood rat (*Neotoma fuscipes, N. lepida, N. albugilia;* all called *qawal*), especially common in oak woodland, chaparral, rocky cactus areas, and creosote-bush habitats. Varying in size from five to nine inches in length, they provided a particularly tasty food which the Cahuilla say compared favorably with breast of chicken. Feeding upon seeds, fruits, and green vegetation, they often became a serious threat, exploiting many of the plants necessary for human survival (Booth, 1968:27–31). By reducing rodent numbers through the hunt, the Cahuilla accomplished two adaptive functions—obtaining meat and protecting their plant resources.

The collecting proclivities of some rodents, like wood rats, were also known and exploited. When the need arose, nests of these animals were raided for mesquite beans, acorns, and pinyon nuts which the animals hoarded. This was considered an extra bonus in food collecting, and is an activity recalled with humor by the Cahuilla.

Women prepared these animals by boiling or roasting; sometimes they were skinned, sometimes cooked whole. Occasionally they were covered with wet clay (forming a casing around the animal carcass) and baked.

Several species of squirrel (*Citellus* and *Sciurus; qinqis* and *siqawit*), and chipmunks (*Eutamias* sp.; *ʔulut*) were found in the various life zones, especially in timbered areas, oak woodlands, pinyon-juniper, and in well-vegetated desert sections. Here again, knowledge of squirrel habits and seasonal patterns served the Cahuilla well. Ranging in size from five to seven inches long, squirrels were eagerly sought, providing more meat per animal than small mice, although they were less abundant than mice.

Living in the open and in trees, quick to disappear at the first indication of danger, squirrels and chipmunks were more difficult to capture than mice and rats. They were usually shot or clubbed, although occasionally they were taken in traps and snares.

BIRDS

Many species of birds, both seasonal and permanent residents, were an important part of the Cahuilla diet. Some, like the quail (*Colinus* sp.; *xawit* and *qaxal*), were regularly hunted and provided a significant portion of the diet all year round. Others, such as geese (*Anserinae; siyal*) and ducks (*Anatinae; paatuʔ*), apparently from the Spanish word *pato*), were seasonable and difficult to acquire because they remained in a watery habitat during their migratory stay in the area. Cahuillas have reported that most birds in the area were eaten except for those ritually significant to the Cahuilla, such as the eagle or raven. Birds' eggs also contributed to the diet. Some birds cached nuts and other seeds in trees. These trees were sometimes owned by individual Cahuillas who regularly extracted the stored nuts and seeds.

The favorite and most easily acquired game birds were the mountain and valley quail. Their wide distribution and terrestrial habits made them easy to capture. In the fall, birds in large coveys were easily captured by means of nets, traps, snares, and throwing sticks. Considered a great delicacy, they were cooked by roasting, boiling, or wrapped and baked in wet clay, even though providing only a few morsels of meat per bird.

Birds were a major competitor for fruits, berries, and seeds. They were such competitors that a season's crop could be devoured by flocks of birds if the Cahuilla did not harvest at the proper moment.

REPTILES AND AMPHIBIANS

Numerous snakes (*sewet*), lizards (*mulaq*), and tortoises (*Gopherus agassizi; ayily*) provided food.

Several species of snakes were eaten, a particular favorite being the rattlesnake (*Crotalus* spp.; *mesaxa*). Poisonous snakes were caught by men skilled in handling these snakes. They were prepared for eating by boiling or roasting. Lizards were more commonly sought for food. There were a number of varieties in the area; the large chuckwalla (*Sauromaulus obesus; čaxwal*) was eagerly sought for its sweet and delicate flesh. Lizards, as a rule, were collected by women and children, who pried them out from their hiding places in rocky crags with a hooked stick or captured them in traps where they were clubbed to death. They were also acquired when brush areas were fired. In the early spring, lizards were abundant and provided a source of food during a time of general shortage. The tortoise was captured and roasted, the shell used for making household utensils and rattles.

INSECTS AND WORMS

A large number of insect and worm species inhabited all the life zones, particularly the Lower and Upper Sonoran, and were used for food. Especially important were ants (*Formicidae, ?anet*) and their larvae; grasshoppers (*Acrididae, wi?it*); cricket pupae (*Gryllidae*); cicadas (*Cicadidae, taciqal*); moth larvae (*Lepidoptera*); and worms (*piyatem*).

Ant hills were dug up and the swarming ants pushed into large pits where intensely hot rocks roasted them instantaneously. They were also boiled or parched. Grasshopper swarms were common in the spring, when they massed in great black clouds of flying and crawling creatures which, in some instances, covered a mile or more. The Cahuilla then dug long trenches, filled them with heated rocks and sand, and scooped up and pushed the crawling insects into them. When the grasshopper swarms appeared they voraciously ate every blade of grass, every leaf, every flower, and every seed, leaving nothing but the denuded trunks and branches of trees. Cricket pupae and cicidas also came in large numbers at times, and were eagerly gathered and roasted as they, too, were considered delicacies. After roasting they were dried and stored for future use, to be eaten without further preparation or as a condiment with other foods like acorn mush.

A worm called *piyatem*—possibly an army worm—was a favorite treat of the Cahuilla. The worms appeared at the surface of the ground in abundance after warm spring rains, and were collected in large quantities, prepared by parching, and stored for future use. Their arrival was celebrated by a first-fruit ritual as were those of the other insects and worms mentioned above.

Wild bee larvae and honey were eaten in historic times. The beehives of imported honey bees were tended by the men and were individually owned. The honey was collected regularly, some always being left for the continuation of normal beehive activity.

FISH

Fish (*kiyul*) were occasionally caught in mountain streams and small lakes and obtained by trade from neighboring groups. A remarkable report was given to Florence Shipeck by a coastal Diegueño woman (personal communication), who stated that some Cahuillas had fishing rights in the San Diego bay area, coming annually to acquire seafood for themselves. Similarly, inland Luiseños came to the coastal areas to fish and collect sea food (Macario Calac, personal communication).

Perhaps three or four hundred years ago fish played an important part in the Cahuilla diet. Traditional oral literature describes fishing techniques and the use of fish nets for taking fish from the now desiccated Lake Cahuilla. This information is backed by archaeological finds of fish bones in association with arrowpoints which I have seen in private collections, suggesting that the bow and arrow were used to capture the fish. The famous Cahuilla fish traps remain a problem of archaeological interpretation (Treganza, 1945:285–294).

CARNIVORES

There are approximately a dozen species of carnivores inhabiting the life zones of the Cahuilla that provided significant ecological advantages and disadvantages to them.

Their primary advantage was maintaining the population control of rodents who could seriously deplete the plant resources of an area. Furthermore, the larger carnivores, such as mountain lion (*Felis concolor; tukwet*), bobcat (*Lynx rufus; tukut*), and coyote (*Canis atrans; ʔisily*), fed upon the sick and old grazing animals in the area (deer, antelope, and mountain sheep), and acted as scavengers to eliminate putrifying carrion, a possible source of ptomaine poisoning for other biota. This also benefited the game animals, because healthier and more agile animals were left to produce offspring (Booth, 1968:79). Some of these same animals provided serious disadvantages, competing for the available food supply: animal and vegetable. The bear (*Ursus* spp.; *hunwet*), for example, ate berries, fruits, and the tender shoots, and occasionally attacked humans and other animals.

Large carnivores, such as the bear and mountain lion, limited the activities of humans, occasionally maiming or killing them, so that the hunter was wary and cautious.

Most of these animals were forbidden as food. When eaten, they were reserved for old people or shamans. Only they could dare to eat the flesh, because they had access to supernatural power; they were protected from the animal's harmful attributes stemming from its association with spirit beings. The hunters also feared that in killing these animals they might be killing a transformed *puul* or shaman. In such instances, the animal was adequately warned that he was to be killed and was given opportunity to leave the scene before he could be killed.

Other carnivores, such as the badger (*Taxidea taxus, hunal*), were known to be dangerous because of their aggressive nature and dangerous claws which precluded them from being hunted very often, although they were considered a very palatable game food in contrast to some other carnivores. Other less dangerous carnivores such as the skunk (*Spilogale putoris* and *Mephitis mephitis, teqwel*) and raccoon (*Procyon lotor, ayalal*) were occasionally killed for food. Coyote and fox were hunted to obtain the skins, which were used to make ceremonial objects.

In historic times other large animals such as wild horses, donkeys, and burros became the object of predation by the Cahuilla.

PETS

Animals, birds, and reptiles were kept as pets in Cahuilla households. Evidence of the popularity of these animals is contained in
Cahuilla oral literature which explains their special qualities.
Dogs (*Canis* spp., ?*awal*) were special favorites because they were
thought to communicate with men. In legends they were referred
to as "people" who had been transformed for one purpose or another, usually to deceive or spy on someone, or to test them. Dogs
in this conceptualization had souls like humans and understood
what humans said (Hooper, 1920:361); thus they were capable of
being messengers of the shamans. The Cahuilla creation story
states that *Mukat* appointed the dog to guard the home and protect the people (Hooper, 1920:361). Other pets were also used by
the shamans (*puvalam*) for information.

Dogs were used in hunting, but it is not recalled how they
functioned. They may have served to discover the presence of
game, or aided in the chase. However, their primary adaptive
function was as watchdogs, a significant role in a society needing
warnings of impending dangers from predators (animal or human), and as scavengers, because hygienic techniques were useful
for clearing the refuse from around home sites. In addition, in
rare times of famine conditions, dogs were eaten as food.

Informants have recounted instances where dogs and other pets
were used to train young hunters in the ethological lore of animal
behavior. Children were taught proper attitudes toward animals
by having pets. For example, their animals were treated with care
and respect although there was no undue affection displayed toward them by their owners.

TECHNOLOGY OF THE HUNT

A detailed reconstruction of the technology used for the capture
of game animals and birds is difficult. With the advent of stock
raising and agriculture, hunting activities largely passed out of
use. However, because old people participated in, or heard about
the hunt from their parents and grandparents, the main outlines
can be reconstructed.

The bow and arrow and the throwing stick were the primary
weapons for killing game. Two types of bow were used: the self-
backed and the sinew-backed bow, both types ranging from three

to five feet in length. Bows were usually made of willow, mesquite, or the stalks of palm fronds; arrows were made of cane, sagebrush, and arrowweed, and tipped with stone or wooden points of various sizes and shapes depending on the kind of game sought. Although the bow and arrow were used for killing birds and small game, the weapon was effective when hunting large game animals. The tension of the bow was sufficient to propel an arrow at ten-to-twenty-yard range to kill a deer. The arrow tips were dipped in poisonous concoctions made from the venoms of black widow spiders, rattlesnakes, and fetid meat. Although the animal might not be killed by the penetration of an arrow, it would eventually die or become incapacitated from the poison.

The throwing stick served for killing various types of game, and was especially useful for killing rabbits. Considerable throwing skill was required. The stick was thrown close to the ground to break the legs of the animals or stun them. Rocks were also thrown at game. A good eye and throwing skill were encouraged in every hunter, and when a rabbit stick was not available, appropriate throwing by hand or a sling would be used.

Fire was also used for killing game. Nests were burned and clumps of bushes or trees were set on fire to flush the game out. The game was clubbed, netted, or shot with bows and arrows as it fled from the burning area. Some were asphyxiated or killed in the fire.

Another common method used for extracting small game from their burrows was to make a great deal of noise to frighten them out, or to use a simple stick for prodding them out. A stick was also used to insert into the nest which, if twisted quickly, caught in the fur of the animal, enabling the hunter to extract it.

Several kinds of traps were used: spring pole snares and deadfalls with seed triggers were the most common. Box traps were used in recent years for quail and whatever other small game might be captured. Narrow-necked pots were buried on game trails and near feeding areas and sometimes partially filled with water to drown the animals who fell into them.

Pit traps were also used. A hole two or three feet wide was dug and covered over with a delicately balanced lacery of sticks and grass so that small game would be trapped. The task was not as physically demanding as other kinds of hunting, therefore trapping was usually done by old men and women.

The discussion on the hunting of large game animals reveals the effectiveness of cooperative effort of several or many men who acted for running down the game in relay fashion; no further summary is needed here other than to comment on the use of various methods.

Decoys and game calls were used for disguise of the hunter, enabling him to get close to his prey. Knowledge of calls and skills in imitating game was a highly developed art and is frequently recalled when recounting the special qualities and abilities of an individual hunter.

Nets were, of course, a very significant part of the capital equipment. They were made and owned by the men and placed along game trails for whatever small game or birds would be caught within. The nets were especially productive when used in conjunction with a communal drive. A number of people acted together to drive the animals into the nets.

Flares were used in night hunting to attract birds, and hunting blinds were constructed of rocks or brush, behind which the hunter could conceal himself until the game approached.

All in all, the Cahuilla male was a very skillful hunter who used his intelligence and knowledge of the habits of animals to acquire what he needed for food.

MEAT PROCESSING AND CONSUMPTION

Virtually every part of the game animal was utilized for food, or fashioned into tools and clothing or other useful articles.

Butchering and skinning were done by men, and the cooking by women, except on certain ritual occasions or while the men were on hunting or trading expeditions.

All the meat of animals was used; the meat was roasted, boiled, or cut into strips to be dried as jerky. The jerky was either chewed directly or simply recooked in water to soften. Usually game was skinned before cooking, but sometimes not, because the fur and skin, acting as a protection against the heat of the coals, enabled the cooked meat to be lifted directly from the charred skin and eaten. Thick, soft clay was frequently molded around the carcasses of small animals, fur, skin, and all, and the packet put directly into the coals. After roasting in the fire, the clay container was broken open and the meat neatly removed. Marrow was acquired by cracking the bones; the bones were crushed and ground into a powder which was mixed with other foods; the blood was either drunk fresh or cooked and stored in a leather pouch or in sections of gut.

Bones were used for making tools, hides were tanned. Some

rawhides were cut into strips (for example, rabbit skins) and wound with twine to make blankets. Hides were used for making clothing, ritual regalia, and quivers for arrows. A special meat-processing technique was used in preparing meat for old people. A multiridged metate was used to grind the meat, making it easily swallowed and digested.

5

Settlement Pattern

INTRODUCTION

An analysis of Cahuilla distributions will further indicate the relationship of the Cahuilla to their environment. First, a discussion of the social environment (the neighbors) of the Cahuilla will place them in social space. Second, a discussion of the sib territory, village locations and their relocations over time will indicate other relationships between spatial distributions and environment. An estimate of population density and factors responsible for population equilibrium will further place the Cahuilla in perspective as part of an ecosystem.

SOCIAL ENVIRONMENT

The Cahuilla were located in the geographic center of Southern California (see map on page oo). This area, thus situated, was bisected by the major trade route, the Coco-Maricopa Trail; and at the periphery of two others, the Santa Fe Trail which went from what is now the city of Needles through the Mohave Desert and the Cajon Pass; and the Yuman Trail, leading from the city of Yuma and crossing the Borrego Desert to San Diego. This advantageous location gave the Cahuilla access to resource materials through trade, intermarriage, or ritual which otherwise might not have been available to them. Examples of trade items were shell beads and asphaltum from the coast, pottery and agricultural products from the east.

Geographic features separated the Cahuilla from most of their neighbors: the Colorado Desert to the southeast separated them from the Yuma, Halchidoma, and Kamia; and hills and mountain

68

country separated them to the north and south from the Serrano, Chemehuevi, Diegueño, and Luiseño. No distinct topographic features separated the Cahuilla from their western neighbors, the Gabrilieno. The Cahuilla to a lesser or greater extent interacted with all these groups through intermarriage, trade, ritual, and war. With the Chemehuevi, Serrano, Luiseño, and Gabrielino, the Cahuilla shared the Shoshonean tradition, and it is this group Kroeber referred to as the "Shoshonean wedge" (1925:578–580).

Taken as a group, the Serrano, Diegueño, and Luiseño were the ethnic peoples with whom the Cahuilla interacted most intensively. These groups shared a similar ecological base, subsistence system, social and political structure, and belief system. It was with these groups that they exchanged the greatest number of foods and goods, and with whom they were most frequently in competition for similar resources.

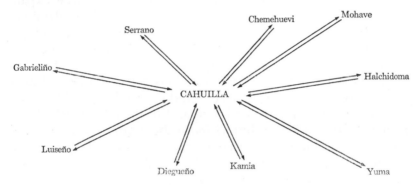

Figure 2. Schematic Diagram Showing Intertribal Relationships with the Cahuilla.

The Chemehuevi, although a part of the Shoshonean tradition, were both geographically distant and culturally different because of the more arid desert conditions in which they lived; thus, Cahuilla interaction with them was less than with other groups. The Cahuilla did intermarry with them and exchanged goods, but their role as an intermediary between the Cahuilla and the Mohave was probably more significant. There was little of advantage to the Cahuilla in the Chemehuevi territory; however, it is possible that agricultural technology or products and such things as pottery and other trade goods reached the Cahuilla by means of Chemehuevi intermediaries. This will be discussed at further length in the section on economic relations.

Another distant, desert-oriented group was the Kamia whom

the Cahuilla occasionally visited, but their relationship was generally felt to be hostile (Gifford, 1918:9; Forbes, 1965:80). They possibly received some agricultural technology or goods from the Kamia.

The Gabrielino, who lived on the Pacific Coast, were the most powerful of the Shoshonean groups and were probably very influential in the diffusion of ideas to inland peoples (Kroeber, 1925: 22). They are frequently mentioned in Cahuilla oral literature. The Cahuilla visited the Gabrielino often, bringing foodstuffs and natural resources, such as obsidian and salt, to exchange for shell beads and asphaltum. Intermarriage and ritual reciprocity between these two groups are recorded. The powerful military competency of the Gabrielino undoubtedly limited territorial expansion of the Cahuilla because their easternmost villages were adjacent to the Cahuilla area.

The Colorado River peoples also limited the Cahuilla expansion eastward, although the dry desert conditions were probably as much a deterrent as its occupation. It was with the Halchidoma and the Gabrielino that the Cahuilla formed an economic military alliance which stretched from the area that is now Los Angeles to the Gila River in Arizona. Consequently, the Cahuilla had access to a very broad ecological and cultural zone. The other Yuman tribes, the Mohave and Yuma, did not have much direct contact with the Cahuilla, but visits to these groups are recorded (Garces, 1965:45; and Spier, 1933:9, 42, 172, 333). Their relations were alternately hostile and friendly. Apparently the Cahuilla were generally hostile to the Yuma because there are several recorded instances of attempted attacks on Yuma settlements, but they did receive some agricultural products in trade, and apparently there were occasional marriages between members of the two groups.

The Mohave to the north seemed to have had little direct contact with the Cahuilla although Mohave oral literature mentions specific topographic features in the Cahuilla area. Also Cahuilla pottery designs bear a marked similarity to those made by the Mohave.

SIB AREAS

The 2400-square-mile territory occupied by the Cahuilla was clearly demarcated from the areas occupied by neighboring groups. Within this realm, the land was divided disproportionately into ten or twelve distant geographical areas, each area claimed in perpetuity by a corporate group—the sib.

Villages within each sib area were occupied year-round, individuals or groups leaving only when necessary for hunting, gathering, visiting, or trading activities. The most extensive leave-taking was associated with harvesting or collecting of basic food staples such as acorn, mesquite, or pinyon. At these times perhaps one-half or two-thirds of the population moved to the collecting area and camped from one to several weeks. Some exceptions occurred when food resources were very close to the village, requiring only an absence of a day or more. This varied when a village group moved to another locale for a season in order to escape extreme temperatures. In the Palm Springs area one lineage is said to have occupied Palm Canyon in the winter and Chino Canyon in the summer because it was more comfortable to live there during the searing heat of the summer months.

It was sometimes necessary to relocate a village because of flash floods (which, on occasion, wiped out whole villages), fires, faulting, epidemics, and interlineage feuds. On such occasions, the village was founded on a site within the boundaries of the sib of which it was a part. Occasionally, though, villages were moved into completely foreign areas which could result in armed conflict.

When a village was moved to a new location, the people continued to claim ownership and exploit the biotic resources of their former land for a considerable time. This claim provided a guaranteed food resource for the village while it was adjusting to a new econiche, making the shift less stressful. When the new location was occupied for an extended time the previous area might be taken over by a new group.

The arrangement of the buildings within a village area was determined by ecological factors and a desire for privacy, but there seemed to be no standardized arrangement. When a village was located along a stream, the buildings were generally extended along the sides of both banks. An example of this arrangement occurred in Palm and Andreas canyons. Where several springs were located within a canyon, individual or extended family households were scattered at some distance from one another but in clusters near to the spring. A third arrangement was adopted in the desert areas where houses and other buildings were grouped around a spring in a two-to-three-square-mile area, the houses some thirty to sixty feet apart. A lineage of perhaps twenty-five to fifty houses might be scattered over a three-to-five-mile area.

From Cahuillas and the writings of Kroeber (1908 and 1925), Strong (1929), James (1960), and Barrows (1900), it is possible to get a fairly clear idea of the ethnographic details of Cahuilla structures built for living quarters, community ceremonies, or sweat baths.

In some instances caves were used for living quarters with brush shelters added in front to make the area more commodious. Calistro Tortes of Santa Rosa reported that the mountain Cahuilla frequently made houses from slabs of incense cedar bark, which could withstand hard winters, and could be reoccupied summer after summer during hunting and gathering periods.

Houses in desert regions varied in size and shape depending upon the family's needs; most were dome-shaped, although some were rectangular. Some were large (fifteen or twenty feet in length and perhaps as wide); others might be described as small brush shelters. The roofs were supported by stout, upright, forked posts well set in the earth, and the walls and steeply-pitched or dome-shaped roofs thatched with whatever material was available—palm fronds, arrowweed, willow withes, tules, or other pliant shrub material. Some were wattled, plastered with adobe mud, or banked with sand. Kroeber stated (1908:64) that the Cahuilla house was distinctively an airy brush house. A hole or holes were left open at the roof peak for smoke to escape. Furthermore, most living complexes were a cluster of two or three houses interconnected by ramadas or thatched arbors and wind breaks, which sheltered the people from the intense summer sun and winds while they worked on domestic chores.

Barrows describes the inside of the houses this way:

At one side of the door within lies the woman's broad metate and her mortar for crushing seeds, both kept covered with a mat or cloth. At the other side of the door stands the brown tinaja or water jar . . . brought full each morning from the spring. In the center of the floor is the hearth with its few blackened cooking pots; perhaps a beautifully woven baby hammock swings from the ceiling, and in one corner are the saddle and reata of the man. Bunks of poles are sometimes built against the wall, but in the more primitive homes the usual bed is simply an untanned rawhide and a blanket spread on the floor. Supplies of food are kept in earthen ollas or beautiful grass baskets, and pieces of jerked meat and bundles of herbs, together with innumerable household articles, are tucked into the sides of the thatching. There is little to become disarranged, and the interior of a jacal is usually tidy and clean. In the summer the furniture is moved into the patio (1900:40).

The largest structure in a village, the ceremonial house, was usually centrally situated and near a permanent source of water.

The lineage leader, or *net,* made this his home to be on hand to protect the ceremonial bundle and to supervise the various activities which occurred daily: political meetings, curing rituals, and recreation. These dome-shaped structures were as large as fifty feet in diameter and constructed of the same materials and in the same manner as other houses. The interior was divided into sections: one was the sacred sanctuary where the ritually significant *maiswat* (ceremonial bundle) was kept; another area was devoted to the dance floor and seating room for the congregation. Attached to the house was a cooking area as well as an outdoor, fenced-in dance floor directly in front of the building.

Each village also had its own sweathouse, which was situated next to a stream or pond. It was used, for the most part, by adult men for sweating, as well as for a men's club. Here community opinions were formed and decisions made.

Clustered about the individual homes and the ceremonial house were granaries where various seeds and foodstuffs were stored, such as acorns and mesquite. Each of these contained several bushels of food after the harvest season. They were typically made of arrowweed or willow withes and sealed with mud. They were placed on platforms high above the ground, on the tops of houses, or on the tops of boulders, beyond the reach of rodents and other predators. The lids were held in place with rocks or large stone slabs.

The buildings in the village were interconnected by pathways, clearly visible in village sites even today. In addition, each of the distinctive topographic features within a village area were given special names. For example, over a hundred such names have been collected for the Morongo Reservation. Another significant feature of many villages was water wells varying in size from minor depressions to walk-in-wells some thirty feet deep, which had been dug into the sand. In villages situated along streams, water was often diverted into trenches so that it was more accessible for household use, and, occasionally, for agricultural purposes.

VILLAGE LOCATIONS

Villages were situated in areas which took maximum advantage of basic resources: climate, water, food, and materials. In the Upper Sonoran life zone they were situated in well-watered canyons or on alluvial fans near streams or springs. These sites were also areas where plant foods and animals were available within a relatively short distance of the village. It has been estimated that

80 percent of the edible plant foods were within a two-to-five-mile radius of most villages. In the eastern desert region a slightly different pattern occurred. Here the villages were located at the lower end of alluvial fans where a sufficiently high water table enabled the Cahuilla to dig shallow wells to reach a dependable water supply and also to be near large clumps of mesquite.

The judicious choice of village sites was also important for protection from environmental exigencies such as flash floods and strong prevailing winds. Villages were located, wherever possible, away from flood channels and out of the path of strong, prevailing winds. Also, there was a need for protection from hostile neighbors. The canyon locations provided natural defense because narrow defiles at the heads of canyons could be guarded fairly easily against sudden attack, and precipitous walls were good barriers against mass invasion.

Once established, these villages were considered as permanent by the Cahuilla, the sites being the exclusive property of the specific lineages occupying them. Once a space was occupied it belonged to an identifiable sib and ranged from seventy square miles to over six hundred square miles in area. Characteristically, they were arranged in an uneven wedge shape, each including several life zones and providing access to the biotic potential of these zones. Geographic features such as mountain ranges and sparse desert areas provided natural boundaries for these groups. Further, each of these sibs was divided into smaller corporate groups or lineages, each occupying its own village site. It is estimated there were some forty-eight to eighty of these villages. Most villages were located in the Upper Sonoran zone or on the alluvial fans in the Lower Sonoran zone at varying distances from one another, depending upon the availability of water within the particular territory. In the desert areas near the foothills of the Santa Rosa mountains these lineage villages were sometimes only a half-mile from one another, whereas in other areas they were situated several miles apart. The average distance was two to three miles. Each of these discrete units had access not only to the biotic resources immediately adjacent to their village but also to specific gathering areas within the larger sib territory. Specific camp sites in gathering areas were claimed by lineages and were visited periodically by the same families, so the settlement situation of an acorn grove or pinyon forest tended to parallel that of the village, with each family being separated from other families to a greater or lesser extent.

Villages within sib territories were connected by a complicated but well-defined trail complex making movement from village to village relatively easy; these trails also connected the villages to gathering and hunting areas. There was an intricate system of trail complexes interlacing the entire Cahuilla area. The trails were carefully maintained by clearing away brush and rocks, and were assigned different functions. There were hunting trails in contrast to visiting trails, trails for trade to other sib and tribal people, and trails for the exclusive use of people within a particular lineage. Furthermore, it was essential for everyone to know not only the differences between the trails, but also all the identifying trail markers in order not to trespass onto land belonging to other groups.

Population movements within the sib territory beyond the village areas were situational, usually involving only a small number of people within a given time. Collecting food plants required small groups of people to move throughout the area periodically on overnight trips, whereas game hunting required groups of men to go on trips which often lasted several days. The gathering of plant foods, such as pinyon, acorn, and mesquite, required as many as half the village population moving to the area to camp for weeks at a time. Many times during the year individual families visited other villages within the sib territory to discharge their affinal obligations, and political and ritual leaders went to other villages to attend political and ritual affairs. These visits, such as the expeditions to Catalina Island and the Gila River in Arizona, crossed tribal boundaries.

Throughout the sib territory there were numerous sites which, because of the presence of water or natural shelter, were used as overnight camping areas. Each of these places was given a name, and, like the trails, their precise locations were well memorized.

In addition to various sites characteristically used by the sib members, others were considered private, and restricted to specific individuals because of ritual or sacred connotations. Such areas, frequently marked by petroglyphs and pictographs, were places known to be dangerous because of the presence of powerful beings. Shamans and other ritual leaders frequently had sites of this kind for their own exclusive use, where they carried on esoteric activities.

POPULATION

Epidemics at the time of contact decimated the Cahuilla people very rapidly. Population estimates are also complicated because few mission records of births, baptisms, and deaths provide reliable figures. I have used lineage counts, inferences from historic records, suggestions derived from the rather sparse archaeological records, and data collected on neighboring groups, as well as other California Indian populations, to estimate demographic variables.

A conservative estimate of the aboriginal Cahuilla population is 2500 (Kroeber, 1925:692). Hicks (1961) suggested the Cahuilla population at 3600, basing this figure on an estimate of 48 lineages comprising an average of 75 people per lineage. If one adds this count to the estimates for the Cupeno, who have been included as Cahuilla peoples, a population total of some 3900 people is possible.

There is other evidence to support an even higher population. There were probably more than 48 Cahuilla lineages, the number 48 being based on evidence provided by Strong (1929: *passim*) whose informants recalled lineages existing around 1875. And yet, by 1875, European-introduced diseases had reduced the Cahuilla population to a fraction of its former numbers (Beattie, 1939).

Taking all the varying sources together, it is probable there were as many as 80 lineages prior to contact. If Hicks' estimate of an average of 75 people per lineage is used, then the figure could have been as high as 6000. However, other evidence suggests villages may have had more than 75 people per village.

Another area supporting evidence for larger numbers comes from government census figures of Indian villages in the 1850s in which several villages were said to have numbered from 150 to 300 persons (Harvey, 1967:190). Although these large concentrations could be due to resettlement into central areas because of historic factors, the evidence is consistent with other reports of Cahuilla villages about this time. Caballeria, for instance, has suggested that 200 persons per village was typical (1902:46). Recent estimates of neighboring tribes, the Luiseño and the Diegueño, whose ecologies were somewhat similar to that of the Cahuilla area, are also in line with the above estimates. White (1963:104) has reported that among the inland Luiseño groups, a population of 200 per village was felt to be a reasonable figure. Florence Shipek surveyed Spanish accounts of the coastal and inland Diegueño and found that a similar figure is representative of that area. Taken together with other studies of California Indian populations (Cook, 1955), this suggests that Kroeber's counts of several California Indian groups should be doubled.

The most recent estimate of Cahuilla population in historic

times, as given by Harvey (1967:191), cites 2500 to 3000 in the early 1850s. Harvey goes on to say that his figures are more conservative than those made by observers at the time. Thus, in 1850 the Cahuilla population was very probably equal to or more than the totals given by Kroeber for precontact times. Cahuillas were already well acquainted with Spanish and Mexican cultures, were working in towns and on ranchos, and had been exposed to European diseases with regularity for several generations; therefore, it is extremely unlikely that these 1850 figures reflect their original numbers.

Many sites rich in archaeological residue suggest intense occupation for long periods of time, yet have no lineage name attached to them; this further supports an increased population figure. There are several canyon areas within the stated boundaries of the Cahuilla that meet these criteria but are in no way accounted for in the historic records. Furthermore, there are numerous archaeological sites on the northern part of what was Lake Cahuilla several hundred years ago which, because of the lacustrine ecology, could have supported very large populations. Such data support the thesis that many more than 2500 people occupied the Cahuilla area.

Finally, given these various data, the extrapolations necessary for coming to a conclusion about the original population must be deferred until more evidence is available. Ten thousand people might possibly have occupied this area at a time when more lacustrine conditions prevailed. I suggest, however, that the figures of 5000 to 6000 are easily validated. This speculation means that the Cahuilla maintained a man-land ratio of two-plus people per square mile. However, if the areas of use were to be included, this would be a much higher figure because a large amount of the square mileage in the high mountains and the desiccated desert regions was of little use for food exploitation.

FACTORS CONTRIBUTING TO
POPULATION VARIATION

To flourish, a population must remain in balance with ecological conditions. In human populations this equilibrium is usually maintained by institutional means. Some significant demographic factors were birthrate, famine, malnutrition, disease, and physical trauma. Institutional controls were warfare, birth control methods, medicinal curing and ritual.

Bartholomew and Birdsell (1953:474–478) suggest that most hunting and gathering societies utilize about 30 percent of their potential, and a starvation period once a generation is sufficient to maintain demographic equilibrium. Although there is little evidence of protracted famine periods among the Cahuilla, reports of extreme droughts, severe periods of cold weather, and other natural catastrophes mentioned previously are consistent with Bartholomew and Birdsell's estimates, and it is likely these acted to hold down population densities at a level sufficient to adjust to minor fluctuations in food potential. In these times, young children, older people, and the injured or sick would suffer a lowering in their resistence to these harsh conditions, and there was undoubtedly a concomitant increase in mortality.

Little factual information is available concerning disease as a population control mechanism, and it may not have been significant. Dunn (1968:225–226) suggests contagious diseases are not, as a rule, a prime factor in population control in hunting and gathering societies because the groups tend to be small and contacts with other peoples limited. Moreover, Dunn states that dwellings are both rudimentary and temporary and that the dietary range is usually sufficiently great to provide the necessary vitamins, minerals, and proteins for health. However, in the Cahuilla instance there were frequent visiting patterns with neighboring populations, so contagion could very likely spread widely and quickly, had it occurred. The deliberate burning of houses and personal property after the death of an individual, as well as the healthy diet, may have tempered the effects of contagion.

There is little available evidence concerning disease among the Cahuilla. What is presented here comes from an analysis of curing practices and oral literature. Diseases frequently mentioned by informants are bronchial infections, gastrointestinal disorders, tuberculosis, hepatitis, infections in wounds and sores, blood poisoning, rheumatism, and arthritis. Trichinae and tularemia may also have caused health problems because of ingestion of poorly cooked meats or by handling game that had been infected. However, the Cahuilla have traditionally cooked their meats well, and we have no data concerning tularemia so these may not have been significant. Spoiled food, polluted water, or the ingestion of parasites may have been a significant factor in the death of infants, but again data is lacking to support this contention. Cahuilla mortality rates may possibly have been caused by the presence of genetically determined diabetes, as present-day populations indicate a high rate of diabetics among the people; the complications associated with this malady, such as infant mortality, blindness, and gangrene, may have been important factors in the past.

Dunn (1968:224) states that "Accidents constitute a major cause of death in hunting and gathering societies." But again there is no specific data available. However, considering the diverse terrain and constant activity of the Cahuilla hunter-gatherer, it is easy to assume that accidental and traumatic death was a frequent occurrence. Complications arising from serious accidents, such as falls, broken limbs, and severe wounds, could have been responsible for many deaths. Deaths due to exposure or to natural catastrophes are remembered by the Cahuilla.

The most frequently mentioned causes of traumatic death were attacks by bear, mountain lions, bites from poisonous snakes, and insects such as black widow spiders and scorpions. A less frequent cause of death was warfare or interpersonal conflict. The institution of warfare is to be discussed later, so it is sufficient to say here that there are numerous accounts of entire populations of villages being killed in some of the battles, and these disasters are frequently recalled in the oral literature. Most instances of intervillage conflict appear to have killed or maimed only a few individuals. Interpersonal feuding which resulted in murder and assassination are also mentioned with some frequency.

Population density was also affected by customs associated with procreation and childbirth. The Cahuilla were consciously aware of problems imposed by having too many children too close together, because nursing was imperative in their way of life for nurturing babies as there was not much food which was digested easily by the newborn. Although mothers or other persons caring for infants in aboriginal times sometimes premasticated foods to feed infants, breastfeeding of an infant was still necessary. Most babies were nursed for several years. Some instances are recorded of children still nursing when they were seven years old.

These factors, together with the rigors of supporting a large family in the hunting-gathering economy, encouraged the deliberate spacing of births. Thus, sexual restraints were maintained by a rule that sexual activity should be curtailed while a wife was nursing her baby. This was supported by a belief that sexual activity would be harmful to the mother's milk, decreasing its nutritional quality.

Infanticide was not condemned among the Cahuilla, but instances of private and individually determined infanticide by suffocation are recalled, and this was made possible because the mother usually bore the child in private without assistance. A more frequent cause of infant mortality when children were born too close together was that the second child might, because of in-attention and inadequate nursing, become sick and die. It is said that the first child received the dominant attention in such an instance.

Abortion, miscarriage, and stillbirths also controlled population density. Abortion was sometimes induced by drinking a herbal concoction or by strenuous physical activity. Accidental miscar-riage, miscarriage due to malnutrition, or other factors probably occurred with considerable frequency in aboriginal times; al-though here again there is no data on which to rely, except that during the past several generations there have been a large num-ber of miscarriages. Whether this is representative of the aborig-inal times or due to changes in diet or to other reasons is not known.

Cahuillas recall that birth contraceptions were induced in former days by chemical means, as certain chemicals and other substances alter the ovulation process; this should be considered as a possibility.

Factors controlling population density were also adaptive in contributing to the survival of robust individuals. Cahuilla ro-bustness has been observed by many, Barrows (1900:81) being but one. There may have been a disproportionate contribution to the gene pool coming from persons successful in the hunt. These men were able to support more wives and were, therefore, able to maintain a better nutritional balance. They, therefore, increased the survival of their children as contrasted with those of less skilled, less physically robust members of the community. This process has been suggested in other contexts by White (1963:160) with the neighboring Luiseño and by Laughlin when speaking of skilled hunters in general.

As a rule they appear to be well informed, to have better memories, more equipment or material goods, more wives including access to women who may not formally be their wives, to be above average in physical constitution, and—directly as a consequence of their superior hunting abilities—to have a better food supply than those less well endowed. A multitude of consequences follow. The wife, or wives, of a headman are better fed and more likely to carry a pregnancy to full term, and any infants are likely to be better fed and therefore more likely to survive to reproductive age than those infants that are less well fed (1968:317).

PERSONAL HYGIENE AND THE
CONTROL OF DISEASE

Factors of personal hygiene which were relevant to health were focal points in the Creation myth itself. For example, when *Menil* (moon maiden) left the earth, she instructed the people to bathe every day: "In the evening you will see me in the west, then you must say ha! ha! ha! ha! and run to the water to bathe. Remember this always" (Strong, 1929:138).

In a similar fashion the proper disposition of fecal matter was directed by the implicit warning that it was the acquisition and dispersal of Mukat's fecal matter which resulted in his death. Defecation and urination were done privately and discretely. Fecal matter was buried because of the possibility of ill use for sympathetic, magical purposes.

Bodily cleanliness was emphasized, regular bathing and sweating in the sweathouse were commonplace. There was great concern for the proper cleaning of cooking utensils, mortars and manos, baskets, ollas, and so forth, because the presence of foreign particles on any of this equipment was considered a great disgrace. Similarly, there was a general avoidance of spoiled plant and animal food. Personal clothing was also washed frequently, using plant substances containing saponin to produce a creamy lather. Certainly a major factor in the control of disease was this caution surrounding personal hygiene.

SUMMARY

The Cahuilla have been located in space, and their use of space has been outlined. They were at the center of a wide-ranging trade system, and were surrounded by cultural nationalities of varying cultural backgrounds and ecological circumstances. These factors affected Cahuilla cultural development.

The Cahuilla area (2400 square miles) was divided into sib territories ranging from 70 to 600 square miles, each ranging from the Lower Sonoran to the Canadian-Hudsonian life zones. Topography, climate, location of water resources, and the nature of neighboring groups influenced the Cahuilla settlement pattern.

Cahuilla settlement patterns were related to their environmental circumstances. Villages were located within the sib territories in areas which provided a majority of food resources, and they were situated to take advantage of climatic factors such as water and wind patterns. They also were affected by topographic features which provided natural boundaries for discrete groups. Social distance was maintained between the groups and very likely helped to keep peace and control disease.

The Cahuilla remained in one permanent village the year round, from which individuals and groups left for specific subsistence, ritual, and trading activities. The Cahuilla population is estimated at five to six thousand persons, or roughly two-plus persons per square mile. Factors affecting this population density were culturally and ecologically induced. Occasional drought, disease, traumatic accident, birth control, and other institutionalized behavior patterns acted to keep the population in balance with its environmental potential.

6

Social Structure
and Organization

INTRODUCTION

An analysis of social structure and organization provides the framework of ideal and real actions, therefore an outline and discussion of the system of social guidelines by which Cahuilla behavior is determined or assessed is necessary to understand the interaction between ecological circumstances and the Cahuilla society. The sociopolitical structure of the Cahuilla will be described, analyzing separately the Cahuilla cultural nationality, the moiety system, the sib and the lineage. Ascribed and achieved status operating within these frameworks, particularly at the lineage level, will be discussed. Particular attention will be given to statuses connected with political-religious or economic activities. The marriage and the kinship system, which are exceedingly complex, would require a separate paper to describe adequately. Consequently, the system will be summarized and generalizations made relative to ecological integration.

CAHUILLA GROUPS

Gifford (1918) and Strong (1927) described the Cahuilla as having marriage regulating moieties, with ceremonial reciprocity, and politically autonomous patrilineages. Each lineage had its own food-gathering areas, lineage chief, ceremonial house, and ceremonial bundle. Descent was traced carefully for five generations and the lineage was exogamous. The ceremonial bundle was held in great esteem and handled only by specific persons. It was "owned" by the lineage leader, who could use it to enforce his judgments through supernatural means. The bundle was passed from father to son in a direct line of descent. Strong stressed the significance of a ceremonial complex (house, bundle, ceremonial office) stating that it is the "most important factor in aboriginal society in Southern California" (1927:34).

I have elsewhere suggested (Bean, 1960:111–119) that a redefinition of Cahuilla social structure was in order. I pointed out that in the San Gorgonio Pass area a larger grouping existed than the

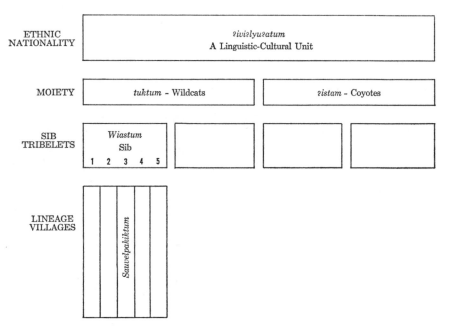

FIGURE 3. Cahuilla Social Organization.

localized lineage Strong and Gifford suggested as a maximal unit of Cahuilla organization, namely, a sib composed of several lineages. The sib occupied a specific territorial area and had political unity. Economic cooperation, in the sense of sharing hunting and gathering lands, ceremonial reciprocity, and linguistic unity further characterized its internal structure. The sib was composed, however, of separate, independent, localized lineage units, each with its leader, ceremonial house, ceremonial bundle, and specific locality after which the lineage was usually named. Since that time, there has been further confirmation of this kind of organization; five such groups have been identified, and several others, for which only partial evidence exists, have been located. On the basis of this information, a reconstruction can now be made showing that the maximal political and economic groups in Cahuilla society were characteristically the sib, rather than the lineage, although the lineage was the basic corporate unit of organization.

CULTURAL NATIONALITY AND MOIETY

The maximal level of social identification among the Cahuilla was the *ʔiviʔlyuʔatum,* a linguistically and culturally defined group. *ʔiviʔlyuʔatum* refers to persons speaking the Cahuilla language and recognizing a commonly shared cultural heritage. I refer to this as a cultural nationality, a term adapted from Kroeber's ethnic nationality (Kroeber, 1962). There is no indication that the *ʔiviʔlyuʔatum* united for any activity as a single unit prior to white contact, although some extensive organization took place shortly after contact under the leadership of such historic figures as Antonio Garra, Juan Antonio, and Cabezon. Membership in the *ʔiviʔlyuʔatum* was determined by birth and socialization. All members of a subsidiary group who spoke the Cahuilla language were referred to as *ʔiviʔlyuʔatum,* as contrasted to other cultural nationalities such as the Luiseño and Serrano who bordered the Cahuilla. Cahuilla culture and history was also seen as distinct from these other groups, so that a Cahuilla was never in doubt about his membership within this cultural nationality.

A more precise membership criterion existed at the next level of group identity. The Cahuilla were divided into two moieties named *tuktum* (Wildcats) and *ʔistam* (Coyotes). Every Cahuilla was a member of the moiety of his or her father, and although the moiety had no territorial boundaries it was a real social entity. The primary functions of the moieties were to regulate marriage and ritual reciprocity. Exogamous marriage rules were very strict, being maintained to the present by some families, although they had broken down considerably in some groups by the time Strong visited the Cahuilla in 1928. The moiety was a kin group wherein common descent was recognized by the members referring to one another as *kilyiw,* a term implying genealogical relationship and obligation. The moieties also provided an economic and ceremonial function at most Cahuilla rituals, at which intermoiety cooperation was mandatory. This was particularly true at funeral and mourning ceremonies, because certain components of ritual activity were owned by each moiety which had to be integrated to complete the performance. According to Cahuilla world view, the very existence of mankind and the ecosystem of which an individual was a part would not be sustained without this ritual reciprocity.

The institutions of marriage and ritual, closely linked with moiety reciprocity, operated to bring groups together frequently, and set the framework for alliance systems which encouraged social interaction on a long-range basis.

It is impossible to appreciate Cahuilla social organization and economic or religious life without first recognizing a pervasive concern with social dichotomization. For all the Cahuilla-speaking people, as well as for most of their neighbors, the universe was classified into one of two mutually exclusive groupings: moieties. Wildcat and Coyote moieties were groupings in the social world, and the beings or creations of *Mukat* and *Temayawut,* the two creator gods, were the dichotomizations in the cosmological realm. This dichotomy is the essence of the operational-instrumental life. Its consequences were immediately related to ecological-subsistence needs.

As has been pointed out, every Cahuilla lineage or sib was a member of a moiety. They were distributed in space so that most sibs of one moiety immediately bordered a sib of the opposite moiety. Thus, within either moiety several significantly different ecological niches were occupied. Therefore, through the institutions of ritual and marriage, subsistence goods of these various areas were distributed throughout the area as a whole, as considerable quantities of foods and goods were reapportioned to members of the opposite moiety at rituals. The economic significance of this exchange at ritual occasions was cited by numerous Cahuillas who were consciously aware that ritual occasions served as a food redistribution device, protecting various groups against food shortages. Food distribution across moiety lines was also brought about by marriage rules. Each moiety was a source of wives for the other because each sib was bordered by a sib of the opposite moiety. Thus, moiety locations were conveniently situated for the acquisition of wives, as well as the ceremonial-economic reciprocal activities. Marriage rules will be seen to have significant economic consequences.

THE SIB AND THE LINEAGE

The sib was composed of a number of lineages, varying from three to ten. These sibs appear to have been dialectically different groups. Each group was named, and claimed a common genitor to which all others were related in varying degrees of patrilineality.

The sib was a political unit, an economic-corporate unit, and a ceremonial unit. Seven such groups are identifiable from the ethnographic data; however, it is possible that several others existed in the recent past. Traditionally, a single lineage was the parent, from which all others were segmented. This condition was symbolized by the term *ʔa čaʔi,* which means the "first" lineage. The degree of segmentation varied, however, from sib to sib, and in some, such as the *Wanikik,* it seems to have been on the verge of a split into two sibs at contact. Each *Wanikik* lineage had acquired its own ceremonial house, a ceremonial leader, and a ceremonial bundle. The presence of all of these components in one lineage is referred to as lineage maturity. In some other sibs with fewer lineages, the same conditions existed. In the sibs where each lineage had all the components, the *net* (leader) of the *ʔa čaʔi* lineages was recognized as a nominal leader over all the lineages, but his authority over all sib members was based on respect rather than on real sanctioning powers. He was, however, a mediator in intrasib disputes, and his opinion was highly regarded.

When the sib acted as a political or economic unit, the *net* presided over a council of lineage leaders (*netem*). Political cooperation on the sib level seems to have been relevant on several occasions: when sib territory was being exploited by nonsib members, the sib united for the protection of its resources; when large communal hunting activities were undertaken, members of several lineages were united; when intrasib conflict arose concerning land tenure, or at times of impending or real disaster, all the political leaders and religious practitioners assembled to combine their knowledge, strength, and supernatural power to deal with the disaster or settle the conflict (this is reported in instances of floods, droughts, earthquakes, and epidemics); when a large labor force was required to control wild food resources by burning food areas, members of several lineages cooperated as a single unit; when lineages had ceremonies, the sib members contributed food, and performed ceremonial activities, because some sibs had not developed a full complement of independent lineages.

At any one point in time, the sib system was in varying degrees of segmentation. For example, the principal lineage owned the office of ceremonial leader, and the group house was in the village of this lineage, whereas other lineages, which had splintered and established separate villages (usually only a few miles away), returned to the parent lineage for ceremonies. In these instances, ceremonial offices were usually distributed throughout the sib in separate lineages. For example, the parent lineage had the office of *net,* or ceremonial leader; another lineage, his assistant (*paxaaʔ*); another lineage, a ceremonial singer (*haunik*), and so on. Each village, as a result, had separate locations and distinct food-gathering areas, but the lineages acted as a single unit in ceremonial affairs, some political affairs, and some economic affairs.

In recent times, the procedure seems to have reversed, further attesting that kinship was highly relevant to Cahuilla social activities. When some lineages disbanded and no longer had ceremonial paraphernalia or leaders, a lineage retaining its structure (bundle, ceremonial leader, group house) incorporated individual members of those lineages, which had been a part of their sib, into their ritual affairs.

Each lineage, regardless of its degree of dependence on the parent lineage, was, for the most part, economically independent. The bulk of the area between lineages was open land and could be used for hunting and gathering by any sib member. Hunting areas seem less associated with lineage ownership concepts than the areas where dependable and basic crops were present. In the instance of the oak groves, individual trees and small groves were owned by individual families and inherited in a patriliny.

THE *MAISWAT*

A proper discussion of Cahuilla religious or social life is impossible without first defining the role of the *maiswat,* or ceremonial bundle. Each lineage or sib had such an object. The *maiswat* was first created by *Momtakwit,* the first *net* in Cahuilla history, and the reeds from which the wrappings were made were acquired by *ʔisily* (Coyote) who served as the first *paxaaʔ*. Thus, the sacredness of the bundle was emphasized by tradition.

The *maiswat* was a reed matting of four or five feet in width, fifteen to twenty feet in length, and enclosed ceremonial objects such as feathers, shell beads used in ceremonial exchange, a bone whistle, a curved stick, tobacco, and other ritual items. Within the bundle a supernatural power (*ʔamnaʔa*), suggestive of the creator, existed which communicated with the *net*. *ʔamnaʔa* was spoken to in an esoteric language and regularly fed tobacco. No important community activity could take place, nor could the bundle be handled without consulting *ʔamnaʔa* about the activity and purpose. For example, if a *net* planned to move the bundle, unwrap it, or even enter the *kišʔamnaʔa* (ceremonial house), *ʔamnaʔa* must be informed. The bundle was kept in a special place, usually a special room attached to the *kišʔamnaʔa,* or in a secret hiding place such as a dry cave. It was brought to the *kiš?amna?a* only when a ceremony was to begin.

The *maiswat* served as a symbolic representation of the lineage or sib. It symbolized all Cahuilla life: the religious, the political, the social, and the economic. As a sacred object, it connected the people with the "beginning" and their creation: the time when all the good things of life came; when food was created; when their ceremonial and political structures were given to them as well as the territories they occupied; the songs they sang; and all other things from the past. In the present world, the *maiswat* supported the adjudicative and administrative roles of the *net* and *paxaa?*, for they could call upon its powers as a sanctioning device to punish deviant behavior. It was integrated into the economy, brought into play when the community performed its annual rites of increase, and its possession reaffirmed the right of the people to live in the land whose resources they exploited.

The *maiswat* also represented the values of Cahuilla society. Those who were allowed to see the *maiswat* were men who had reached old age, those who had acquired an important position such as the *net* or *paxaa?*, or those who through their personal worth had achieved high status and recognition by their use of supernatural power. The *maiswat* was used to control the behavior of those in high status positions. If *?amna?a* was offended by an improperly performed ritual, the ceremonialist was punished. A *paxaa?* of a given ceremonial house is recorded to have served the same role at another. He died a half year later because he had offended *?amna?a* in his own house. If the *net* or *paxaa?* did not perform their proper function, they or their family were punished by *?amna?a*.

ADAPTIVE FUNCTIONS OF
CAHUILLA PRINCIPLES OF ORGANIZATION

The lineage principle can be seen as ecologically advantageous in several ways. The lineage principle defined group membership, and food-producing areas were often owned by lineages; therefore, members of respective lineages were able to maintain day-to-day and season-to-season control over food-producing areas. The careful delineation of groups within geographical areas minimized the possibility of conflict over valuable food resources. Further, it guaranteed that some food-producing areas were exclusively and always available to particular groups of people. Thus, the lineage functioned as a corporate entity. The Cahuilla emphasis on patrilineages perhaps served as an adaptive function with respect to their orientation toward hunting. This will be discussed further in a later chapter.

The segmental nature of the lineage system provided a further adaptive component for the Cahuilla social structure. For example, when circumstances limited food supplies, a group could split from the lineage and establish itself as a separate economic group; on the other hand, two lineages could merge by recognizing common origins, maintaining kinship ties and rituals when convenient because of the ecological circumstances of the system. This can be recognized in the sib structure. The sib principle allowed the segmentation of these groups to form larger corporate groups. This permitted social groups to expand or decrease as ecological conditions required. The manpower resources of several lineages could be called together for any purpose, thus increasing the power potential of any sib. For example, the leaders could organize the men of several lineages to defend sib properties from exploitation by neighboring groups when necessary. Sib boundaries were extended to maximum logical limits imposed by ecological circumstances.

The moiety principle set up a dualistically based, reciprocal social system which acted adaptively. It regulated marriage, requiring that each Cahuilla lineage exchange women with another lineage of opposite moiety. This guaranteed the spread of economic-political alliances to several other groups and set up long-range reciprocal acts which operated to redistribute foods and goods among several econiches. This process was further intensified by the rule that Cahuillas might not marry anyone who was related within five generations in either the father's or mother's line. These rules are discussed in the forthcoming section.

Ritual reciprocity was also a necessary consequence of the moiety principle. Each lineage at some ritual occasions was required to invite lineages of the opposite moiety to fulfill the obligations of ritual conduct. The accompanying economic exchanges were thereby adaptive. These are discussed in greater detail later on.

MARRIAGE AND ALLIANCE

Marriage in Cahuilla society was primarily a concern of the lineage and family. The marrying individuals were restricted in their choice of partners by two rules: moiety exogamy had to be observed; and no one could marry anyone related in the opposite moiety with whom a genealogical relationship could be traced within five generations. These two rules had significant ecological consequences. Not only was a lineage female sent to another lineage of opposite moiety which was in a different geographic area, but the five-generation rule prevented two or three lineages from clustering their women among themselves. These rules extended the marriage alliances throughout all the possible ecological zones in the Cahuilla area. Members of each lineage had marital alliances with most of the other sibs, and therefore most of the resources within the various ecological niches of the Cahuilla area were, to some degree, available to each lineage.

The families of the marrying pair were, of course, the most immediately concerned about the alliance. Spouses were selected by the parents, using several criteria for their selection. The most important criteria was the food-producing capabilities of the spouse. An ideal spouse was one who was responsible to kin obligations, respectful of elders, skilled and diligent in economic pursuits, or showing potential leadership abilities associated with ritual or curing. Physical strength and hunting skill were of paramount importance in a young man. His value as a spouse was increased if he was in line to inherit political or ceremonial roles, or if he had shamanic potentialities. The young girls were chosen and remained spouses if they were hard working, could get along well with their in-laws, prepared food efficiently, and bore children, especially male children. A less formal criterion, but one of significance, was the reputation of the family. For instance, individuals in families of the same social rank tended to marry with one another. Past relations between families were also important; if they were not on good terms with one another, a marriage was unlikely.

MARRIAGE AND KINSHIP

When a marriage was arranged, the boy's family presented a sizable gift of food and goods to the family of the girl. The girl was brought to the house of the boy's parents. If she was too young to become a wife, she was raised by her future husband's mother. If she was found acceptable upon adulthood, she would then marry the boy and reside at the boy's parents' home until children were born, after which the couple established a separate residence nearby. The marriage was not considered final until the birth of a

child. If the girl was already of marriageable age, she simply was
brought to the boy's home, a brief ceremony ensued, and the
couple established residency.

The marriage established a long-range economic and social alliance between two families. Reciprocal exchange of gifts of food
and other items was a highly valued and rewarded activity, the
responsibility of which was constantly pointed out to the young
couple. Prior to a boy's marriage, economic reciprocity with affinals was already well developed: a young unmarried man was expected to give his first game to his maternal grandparents. A
young man was expected to furnish game to the bride's family
prior to the birth of children. At all the numerous rites of passage
for the individual, his or her collateral and affinal relatives were
the first to be invited, fed, and gifted. They, in turn, brought
gifts of food and other items. All visiting involved the gifting of
foods—guests were always entertained by being fed—and, upon
departing, a guest was given food to take back to his home where,
if there was sufficient quantity, it was distributed to his other relatives. The flow of economic goods between intermarried families
was thus frequent and of long duration. It was broken only with
great concern or care. Divorce, then, was not an easy thing for a
girl to obtain; numerous instances of runaway brides are documented, after which the brides were returned again and again
before a divorce was acceptable. This interfamily alliance established by marriage was cemented by the bride price and continued
exchanges of food and goods. The only occasions upon which the
bride price was returned was if the bride failed to produce children or if she was incorrigibly nonproductive and lazy. Even death
did not destroy the partnership between families; if possible,
sororate and levirate rules were activated so that a widow(er)
would soon have his wife or husband replaced. A widow might
marry the brother of the deceased husband, but she could also
marry a close relative of the husband if for some reason marriage
with a brother was not possible. Thus, the interfamily-interline-
age arrangements were supported institutionally from disruption
through death.

These extensive kin connections were of great value to the Cahuilla. This is expressed in the frequent statement: "I am related
everywhere." This statement carried with it connotations of pride,
privilege, and power. The value of these alliances was also indicated in the tradition sometimes referred to as "enemy songs"
(*wexily*) which are described in the section on ritual. Each lineage
had an "enemy" lineage which it denigrated whenever possible,

sent misfortune to in time of fear or anxiety, and with whom it was not allied through marriage. If a marriage occurred between members of two such lineages, then the enemy relationship was automatically cancelled. Thus, enemy lineages were usually found at considerable distances from one another.

Although most Cahuilla marriages occurred within the Cahuilla-speaking peoples, there is evidence that marriage outside of the culture was not uncommon and further extended the chains of alliance across more than local ecological boundaries. Neighboring groups—Yuma, Luiseño, Diegueño, Serrano, Chemehuevi, and Gabrielino—are all on record as marrying in, or receiving women as wives from the Cahuilla. Although these were probably atypical arrangements, they further extended the sociopolitical and economic alliances, and perhaps explained in part the generally amicable relationships existing between these cultural groups.

These arrangements for creating kin ties across cultural boundaries aided in preventing open hostility and competition for resources lying between the areas of the two groups as did kin ties within the Cahuilla-speaking area itself.

KINSHIP TERMINOLOGY

Social relationships within the lineage and family were ordered through a kin-based system of status relationships precisely indicating the kin relationship position of each person vis-à-vis some other. Almost all social interaction was with people related to one another. The lack of a kin connection could make interaction exceedingly awkward. Cahuilla relationships were based upon the criteria of age, sex, lineality, affinity, sex of speaker, sex of connecting relative, and perhaps locality. The Cahuilla kinship system is a very exact one which carefully distinguishes a large number of people and minimizes the number of people in one kin category. The system is what anthoropologists usually call a Dakota system with Iroquois cousin terminology. Specialists in the study of kinship find it interesting that all the dimensions that Kroeber (1908) and Tax (1955) consider basic to kinship systems were used to differentiate the various persons in Cahuilla society. Although to an outsider the system may appear burdensome and complex, it is clearly and easily understood by many Cahuilla today.

Each Cahuilla throughout his life was reminded regularly at social occasions of the status relationships of persons with whom he might come into contact and the behavioral obligations consequent with that relationship. The most significant of these obligations was that relating to economic exchange.

The system is too complex to describe in this book. I will demonstrate the relationship of kin terms to ecological circumstances in Cahuilla society by describing terms for lineal and collateral relatives, diminutive terms, and joking relationships.

LINEAL AND COLLATERAL RELATIONS

We have already seen a patrilineal emphasis in Cahuilla society. This emphasis reoccurs in Cahuilla philosophical assumptions and in kinship terminology. For example, in the immediate Cahuilla family the father and mother are contrasted; the father is called *na?* and the mother *ye?*, the sex of the parent being recognized.

When addressing children, the sex of the parent and the child determined the term used. Both parents addressed sons as *maylu?a,* whereas two different terms were used in addressing daughters. The father called his daughter *suŋama* and the mother addressed her daughter as *pulin.* Occasionally, a father might use the special term *kihma* when addressing his son.

In the grandparental generation the important criteria for addressing relatives were generation and sex. On the paternal side only generation was important, the term *qa?* being used when addressing or referring to both paternal grandparents, a devise emphasizing the patrilineage. When it was necessary to differentiate between the male or female grandparent, the speaker added a suffix indicating whether the person spoken to was male or female. Maternal grandparents were named differentially according to their sex. The maternal grandfather was addressed as *qwa?* and the maternal grandmother as *su?*. Sometimes siblings of grandparents were addressed by the same term as the grandparents. For example, the brother of the paternal grandfather and the sister of the paternal grandmother were addressed as *qa?*. Both the brother of the paternal grandmother and the sister of the paternal grandfather were called *kex.* Thus, on the father's side of the family all persons living in the individual's village in the grandparental generation were called by the same term, their corporateness and authority being recognized through kin terms. The persons referred to as *kex* were either outside, or would marry outside, the individual's lineage.

Grandchildren were distinguished according to the sex of the connecting relatives, and the speaker's sex. Both parents referred to their son's children as *qala,* whereas children of the daughters were addressed differently by the male grandparent (*qwala*) and the female grandparent (*sula*). The asymmetry here matches that occurring in the grandparental generation.

Collateral cross-grandnephews and cross-nieces were all called *kexhum.* Sex of speaker and sex of kin were ignored. Terms for collateral parallel grandnephews and nieces were determined by the sex of their parents. If the parent was a male, all grand- nephews and nieces were called *qala.* If the parent was female, they were called *qwala;* if a female, the grandnephews and nieces were addressed as *sula.*

Siblings were distinguished by sex and relative age. Older brothers and sisters were differentiated from younger brothers and sisters. An older brother was called *pas,* the younger brother *yuuly.* An older sister was addressed as *nes,* a younger sister *neʔiš.*

Parent's siblings were differentiated by sex and whether they were older or younger than the father of the individual address- ing them. Father's brothers were differentiated by age. The younger brother was called *mas;* the older brother *kum.* The same principle operated with mother's sisters. Mother's older sister, *nes,* was differentiated from mother's younger sister, *yis.* With cross- aunts and cross-uncles, however, the principle changed. All father's sisters were classified by the one term, *pa;* and mother's brothers were classified as *tas.* Relative age was ignored. Keeping track of the relative ages of men in the father's part of the lineage was important as it established the lines of inheritance and other rights and authorities within the lineage.

Children of an individual's brothers and sisters were differen- tiated according to whether the sex of the connecting relative was the same as the person referred to or different (where it is the same, parallel; where different, cross). Parallel nephews and nieces were differentiated according to age of connecting relative. A man's older or younger brother's child, and a woman's older or younger sister's child were differentiated: man's older brother's child, *taxma;* man's younger brother's child, *kumu;* woman's older sister's child, *mati;* woman's younger sister's child, *nesi.* Sociologically these kin were treated as one's own children. Pa- rental obligations were forthcoming in several social contexts. This role of parenthood did not follow for cross-nephews or cross- nieces who were differentiated by sex of speaker. For a female, the cross-nephew and cross-niece were called *asis.* For a male, cross-nephews and cross-nieces were called *mut.*

Cousins in Cahuilla society were differentiated on the basis of sex and age of connecting relative. Parallel cousins were called by the same term as the speaker's brothers and sisters. The relative age of the connecting relative determined if the cousin should be called older brother or younger brother, older sister or younger sister. Cross-cousins were differentiated from parallel cousins and siblings by the terms *nyúku* and *nyukú*. As in the example of cross-nephews and cross-nieces, cross-cousins lived outside the social context of an individual's daily life, and so the important criteria of age and sex were not attached to them because decisions regarding disposition of property and the like rarely occurred.

The pervasive concern of the Cahuilla for establishing exact behavioral patterns between kin does not operate in the great-grandparental generation. Great-grandparents and great-grandchildren used self-reciprocal terms. One term, *piwi*, was used, generation being the criterion for use of this term.

AFFINAL RELATIVES

The terms used for people marrying into a Cahuilla family reflected the same concerns for age and sex as those above. For example, the wife of a father's brother was called *nes* and *yis,* just like mother's sisters. Sex of linking relative determined which term was used. *Nes* was associated with the older sibling, whereas *yis* was associated with the younger. Thus, a wife of the father's brother was distinguished by the relative age and position of father's brother to the father of the reference person—the "ego."

The husband of a father's sister was called by the same term as mother's brother, *tas.* The mother's sister would probably be married to a male from ego's lineage and might very likely be a parent or parental surrogate, owing to the levirate and sororate rules which operated in Cahuilla society.

Likewise, the wife of the mother's brother was called *pa,* so she was similar to father's sisters. This may have been due to sister exchange in marriage. It was quite common in Cahuilla society for two families to exchange brides. Thus the wife of the mother's brother might have been a sister or cousin to father of the child.

Parents-in-law were called by different terms depending upon the sex of the speaker. Married couples referred to their parents-in-law by different terms depending on whether the couple had children. Before his children were born a man called both parents-in-law *mi kiwa.* After his wife had a child, the parents-in-law were separated by sex, the father being called *qwalhena?*, and the mother *sulhena?*. A woman, before she had a child, called both her parents-in-law *misik,* and after she had a child, she called them both *kalahiyek*. Parent-in-law terms were reciprocal with the child-in-law terms. Parents called their daughter-in-law *misik* before she bore a child and *kalahiyek* afterwards. After a woman bore a child, her father called her husband *qwalahena?*, and her mother called him *sulhena?*.

The presence or absence of children in the marriage was a significant determinant of address. This emphasized the great concern the Cahuilla had for progeny.

JOKING RELATIONSHIPS

Considerable interest has emerged in social anthropology concerning joking relationships. A joking relationship existed when one was permitted, or perhaps required, to tease or make fun of another. These were often reciprocal relationships, but they may also have been asymmetrical. They varied from rather slight to severe breaches of social etiquette. These occurred in Cahuilla society; the patterns of the relationships correlate and reinforce the principles of kin determination, and reinforce basic role relationships and some basic Cahuilla values.

Age, generation, and lineality regularly determined the nature of the joking relationship. For example, ego could never joke with a parent or persons in the generation immediately above ego who was connected to ego by two persons of the same sex. Thus, mother's sister and father's brother were treated deferentially. However, this was an asymmetrical relationship. These people teased ego, but ego could not tease them. The authority of the patrilineage and the older generation was thus demonstrated. The reverse situation occurred with cross-aunts and cross-uncles. Here joking was reciprocal. Diminutive terms were applied here, but not with parallel relationships, a clear recognition that those in ego's group were treated differently and more carefully from those outside. Persons of a parental generation who resided in the same village as ego, or who might potentially live in that village, were treated differently from those of the parental generation who did not or would not live in the village. Those persons senior to ego in age were not dealt with casually or jokingly, but rather they were treated with strict deference rules which applied to the relationship, a constant reminder of the hierarchical arrangement of Cahuilla statuses. For example, a person could

joke with maternal grandparents, but not with paternal grandparents; and only partial joking could occur with a father of a
person's mother. So, whereas the mother's family was dealt with
more casually than the father's, the older male was shown considerable deference regardless of whether he was in one's own
lineage.

Likewise, although a woman could not joke with her mother's
father, he could tease her, his seniority and sex being recognized
in this relationship. Joking relationships were more frequent
among members of the same sex: a woman could joke with her
mother's mother, the relationship being reciprocal; a woman
could joke with her younger sister, but not with her older sister,
because the older sister's potential role as a mother surrogate
was recognized.

Age and authority were also recognized. An older brother could
tease his younger brother, but the relationship was not reciprocal.

Among more distant relatives, cousins of the same sex joked
with one another about sex, but cousins of the opposite sex could
not.

A change in joking relationships occurred with in-laws after
a child was born. For example, a brother-in-law ceased to joke
with a sister-in-law after she had a child.

Parents-in-law differed in their joking relationships. A female
could not joke with her mother-in-law but she could with her
father-in-law. Her father-in-law might joke in return, the relationship being reciprocal.

DIMINUTIVES

Kin terms such as the English terms "daddy," "mom," "pa," are
called diminutives. Such terms occurred in Cahuilla kin terminology. Three are presented here.

1) *Tutu* was used by ego to refer familiarly to *su?* (mother's
mother).

2) *Kwakilye* was used familiarly to refer to *qwa?* (father's sister).

3) *Kexhilye* was used familiarly to refer to *ka* (father's mother,
but not father's father).

This class of terms appears to be limited to collateral, affinal,
or female lineal relatives. Perhaps they referred to people who
were outside the lineage village or those who would move outside.
In any case, the distribution of these suggests again a concern for
separating those males of ego's lineage from other persons. A com-

plete set of these terms must be collected in order to make a final statement.

SOME OPERATING PRINCIPLES
IN CAHUILLA KINSHIP

Proper social and economic role distinctions are reflected in the Cahuilla kinship system. The kinship system extends beyond the nuclear family to embrace relatives five generations removed from any lineally related person; further extensions are accomplished affinally. Several major principles are brought into operation within the kin system itself: sex, relative age, sex of connecting relative, sex of speaker, generation and reciprocity, and perhaps locality.

The reciprocity principle is present throughout the system. Every person that called B "X," B called "Y." Below is a list of all reciprocal terms. Whereas reciprocity is characteristic of most kin systems, the extensiveness of this pattern in Cahuilla terminology is notable.

sula	⇆	*su?*	*mati*	⇆	*yis*
qala	⇆	*qa?*	*nesi*	⇆	*nes*
qwala	⇆	*qwa?*	*?asis*	⇆	*na*
kexhum	⇆	*kex*	*mut*	⇆	*tas*
takma	⇆	*mas*	*pas*	⇆	*yuuly*
kumu	⇆	*kum*	*kis*	⇆	*waxal*
nyukú	⇆	*nyukú*	*takmahiyek*	⇆	*takmahiye*
nyúku	⇆	*nyúku*	*kumuhiyek*	⇆	*kumuhiye*
sulhena	⇆	*sulhena*	*matihena*	⇆	*matihena*
qalahiyek	⇆	*qalahiye*	*nesihena*	⇆	*nesihena*
kexahenak	⇆	*kexhana*	*asiyet*	⇆	*asiyu*
kexahiyek	⇆	*kexhiye*	*mutahena*	⇆	*muthena*
qwalahena	⇆	*qwalahena*			

These twenty-five pairs of reciprocals show that a major factor governing terms is social relationships. This is clear when affinal terms are examined. A given term is based on ego's relationship to the in-law's child rather than to the in-law himself. For instance, the term *qwalahena* refers to the husband of ego's daughter; and reciprocally, wife's father. *Qwala*, of course, is daughter's child (for a male speaker). Thus, *qwalahena* means father of daughter's child, and father of daughter's child reciprocated with the same term.

A reciprocity also occurred with people several generations apart. The Cahuilla practice of referring to lineal relatives five generations away (Gifford, 1922:155–209) as "brother" and "sister" may have been a way of recognizing whether a distant relationship existed. If two individuals called another person "brother" in referring to a great-great-great-grandparent, they would be related to one another within the five-generation limit. A significance of this reciprocal terminology may have been to recognize corporateness, that is, a relationship with persons who were members of the same lineage.

This same sense of corporateness appears in other kin term uses. For example, in the generation immediately below a male ego all children by female relatives were *mut,* whereas children of males were distinguished according to relative age of their parents with respect to ego. For a woman, just the opposite was true; all children by male relatives were called ?*asis,* whereas the children of females were distinguished according to relative age. A locality factor is clear when one looks at the terms for children of siblings. A female, by the sororate rule, would more likely have been physically closer to her sister's children than to her brother's, whereas the reverse was true for a male.

On another generational level, two persons below ego, locality was seen in the use of the term *kexhum;* for a male ego, all a sister's grandchildren were living in a separate village and were called *kexhum;* whereas for a female ego, all of a brother's children were living in a separate village and were called *kexhum.*

In summary, we can see that the sex of the person was significant in the kin term determination and was clearly related to a great concern in society for maleness and descent reckoning through the male line. Relatives in the male line were more particularly designated than those connected through a female relative.

Relative age was related to the concern in Cahuilla culture for tradition and knowledge, power and authority. Great respect was shown for the aged, and their control over economically significant institutions was clear.

The same principles which determined kin relationships (age, sex, etc.) also, significantly, directed the flow of goods, foods, and responsibilities within a group for the economic care of old people, the young, the infirm, and the orphaned. The kinship system was one of mutual-aid. The responsibilities of the kin system operated along age lines. The older brother was responsible for the younger and for the children of the younger brother if the younger man should die or be incapacitated in his economic realm. The system was reciprocal: the younger brother was responsible to the decisions of the older brother and to aid and contribute to his well-being. The older always received benefits from the younger. The aged people were protected by rules which encouraged younger relatives to give their first catch or a portion of the productive goods to their elders.

The kin group or lineage can be seen as a highly regulated corporate system within which the social roles of the group functioned for the maintenance and benefit of the corporate assets. Corporateness, rights, and responsibility within the corporation were determined by the rules of kinship. Most outsiders were nonkin and automatically excluded; a few persons related to the group by marriage (affinals) were brought into the system. Their relationships were formalized and recognized by kin in terms for affinals which, in effect, labeled them as relatives through a member such as the father or the mother of "our son's child."

The structure of kin terminology was consistent with Cahuilla subsistence and corporateness. For example, the biological family was the primary subsistence unit in Cahuilla society, and this group was clearly distinguished in the kin terms. Mother and father, for example, were separated from other kin of their generation; brothers and sisters were separated from others of their generation; and grandparents were also segregated into two types. A similar condition occurred within the patrilineage itself—the members of lineages were clearly distinguished from other relatives who were outside the lineage. Those relatives within the lineage who may have left the locality were distinguished from those likely to remain in the locality, suggesting that locality was, possibly, a basic dimension of Cahuilla kinship determination.

Possible emergency conditions, such as widowhood and orphanhood with their economic consequences, were taken into account within the system. An older brother's social role was that of surrogate father to his younger brother, and an older sister had the mother surrogate role for her sister's children. Further, the changes occurring in kin terminology when a woman had a child was a formal recognition of a permanent and binding marriage contract between two groups. These marriage contracts had economic functions and operated to exploit the ecological potential of the area.

The kin terms also provided guide lines for the smooth running of the lineage system. The differentiation of age and directness of descent so obvious in the kin terms operated to ensure the equitable and clearly defined distribution of corporate goods and regulated decision-making powers within the lineage. Consequently, conflict for power, economic goods and the like were minimized by calling attention to rights and obligations from the very beginning of an individual's socialization process.

The kin system provided operative controls for the distribution of goods by inheritance rules attached to the kin statuses. Older males inherited rights with economic implications, members of a lineage inherited an inalienable right to the corporate lands, and kin obligations within as well as outside the lineage directed the flow of food. For example, a son had obligations to provide food for parents, grandparents, and affinals as well.

The kinship system was adaptive to the ecological situation. The kin were separated on the basis of those who were a corporate group, who together shared a given econiche. They were separated from others who were either affinals or members of one's own sib but not directly related, or persons who were not related at all but simply a member of the Cahuilla ecosystem. These categories carried with them varying degrees of economic reciprocity. The rules associated with the moiety system automatically carried ecological consequences regulating who one would marry and the economic consequences of that marriage. Kin relationships carried with them duties and responsibilities which guaranteed care for the aged, the infirm, and children who had lost their parents. The kin system was a pervasive social welfare group. This operated most clearly within the corporate kin group, but a careful allocation of affinal relationships extended the economic consequences of kinship to many other groups within the Cahuilla cultural nationality.

ASCRIBED STATUS

In contrast to the extensive and precise nature of the kin terminology, other status terms are more general in the Cahuilla language and social sphere. General use categories based on age, sex, and social condition provided a further set of clues as to how the Cahuilla structured their society and regulated their decisions regarding social relationships. The structuring of these statuses is also consistent with ecological circumstances.

In the first years of an individual's life, sex was not a significant criterion for status differentiation. At this time, a child (*kiat*) was cared for by women. Not until the child began to be mobile and of an age where life tasks could be observed and learned was the criterion of sex employed for social differentiation. After two or three years of age, children were called *ʔekikmal* (boy) and *nawiš-maly* (girl). These terms were used until puberty. During these years, the children began to learn the activities of adult life. Instruction and learning were accomplished for the most part by a cooperative effort on the part of older people, older siblings, parents, and grandparents. The child accompanied older siblings or adults in work situations, learning while doing. The tasks of food production began early, and as the child grew older the tasks became more specialized along the lines of division of labor; for example, the boys learned hunting skills with bow and arrow, girls the methods for preparing acorn meal, etc. Children exhibiting special skills were encouraged to develop them.

On reaching puberty, the Cahuilla individual was still not classified as a grown man or woman. They were called *pašwelism*. This refers to young people who have passed the puberty initiation ritual but are still very much under the control and guidance of elders.

Individuals in their late teens or early twenties were referred to as *naxaniš* (grown man) or *ničily* (grown woman), and would retain these terms until the individuals became old men (*naxalu ʔvel*) or old women (*nešlyu ʔvel*). These terms were loosely correlated with reaching grandparenthood or an age of fifty years or more. As with kin terms, age is recognized in these terms. And an increase in age is correlated with a concomitant increase in deferential treatment of those individuals called by the above terms.

Within the nuclear family, status terms differentiated boys and girls. The term *nawitaly* (little girl) was used as an affectionate term by parents when addressing a girl. This term was likely to be used throughout that individual's life by her parents. It was a term reserved for relatives rather than nonrelatives; more distantly related people referred to a girl as the *nawišmaly*. The term *ʔekwatal* was the equivalent of the above for boys. When parents wished to distinguish between children of the same sex but of different ages, they differentiated by the criterion of age, adding a suffix indicating that the individual was younger or older.

The statuses of husband and wife were indicated by the terms *wilʔisiw* (husband) and *kinʔi* (wife). The status of divorce was indicated by the term *kiŋiʔa*. All in-laws were indicated by the term *naxwaʔa* or *naxwaʔlem*, and a complicated set of affinal terms were used, most of which indicated the nature of the relationship in terms of the children of the couple.

Changes in life circumstances were, of course, also indicated.

There were kin terms with affixes distinguishing relatives who were dead, and special terms were employed for statuses involving work roles. An orphan was called *leepi* (Spanish). There does not appear to be a Cahuilla term for this status, and it may not have been a sufficiently meaningful condition in Cahuilla society for it to be given a special term.

ACHIEVED STATUS

There were a number of statuses in Cahuilla society based on special relationships between individuals, special skills, and associational activities. A head man, a leader, or one who made decisions was called *čimlyuka* or *čimiyunuenkalat*. A person who was a partner or involved in a work relationship with another was distinguished by the term *taxliswet* (apparently the same term as "person"), and any member of one's moiety was, of course, *kilyiw*, as was anyone with whom the individual could trace a direct relationship on either side of the family. *Kilyiw* was also classed as companion or friend, except nonmoiety kin of husband or wife.

Other status terms were applied to persons on the basis of special skills, such as basketmaker and hunter, a recognition that labor specializations were encouraged and rewarded in Cahuilla society. Other positions in society are not recalled, but when used in the dimly remembered past they were terms such as "leader of the rabbit hunt."

The most significant statuses other than those based on kin were those based on political, judicial, economic, and religious activities at the level of lineage or sib organization.

THE "NET"

The *net* was the key individual in Cahuilla society, corresponding to what is usually called "chief"; Strong has incorrectly described it as a ceremonial leader (1929). The status was usually inherited, preferably from father to eldest son, and was carefully maintained as nearly as possible within a direct line of descent. For example, if the *net's* eldest son was not equipped for the role, it could go to his father's younger brother, first cousin, or youngest son. The responsibilities of this office pervaded all Cahuilla life. The *net,* as a ceremonial leader, was responsible for the correct maintenance of ritual and the proper care and maintenance of the ceremonial bundle (*maiswat*) and ceremonial house (*kisʔamnaʔa*). Without these, the structure and support of the group would have disintegrated, because the ritual activity kept the environment in proper balance. The *net* also served as an economic executive, determining where and when people would go to gather foods or hunt game. He administered first-fruit rites prior to gathering of acorns, mesquite, and other staples, and he collected goods which he stored for future ceremonial use, exchange with other groups, or emergency rations. He was responsible for remembering group boundaries and individual ownership rights, so that when conflict arose between individual families, or within lineages or sibs, he could adjudicate them. When two individuals were unable to resolve a problem between them or among their particular family leaders, they could bring their dispute before the *net*. He heard both sides of the issue and made a decision which was then binding upon the conflicting parties. The sanctioning authority behind his decision was *ʔamnaʔa*. When the *net* felt further community help was needed he called upon the *paxaaʔ* and the *puvalam* (or shamans) who met with the *net* and provided advice. These decisions ranged from what to do with malevolent shamans to disagreements over bride price.

Beyond the lineage or sib level, the *net* met with *nets* from other lineages concerning land use, boundary disputes, disputes between lineages regarding marriages, warfare, and ceremonial decisions. His authority, like that of *ʔamnaʔa* and the *paxaaʔ* (the *net's* assistant), was wrapped in the cloak of history and sanctified by tradition: the story of the first *net* who managed the first ceremonial activities after the death of the Creator was retold at each mourning and funeral ceremony, thereby reinforcing the role.

THE "PAXAAʔ"

The *paxaaʔ* was the ceremonial, administrative, and adjudicating assistant to the *net* with whom he worked very closely. The two positions were complementary because both were essential for the maintenance of the economic, social, and religious structure of the Cahuilla. The *paxaaʔ* was an integral part of all ceremonial rituals and functions (birth, puberty, first-fruit rites, death, and others), and no other person could assume his specifically defined duties, or office (which tended to be hereditary). The *paxaaʔ* participated fully in the economic phases of community life, often organizing and leading certain community hunting parties (usually ceremonially instigated), and gathering and distributing the food throughout the community.

In addition to being an administrator and a ceremonialist, the *paxaaʔ* was responsible for proper order of ceremonies and ensured that certain ritual acts were properly performed. If anyone misbehaved at the rituals great harm could fall upon the people in attendance; consequently the *paxaaʔ* sought out and punished anyone who transgressed. When a political or ceremonial decision had been reached, it was the responsibility of the *paxaaʔ*, as the *net's* messenger, to communicate the decision to the people. He informed the ceremonialists what and when to perform, and contacted the people who were to contribute food. He instructed the people what to bring, and he saw that his instructions were followed. When food was distributed to guests, he maintained protocol in the proper distribution of food and gifts to the guests. These were important functions because it was necessary that respect relations and obligations were maintained between ceremonial groups. The distance the guest had traveled, his age and family, all had to be considered when inviting people to eat.

The *paxaaʔ* had to be a man who inspired respect and fear among the people; a person who would be obeyed without question when he commanded. His power was justified by tradition, as it was Coyote (*ʔisily*), one of the culture heroes of the Cahuilla, who served as the first *paxaaʔ*, who assisted with the funeral ceremonies for the Creator, and who went to the sea to gather the materials from which the first *maiswat* was made. Like the *net*, he was able to call upon the power of the *maiswat* to implement his power, thus utilizing this power to punish a wrongdoer by death or disease.

The *paxaaʔ* was also involved in political decisions by sitting with the *net* in tribal meetings and later communicating decisions of a political nature to the group.

THE "HAUNIK" AND HIS RITUAL ASSISTANTS

One of the most revered men in Cahuilla society was the ritual singer, or *haunik*. His talent as a performer and ceremonialist was a matter of religious and aesthetic interest. He possessed and performed ceremonial songs utilized at rites of passage and intensification. He was the "song" leader. The song cycles were of great length and complexity. It was not unusual for a singer to perform a twelve-hour cycle. He knew at least two of these cycles for death ceremonies alone, one for male funerals and one for female funerals, aside from a multitude of songs for other occasions.

The *haunik* was always a man, but might be of any age. Some men acquired the proficiency to perform while young, others passed middle age before they were asked to lead a ceremony. He was usually taught the songs by his father, the status passing from father to son. This was not rigidly required, however, and a *haunik* could teach anyone to carry on his position. He usually sang with three assistants, accompanied by the audience. The *haunik's* assistants sang, danced, and performed dramatic roles described in ritual song texts. Various members of the community, as well as guests at ritual occasions, were called upon to assist the *haunik,* as ritual occasion demanded. The *haunik* sang at all community ceremonies which occurred at the *kisʔamnaʔa,* and also at rites associated with puberty, and the burning of personal property of the deceased.

The *haunik* was a teacher to the young people in his lineage. At puberty ceremonials he taught young people songs associated with their lineage and instructed them in proper adult behavior.

The training of a *haunik* began informally. An interested, talented young person could learn much of the procedure at an early age by attending ceremonies. As he learned the song texts and demonstrated ability and qualities necessary for the role of a *haunik,* he would receive private instructions from the *haunik.* As his protégé's proficiency was recognized, he would be included as one of several assistant singers to the *haunik;* later, following the death of the master *haunik,* one of the assistants would become the leader of the singers.

The *haunik,* responsible to his own *kisʔamnaʔa* to perform sacred songs, received no formal remuneration for his service. However, when he sang in another *kisʔamnaʔa,* he was paid for his services by the owners of that ceremonial house. He then shared his remuneration with his assistants. Formerly he was paid in food or goods, whereas today he may be paid with cash or cloth.

This responsible role was often refused by the son of a *haunik.* It was a difficult role requiring a quality voice, excellent memory, and years of hard learning. It was also a dangerous role; a bad performance would bring both supernatural and community censure upon the *haunik.* The personal inconveniences were great. In addition to certain ceremonial dietary restrictions, a singer performing a song cycle (often stretching over twelve hours) was required to sing without error the entire cycle before stopping. If he made one mistake, the song cycle had to be started again from the beginning. The *haunik* could not leave the house even for natural functions.

"ŋEŋEWIŠ" (DANCERS)

Integral to most ritual performance, dancing portrayed dramatic persons and events in Cahuilla history and cosmology.

Childhood training began with observation and private instruction. During the boy's initiation ceremony, the especially talented were taught choreographics and symbolic dance meanings, and then brought into the formal performances.

The dance performances were complex events that ranged from the swift, elegantly performed eagle dance (simulating an eagle's flight) to ponderously careful and dramatically significant war dances, to emotionally meaningful dances associated with burying images of the dead. These required choreographic talent, stamina, and a sense of mimicry, rhythm, timing, and imagination.

Members of the community were acutely aware, as were singers, of the formal dance system requirements. They therefore evaluated, criticized, and aesthetically compared dancers. Famous dancers were highly praised, well rewarded materially, and sought for religious and secular dance occasions. They were variously costumed, most frequently in eagle feather skirts, and headgear of fur, hawk, or owl feathers. The bodies were usually painted in ritually meaningful designs.

Women also danced at ritual and secular occasions; their less complex choreography reflecting the quiet and unobtrusiveness Cahuilla society expected of women. Women's dancing, like their singing, usually supported the males. In some rituals, for example the *nukil* and the girl's puberty rituals, there were specifically female dance roles. The modest, quiet, soft, and elegant steps contrasted startlingly to the often vigorous, rapid, and powerful dance steps so characteristically masculine. Women rarely costumed in any special way, though garland headdresses were permitted. To my knowledge women never donned ceremonial feather gear like the men. No doubt this was because of the general female abstinence from ritual and powerful materials.

THE "PUVALAM" (SHAMANS)

Two other statuses (*puul* and *pa?vu?ul*) fell within the category of *puvalam*. These were "shamans." The two statuses differed in degree rather than kind.

The dramatic role of *puvalam* in Cahuilla society was noted by the first students of Cahuilla culture. Barrows found "the medicine men among the Cahuilla seem to form a special class, having undergone preparation and initiation that makes them exorcists and men of influence for life" (Barrows, 1900:75). Kroeber (1908), Hooper (1920), and Strong (1929) also discussed the *puvalam*. Yet Williard Park, in his survey of shamanism in western North America, wrote that:

Information is vague or entirely lacking for most of southern California. From the data, it appears that animal spirits play a role in giving shamanistic powers. Among the desert Cahuilla shamans are supposed to derive their powers from *Mukat,* the creator, but power is conferred through the medium of guardian spirits. These are probably the animals such as owl, fox, coyote, bear, and others that act as messengers to shamans (1938:48).

We can clarify the situation now by describing the sources of supernatural power, and how the *puul* functioned and demonstrated his power in society, and by describing their relationship to Cahuilla religious, political, economic, and social institutions.

Possession of supernatural power was necessary for becoming a member of the powerful and somewhat secret society of *puvalam.* Power was acquired by one of several means: an individual could be born with the power, it could be passed to an individual by another *puul,* or it could be given to him by a spirit being. The power often came to a child or man in "dreams." Some children were born with the "call" while other individuals were visited as a young man or later in adult life by a "spirit." Some *puvalam* could predict when a child was going to become a *puul,* or a *puul* might favor a young boy and pass his power on to the boy. In either instance, when the candidate received a dream or call, it was then mandatory that he assume that position or risk some misfortune such as death or disease. Despite this great danger, a number of instances are recalled where the individual did not assume the position, at least publicly. Some of them became *neŋaŋaniš* ("secret witches"); others apparently had the call, refused, but did not succumb to the predicted misfortunes. Several men in recent years have refused the call. They were usually men of "quality" and respect in the Indian community. One, for example, was an important political leader, holder (keeper) of a ceremonial bundle. He was an honored and well-loved man—considered to be one who had probably been called but refused the obligation because of its arduous demands.

If the individual accepted the call he was explicitly instructed, by a *teyewa* (a "familiar"), as to how he should manifest his power. The candidate received instructions, songs, dances, and varied esoteric knowledge providing him with special power. An individual often had one or more such relationships with powerful beings concurrently. As the *puul* increased in age, his power usually increased, almost as if the very act of living out a long life implied the possession of power. The *teyewa,* representing the "spirit guardian," resided in the *puul's* body. Represented by an

animate or inanimate object, such as a lizard, snake, seed, or cactus thorn, it communicated with the *puul* and was employed in
the performance of acts demonstrating supernatural power. The
teyewa was treated with extreme care and respect by the *puul*
and his family. For example, the children of a *puul* who were playing with a lizard of the variety employed by their father were
carefully instructed not to hurt or play with the animal as harm
might come to their father.

Upon receiving instructions from the guardian spirit, the young
man informed his father, who informed the *net* that his son had
received instructions from a guardian spirit. The *net* interviewed
the candidate. If he felt the candidacy was legitimate, the *net*
contacted the *paxaaʔ* and various *puvalam,* who talked with the
boy and came to a final decision concerning the validity of his
candidacy. Upon their approval a ritual of installation was arranged which lasted for three days. This ritual was conducted in
the *kisʔamnaʔa* by the *net* and *paxaaʔ*. The family of the claimant sponsored the rite by furnishing food for the event and the
candidate's lineage members, as well as others who had been
invited to attend.

At the ritual the claimant performed his songs, danced, and
otherwise executed acts to demonstrate his power. Occasionally,
at these installation rites the older *puvalam* attempted to match
their power against that of the novice in order to harass or harm
him, thereby testing the efficacy or strength of his power. At the
conclusion of the rite, if the claimant had successfully demonstrated his power, he was publicly accepted as a *puul*. Others then
knew his songs and were able to accompany him when he sang in
public. Although accepted as a *puul,* it remained for him to validate his power through continued works in order to gain prestige and remain a *puul*. If he was installed but afterwards did not
demonstrate his status, he was considered to have lost his power
and status as a shaman. The *puul's* songs, in contrast to those of
the *net* and *haunik,* were individually owned, belonging only to
him. They were sung only with his permission and under his
direction. These songs represented the personal relationship between the *puul* and his spirit guardian. The individual nature of
these songs allowed for a wide range of aesthetic expression. As
a *puul* developed his powers, he was tested by his sponsor. If he
had been given or offered the power to cure a particular disease,
for instance, his performance was tested for proper procedure. If
he failed, the spirit guardian took away the *puul's* power.

The economic activities of the *puul* were critical. He was able to "create" food. When there was a scarcity of food or when there was a prediction of scarcity, the *puul* drew a miniature food-producing tree such as an oak from his hand during a public performance, thereby magically ensuring that the season's acorn crop would be plentiful. This act was described by Victoria Wierick as follows: "When the witch man made acorn trees in his palm, he got hot coals in his hands and he held it there and it came like a weed grown in the ground. It grew that high [about two inches]—this would make food come when there was no food. There are none of them that way any more" (personal communication).

The *puul* was also expected to control rain or other natural elements to preserve or help crops. For example, if the rain occurred in the fall or early summer, before the people could gather the acorns or mesquite, the whole crop might be destroyed. The people then called upon the *puul* to perform special rites to predict whether rains or other natural elements would be damaging to crops. If they were, the *puul* would be called upon to stop them. The *puul's* power was also used to discover the location of animals for the hunter and to encourage the animals to make themselves available for the hunter.

The treatment of disease was another major function performed by the *puvalam*. Medical problems were caused by: natural causes such as wounds, snakebites, accidents; "witching" by other *puvalam;* supernaturally caused punishment due to the infraction of rituals and taboos; soul loss; and malevolency of spirits prior to a death ceremony. The *puul* was also responsible for ensuring that an individual thought to be dead was not simply in a trancelike state.

The *puvalam* cured diseases by sucking disease objects from the patient's body and blowing to send away evil. These acts were accompanied by songs and natural methods such as the use of herbs and massage. If there was a question about what had caused a disease or how to cure the disease, the *puul* consulted his spiritual sponsor. He would then extract the disease. If he could not determine a course of treatment, he would ask another *puul* to aid him.

The relation of *puvalam* to the religious, economic, and political structure was considerable because of the great power at their disposal. In addition to the functions already mentioned, the *puvalam* were involved in all ceremonial occasions, not in a formal ceremonial role such as that of the *net, paxaaʔ,* or *haunik,* but nevertheless as necessary functionaries. The *puul's* principal activities at these rituals was to perform the "witch dances" at which a number of *puvalam* from various lineages participated. These *puvalam* aided the ceremonialists in keeping away ghosts, malevolent spirits, or any other evil which might be present at the occasion and interfere with the ritual. For instance occasionally a *puul* or someone else might have utilized a ceremonial occasion to harm someone. He could do this by hanging an object someplace in the *kisʔamnaʔa* where the intended victim would touch it, thereby harming him. It was the function of *puvalam* to rid the *kisʔamnaʔa* of such objects. Many people attended these rituals from diverse groups, so the opportunity and likelihood for social disequilibrium was very high. Competitive games, economic exchanges, and the like were occurring at the same time as ritual action. These actions of the *puvalam* placed visitors on constructive notice that personal conflicts were to be repressed or held at an acceptable level of expression. Sociological equilibrium was thus ensured.

The *puvalam*, albeit informally, played a significant political role. When there was an important political decision, the *puvalam* met with the *net* and *paxaaʔ*. When an important man in the community was to be censured, or a legal dispute arose which had repercussions beyond an individual or family level, these men were called upon for their opinion and support. They also acted to punish offenders on behalf of the lineages.

The maintenance of one's status as a *puul,* unlike that of the *net* and *paxaaʔ*, was subject to unexpected or rapid fluctuation, either decreasing or increasing in power within the community. A *puul's* status was, in effect, under constant question by other *puvalam* and the community at large. He had, therefore, to reaffirm his status by public and private demonstrations of his power.

An example of the manner in which reaffirmation was accomplished at such occasions was the "witches' dance" when the *puul* removed his *teyewa* from his throat or nostrils. Then he might eat hot coals, pull out his entrails and reinsert them, pull out his hair or his nose and return them to his body. At these performances extreme respect was required of the audience. People were forbidden to appear startled or to express anxiety at the demonstration because it might disturb the careful performance and cause the *puul* to die. No one should cry out or talk until the familiar had been returned to the body because the *puul* was particularly vulnerable at that time. The *puul* himself, however, while conducting his ritual (often a long performance

containing a series of songs and dances) could stop the performance if a mistake had been made, or if he felt that someone was
there to harm him. Another activity which enhanced his status
was his right to see and handle the *maiswat,* and, as mentioned
previously, to perform at ceremonial occasions. Aside from these
public demonstrations, his other activities (curing and divining)
were constantly being assessed by community opinion. Activities
which were performed in private were publicized by him. Some
puvalam transformed themselves into animals, such as bear, coyote, or mountain lion, to facilitate hunting or to move rapidly
across great distances. These individuals were in a special category, *paʔvuʔul,* discussed later. Communication with animals and
the ability to endure hunger and thirst for long periods of time
added to the *puul's* power demonstration.

The *puul* was also a diviner. He could understand signs given
by birds, animals, and celestial bodies. He could predict such
things as impending illness or certain death. The *puul* knew, for
instance, that a soul was lost when he saw a falling star, and he
could proceed to discover whose soul it was and return it to the
person before one of several soul-catching beings found it. At
such a time the *puul* would call all the people together and perform a rite to get the soul returned safely. *Puuls* also saw impending disaster—a flood, drought, famine, or epidemic might be fore-
seen, requiring the gathering together of the people and the
puvalam to offset malevolent spirits. By utilizing the combined
powers of the *puvalam* and the *miaswat,* disasters were sometimes
averted.

Victoria Wierick remembered a prophecy of a *paʔvuʔul* which
dramatically demonstrated the accuracy and predictive powers
of these men. "One old man saw in a dream that men with skins
the color of the dead, carrying sticks that spit fire, and riding animals like deer pulling objects that had round things that went
round and round [wagons] were coming."

THE ASSOCIATION OF "PUVALAM"

The *puvalam* formed an élite group in society, acting together
with the *net* and *paxaaʔ* as leaders who expressed opinions and
made decisions, especially in times of disasters and epidemics.
As a group they propitiated *ʔamnaʔa* to ensure the community
against danger or to assuage anxiety and suffering. They often
met in the sweathouse, using it as "a sort of clubhouse." The *net*
and *paxaaʔ* were usually *puvalam,* therefore they controlled the
political structure by weaving it into a tightly interacting group,

thereby increasing their power over the community. Thus, an association of *puvalam* cut across sib and lineage boundaries to form an interlineage and intersib association of power-oriented persons.

There was considerable rivalry among *puvalam*. Yet they constantly aided one another in reaffirming their status to the community, because it was only *puvalam* who could knowledgeably define who was a *puul* or who was a fake. Some claimed, it is said, to be *puul* to take advantage of people. An example was given of a man who claimed to be a *puul* and benefited by it. Other *puvalam* denied he was a *puul*. This was an instance where there was no other *puul* in the claimant's community. If a real *puul* had been there, the charlatan would have been killed for claiming the status. Further, if a *puul* behaved improperly while another *puul* was performing, or even made fun of another *puul*, he could be censured. Several *puvalam*, whose combined powers were greater than the transgressor, could join together and take his power away from him. Another manifestation of competition within the group was expressed in formal contests where each would take his turn in demonstrating power, each *puul* trying to outdo the other. A real test of power, it is said, was for a group of *puvalam* to attempt to "kill" a *puul*. If the man was "killed," the *puul* who could bring him back to life was proved the most powerful one of the group.

Other members of the community were ambivalent about the *puul*. He was a highly valued and respected man because his special powers and talents were required in almost every phase of life, from birth to death, in religion, politics, and economics. The status was sought by many because it gave the possessor social prestige, great personal power, and the economic advantages he received from gifts for his curing acts. However, an intense hostility towards these men is manifested in story after story telling of malevolent *puvalam* who killed people, destroyed crops, caused epidemics, and the like. Fear that a *puul* would use his power to harm his people rather than help them was pervasive. All the positive functions that the *puul* was able to perform because of his power could be reversed. When a *puul* was found to be malevolent he was judged by his peers, the *net* and *paxaaᵓ*. Through the institutionalized authority system he was executed, even though this might be extremely difficult if he was an unusually powerful *puul*. The fear of *puvalam* was so intense at times that most tragic events were attributed to these men. Numerous legends were told of magically caused floods which

destroyed villages, epidemics which killed many people, earthquakes that caused rivers to change their course, unseasonable and
torrential rains that ruined crops, and the mysterious disappearance of game. Most of these disasters were the result of malevolent
puvalam. A dramatic example of this fear is reflected in an explanation as to why acorns contained tannic acid. In the beginning acorns were "sweet" and required no laborious leaching
process in order to eat them. Two *puvalam* were fighting and one,
in order to harm the other, "witched" all acorns. Since that time
people have had to work hard to acquire the staple food. A similar
explanation was given for the disappearance of the antelope in
Cahuilla areas in recent times.

The ambivalent attitude of the people toward individual *puvalam*, portrayed in stories about them, suggest that they were
sometimes hostile or competitive people. In the continuation of
the story of the coming of the white man, it is said that if the
puvalam had not been arguing among themselves (competing
among themselves), they would have been able to combine their
power and stop the encroachment of the invading whites who had
taken their land.

However, the pervasive attitude of suspicion, envy, hostility,
and fear did not exclude a positive attitude toward the *puul* as
well. By and large, Cahuillas considered *puvalam* honorable
men, and made frequent statements to the effect that "X" was a
good *puul;* "He didn't take advantage of the people."

THE "PAʔVUʔUL"

The status of *paʔvuʔul* is like that of the *puul* in that he had
more than ordinary supernatural powers. Knowledge of eight
such men who had achieved this status has been recorded, and
they all had one factor in common which was not shared with ordinary *puul:* they were able to change into animal forms. They
were different from the *puul* who could cause disease and slow
death. The *paʔvuʔul* could kill a man instantly by supernatural
means. He knew more complex and difficult cures than others,
and possessed the ability to cure diseases that the ordinary *puul*
could not cure.

When asked if a *puul* was a *paʔvuʔul*, or if a *paʔvuʔul* was a
puul, one Cahuilla said: "Of course all *paʔvuʔul* are *puvalam*,
but a *puul* is different from a *paʔvuʔul*." He explained further
that *paʔvuʔul* were able to change their physical form, and, in
contrast to most *puul*, the *paʔvuʔul* was born that way. The
paʔvuʔul knew he would be a *paʔvuʔul* because when the people

saw him perform these extraordinary acts they knew he was a
pa'vu'ul. Thus, he "knew" and everyone else "knew" by his actions that he was a *pa'vu'ul* rather than a *puul.*

COMPARISON OF ACTIVITIES OF *net* AND *puul*

NET	PUUL
Was group oriented	Was individually oriented
Was traditional	Was innovative
Maintained equilibrium	Created and coped with new things
Had ascribed status	Status was achieved
The status was inherited	Status was individually acquired

THE "TETIWIŠ"

The *tetiwiš,* or dreamer, served as a diviner and occupied another status involving supernatural power. He predicted future
events, found lost objects, located trespassers on sib or lineage
property, and located game animals and new food sources. How
he acquired this power is not clear. He was not formally involved in ceremonial activities, nor were specified songs or dances
or other duties performed by him at ceremonies. It was his responsibility to predict the unknown which, in and of itself, served
as a safety device to lessen anxiety.

In contrast to the *puul,* the *tetiwiš* shared the ability to predict with the *puvalam,* but did not act to change circumstances.
He dreamed that an illness was coming, but he did not call upon
supernatural power to cure the impending disease.

THE "NEŊAŊANIŠ"

There were other persons in Cahuilla society who used supernatural power but did so privately and to achieve personal ends.
These were called *neŋaŋaniš.* They were either men or women
who, in contrast to others with socially recognized statuses,
had no formal position in the social hierarchy. Many women possessed and used these supernatural powers to effect magical control over others or predict future events. A typical example of
their ability to effect sympathetic magic was the burning of a
hair of an individual. The secret use of power was doubtless
related to the subservient position occupied by women in Cahuilla
society.

THE "TIŊAVIŠ"

In sharp contrast to other statuses in Cahuilla society, the *tiŋaviš,* or doctor, utilized no supernatural power for curing. Most
tiŋavis were women, learning their medical lore from other *tiŋ-*

avišlum. There was no formal installation in this status, as a person usually learned gradually through experience, becoming known and trusted through time in the community for his or her skill. Most *tiŋavišlum* were middle-aged or older, and they possessed great knowledge concerning medicinal herbs, the specifics for various conditions or ailments such as childbirth, wounds, broken bones, or intestinal discomfort. The role was economically advantageous. The practitioner was customarily paid for services in food, baskets, or other goods. If the *tiŋaviš* did not know how to cure a disease, he or she called upon the services of the *puul.* There are accounts, however, of a *puul* assigning a *tiŋaviš* to carry out his medical instructions for a patient who might require the services for many days. *Tiŋavišlum* were sometimes reported as suspected of being *neŋaŋaniš* in the sense that they used, or might use, secret magical power.

SUMMARY

The statuses of *net* and *paxaaʔ* in Cahuilla society were greatly sought because they provided sources of power and prestige. Considering this situation, it is certainly no accident that these statuses were crystallized in families.

Two reasons have been suggested for this: the families that acquired this status were loath to give it up, and therefore rigidly protected their vested interests by strict hereditary rules; and the office was so important in maintaining ecological equilibrium that the society could not afford to allow constant jockeying for power through this status. For example, intersib marriage alliances set up long-range, reciprocal exchange patterns. Changing these patterns would necessitate considerable readjustment whenever leadership positions changed. By keeping leadership positions which articulated these exchange arrangements in the same family, a leadership change would be less disruptive to ecological equilibrium than if a leader could fortuitously come from any family. The rigid rules governing inheritance of positions made excessive or injudicious use of power a real possibility. As a safety mechanism, the Cahuilla provided means for politically ambitious individuals to rise through the ranks, creating a constantly circulating system of élite. There were the *puul, paʔvuʔul, haunik,* and *tiŋaviš.* This suggestion is supported by the ambivalent position given the *puvalam.* While they were powerful and respected, and the office was sought by many, it was also the target of considerable aggression, hostility, and suspicion by other members of the community. In contrast, reports of hostile remarks about a malevolent *net* or *paxaaꝰ* are rare.

Another point, with possible analogies to other societies, is that the *puvalam* were often upwardly mobile individuals who came from a lineage or family without the prestige enjoyed by the dominant lineages. They entered into a power structure via the status of *puul*. The individual who moved into and out of another social milieu might be regarded with suspicion and potential anger by his own group, and with a sense of competition by the élite who had already arrived, because he provided a new threat to their status and power. Although it was unlikely that a *puul* would take over a *net's* position, it was possible that an individual could branch off and form his own lineage, thereby setting up an independent religious-political system. Such action took from the vested interests a part of their population and perhaps a part of their territory.

Several generalizations concerning Cahuilla social structure are evident from the preceding analysis. Briefly, they are:

The Cahuilla system of ranking appeared ideally as shown here.

FIGURE 4. Social Structure and Associational Status.

1) The most important status was the *net*, which represented the group as a whole and controlled the welfare of the group through *?amna?a,* and possessed esoteric knowledge which he inherited.

2) Statuses involving political decisions were supported by the acquisition and use of supernatural powers. All statuses having to do with the economic welfare of the people were supported by supernatural power.

3) The same personnel cross-cut the major institutions—religious, economic, and political—religion thereby providing a unifying device for the total system.

7

Other Institutions

INTRODUCTION

Among the Cahuilla law, economy, warfare, and gaming were ecologically adaptive institutions. This chapter will, first, review the source of law and its action; second, discuss the exchange of goods between the Cahuilla and other cultural groups and the role of the trader; third, relate concepts of property and ownership to the environment; fourth, review warfare and conflict with primary concern for the sociology, causes, and methods of conflict; fifth, relate types of games played to the economic needs of the society; and, sixth, review the ecological significance of these institutions.

LAW

For the individual Cahuilla and each Cahuilla corporate group to take full advantage of available resources, a legal system had to be developed so that economic relationships were generally predictable and protected. Consequently, a well-structured and finite system of legal norms and machinery for administering those norms was developed. Dysfunctional deviations from the norm were controlled, and a continuity of social relationships was maintained through sanctions provided by this system. Strong emphasis was placed upon the control of economic resources. Conflict which might be dysfunctional for the economic and psychological equilibrium of the society was usually dealt with quickly.

The structure of Cahuilla law was embodied in oral literature.

This body of knowledge provided the Cahuilla administrators with legal precedent and authority to define correct behavior and punishment for improper behavior. These legal precepts were retained in musical literature, thus the Cahuilla law "existed in the song." Anyone going against the normative pattern was said to be "going against the song." Some of these songs were given to them by the Creator, others were made to accommodate more recent conditions. The force of traditional wisdom was continually reinforced through ritual, story, anecdote, and action. The intensity and frequency of rituals were, therefore, effective reinforcing agents for social control. Thus, the rejection of traditional wisdom, or the failure to remember all conditions imposed by it, resulted in negative sanctions at social and supernatural levels. Conversely, there were rewards in the form of prestige, political power, and access to economic resources for those who obeyed the "songs."

Supernaturally imposed, automatic retribution was expected when actions went against tradition: sickness and death were expected consequences for daring to gather food before a first-fruit ritual had been performed; diminution of a hunter's luck was the result if a wife broke a menstrual taboo. When a misfortune occurred to a person or group, such a cause was sought through dreaming, divination, or the interpretation of dreams by *puvalam* and other older people who were especially skillful in understanding and interpreting traditions.

More direct negative sanctions included individual ridicule, frequent in Cahuilla society. The commonest form was for a lineage to publicly announce an individual's real or reputed antisocial actions in songs, thus bringing shame upon him, his family, and his lineage.

When public offenses such as witching, improper food gathering, and poaching were committed against the lineage as a whole, the *net, paxaaʔ, puvalam,* and other older men called the lineage members together to hear their decision regarding the offender. Banishment, whipping, public stoning, death by being buried alive, or assassination are punishments recalled by Cahuilla.

The *puvalam* frequently acted as socializing agents. If an individual offended the system of rules, a shaman could punish the individual personally, especially if the breaking of the rule offended or had harmed one of his own family or lineage. For example, if a girl did not accept a marriage proposal, or resisted going with a husband that her family had selected, the *puul* sometimes threatened her with witchcraft; or if a woman had harmed her husband by violation of menstrual rules, a *puul*, upon finding this out, could cause her to become sick or die. He might, alternatively, stop the impending retribution of these ritual offenses or cure the symptoms already present.

Within the family itself, decisions and sanctions were made by the older people—the oldest male and the oldest female. Children were usually punished or rewarded by the mothers—most generally by nonphysical means (shaming or praise). Physical punishment was rare, but, when administered, was severe. Thus the legal system synchronized with the status system by channeling force and allocating authority for determining who had the right to exercise physical or social control along lines of sex and age.

Actions frequently recounted in Cahuilla oral literature which required sanction were murder, witchcraft, theft, rape, adultery, poaching, marital conflict, failure to maintain economic reciprocity, and the breaking of taboos. Most of these offenses had economic consequences. Clearly theft and poaching were invasions of economic privilege. Murder obviously had economic implications by destroying the family unit, and witchcraft caused individuals to be removed from subsistence or other activities either through accidents, sickness, or death. The accusation of witchcraft also frequently involved economic activities, because the witchcraft was often expressed in the form of damaging an individual's food supplies or otherwise preventing him from making a livelihood. Marital conflicts also had economic implications in that the amount of a bride price which had to be returned in the instance of divorce was a frequent additional dispute to be arbitrated. In other instances the possibility of divorce broke the economic alliance established between two families by the institution of marriage. Thus, either directly or indirectly, a major concern of the Cahuilla was to maintain a predictable and balanced internal system through the media of law enforcement.

ECONOMIC RELATIONS

An exchange of goods (*tačemnami*—"to trade") and raw materials, especially foods, was necessary for survival because of environmental variations. At any one time a group had a surplus of one or more items which could be exchanged for others. The kinship system was a major mechanism for accomplishing this exchange, and it will be demonstrated later that the ritual system also performed a role for redistributing these resources. Nevertheless, exchange or trade between individuals and groups occurred frequently without the support of kinship or ritual institutions. This is most clearly seen in the trade relationships the Cahuilla maintained with their distant neighbors such as the Gabrielino and the Yuma. The most vividly remembered contributors to the Cahuilla culture inventory were the Gabrielino, who traded their steatite, asphaltum, and shell beads with the Cahuilla for various food products, and furs, hides, obsidian, and salt. There was also a considerable exchange of ideas and nonmaterial cultural items such as rituals, songs, and the like, which are more difficult to isolate as factors of trade than material items. For example, the origin of certain rituals like the *manet* are attributed to the Gabrielino.

The Yuman-speaking peoples on the Colorado River contributed seeds from various plants (corn, melons, squash), gourds for making rattles, and turquoise. Treasure goods manufactured in the Southwest such as grooved axes have been found in Cahuilla sites. Likewise, cultural ideas came to the Cahuilla. The concept of pottery making, agricultural techniques, and songs are examples of elements that were diffused from the neighbors to the east.

Some Cahuilla people had what has been referred to as "special friends" among groups other than their own, who may have been formal trading partners. Most trade was carried on by specialists, with the *net* as a chief trader for a lineage. Trading was done by individual entrepreneurs or groups in expeditions. Traders took goods from the Cahuilla ecosystem to exchange and barter for goods desired by the Cahuilla. These items were then distributed within the Cahuilla system, and the men were paid for their efforts. Patencio (in manuscript) referred to traders as people who were very important, not only for trading but for carrying messages. He said: "They were the newspapers of the people at that time. These people went about everywhere. They were not killed in wars—that was the Indians' agreement."

The exchange of goods between the Cahuilla and their more immediate neighbors tended to occur within the kinship and ritual systems rather than through formal trading relationships. The ecology of the Cahuilla was more like that of their immediate neighbors, so the goods available in these neighboring areas therefore tended to be more similar than different. However, some items were unique to an area such as tourmaline, which was only available in the Luiseño area, and localized foods such as Joshua tree blossoms in the Mohave Desert.

Among the Cahuilla, exchanges occurred between individuals and between various social groups. For example, obsidian in the desert was exchanged for other items, like medicinal plants, unavailable elsewhere.

Craft specialization also stimulated exchange between and within groups. Persons especially skilled in the manufacture of baskets, pottery, bows and arrows, as well as various other utilitarian goods and esoteric items like eagle-feather skirts, frequently made manufactured goods, especially for trading purposes. Such skillfully wrought items were not only sought for their utilitarian value but for their aesthetic qualities as well. The work of these artisans was desired by persons less skilled than they; the Cahuilla did not expect that each individual would be a "jack of all trades." They recognized that individuals differed in their manifest ability and were encouraged to develop their skills.

Usually raw materials and manufactured goods were exchanged for other raw materials and manufactured goods. However, there was a well-developed medium of exchange system using shell beads as "money." What a given number of these beads was worth in relation to other items is no longer remembered—only that there were such monetary units.

In addition to these kinds of exchanges, there was negative reciprocity (Service, 1966:14): theft or the forceful seizure of goods. As will be seen in the sections on war and conflict, poaching or raiding the surplus goods in food-producing areas of other corporate groups did occur.

Another aspect of exchange was gifting. A gifting relationship occurred when a presentation was made without a formal expectation of equivalence. Gifting, frequent among and between Cahuillas and their neighbors, served several societal functions. It was most clearly seen in relation to ritual activities, which will be discussed later. It functioned to establish friendliness and continued social relations between individuals, between family groups, and among lineage and sib groups. Even a casual visit from one household to another was accompanied by gifting. The guests brought a gift, and departed with a gift given by the host. This contributed to a sustained circulation of goods within a village and between villages.

These social relationships had other economic consequences, because the presentation of gifts meant deferring consumption of one's own foods or goods by gifting them to another individual or group. Thus, a form of credit or savings was established between participants of a gifting relationship. As a result, subsistence risks could be spread over a long period of time. As a rule, the gifts given by Cahuillas were food products, raw materials, medicinal plants, and manufactured items such as baskets, bow and arrows, and other forms of capital equipment. Treasure goods such as shells, jewelry, eagle feathers, and objects made for ritual purposes were given. Gifting took place when a Cahuilla family, lineage or sib invited another group to participate in collecting food when it was in abundance. Gifting also occurred when a Cahuilla individual presented foods or goods to the *kišʔamnaʔa*, as will be seen in the chapter devoted to ritual.

CONCEPTS OF PROPERTY AND OWNERSHIP

Concepts of property and ownership were adaptive to environmental circumstances and economic needs. They were supported by ritual and belief. Ownership concepts were associated with territory, food resources, raw materials, manufactured objects, social and ritual privileges, songs, stories, names, and knowledge. These were owned by various groups, and these or individuals were associated with status roles.

All property concepts had either direct or indirect economic consequences, thus it was necessary for the Cahuilla to understand his rights, proscriptions, and relationships to various kinds of property. This understanding minimized conflict when competition over subsistence resources might be activated in times of stress, and to maximize the flow of subsistence goods in a predictable and peaceful manner.

Ownership was recognized by such terms as *nemehana* (it is mine), *čeʔmexanʔa* (it is ours), and *nexanat* (it belongs to somebody—implying you cannot take it, it is owned), and other such phrases which indicate whether these various things were freely accessible or not.

Ownership of the territorial units was established by boundaries (*hemtewataxwa hivay*) which were marked by petroglyphs, stones, or by a specific geographic feature. Ownership of these territorial units was confirmed by oral tradition which established the precise boundaries of each unit; historic rights to the territory had usually been established by a culture hero who named all the various features and sites within the area, and who left signs in the form of petroglyphs, pictographs, and other imprinted features within the area. Ownership of the territory was also confirmed by the willingness to defend it, and permission to use the area was required of all outsiders.

The sib owned a large territory which was jointly owned by all members, but it was at the lineage level that concepts of ownership were most precise. The lineage, itself a corporate unit, owned particular sections of lands within the sib territory, most important of which was the village site itself and the area immediately surrounding the village. Food-gathering and hunting areas were owned by lineage members on an individual or group basis, for example, an acorn grove, a pinyon forest, a clump of mesquite, a hillside covered with cacti or yucca. Moreover, no other lineage within the sib was allowed access to these particular resources without expressed permission or invitation from the *net* or head of that lineage. To violate the proscriptions was to invite severe punishment.

The lineage could also own areas of raw materials such as an obsidian quarry, or a marshy area where valuable raw materials for making baskets or for constructing houses grew. The lineage also owned a body of oral tradition: a series of stories, songs, and anecdotes which only lineage members had the right to tell or sing.

Very special kinds of ownership concepts were attached to the status of ritual leaders. For example, when the office of *net* and the *kiš?amna?a* was owned by one lineage within a sib, then other individual lineages owned certain lineage roles such as the *paxaa?* and the *haunik*, together with the ceremonial equipment associated with that status. The *net* owned symbols of office such as special pendants, and ritual dancers owned their regalia and equipment. The *puvalam* owned their own songs, given to them by their spirit guardians, and the regalia used in their rituals. They also owned patches of land on which useful medicinal herbs grew.

A very special area of privately owned knowledge was associated with ritual leaders. They knew and understood a highly esoteric language which they—and only they—could use in the private chambers of the ceremonial house—and only when they were speaking to *?amna?a* and about the *maiswat*.

Within the lineage, individual families owned individual trees or groves within food-gathering areas or patches of land on which grew valuable food or material resources. These were controlled by the heads of the families in the same way that the *net* or other lineage leaders controlled the use of property within the lineage. The specific nature of property holding within families is not as clearly remembered as ownership concepts with respect to individuals and larger groups.

Individual ownership of goods was keenly developed. Each child, male and female adult, owned property. The kinds of property owned by these individuals ranged from subsistence resources to any item which was open to personal claim. Some food-gathering areas were owned by individuals who had exclusive control. These ranged from food-producing trees such as the oak, particular patches of food-producing plants, areas producing raw materials for manufacture, and many trees which were food caches of woodpeckers and squirrels. If a Cahuilla discovered a small area which produced excellent basketry materials or fine clay to make pottery, he claimed it. These privately owned areas were often kept secret and were marked and protected by ritual or supernatural means so that others would not exploit them.

Equipment used in subsistence and ritual activities were also individually owned. A hunter owned his own hunting equipment which frequently had his private markings on it. A Cahuilla woman owned her own equipment for food preparation (for example, manos, metates, seed beaters) which were often marked to indicate her ownership. Her clothing, jewelry, and baskets were personal possessions. An example of an ownership and trademark in basketry designs was the bent claw of the eagle which was used by one basket-maker. These designs were so well known that even today the maker of the basket can be identified by the individual nature of the design.

The products of the hunt belonged to the hunter, except that various members of the community had the right to share the individual's capture. Young unmarried men were obligated to share their kill with specific members of their own and their future wives' family. Obligations of this nature were associated with specific rituals and will be discussed later on.

Individuals owned shell money in addition to their other goods. Most money was owned by the *net* and was used by him in ceremonial exchanges. Cahuillas recall two names for shell beads (*kičil* and *čuviwunet*), but the distinctions between these names is unclear at this time.

In addition to material items, individuals also owned stories and songs. An individual who composed a song or invented variations upon a traditional song had exclusive ownership of that song, and no one else could sing it or tell the story without his permission. If permission were granted, it was incumbent upon the person to give credit to the person who owned the song or story whenever it was used.

Individuals also owned names and as a person's status changed during his lifetime, he was given a new name to exemplify his new status. These new names could only be used in a later generation at the discretion of heads of families and the *net*.

In a general way, rights to some properties were delegated by sex. There were songs and games and ritual activities in which only men participated, or only women. Men had the right to use songs and ritual equipment and have access to power which was rarely granted to women. There was a very complex cultural inventory associated with such matters. There were special funeral songs performed for women, and special songs performed by women associated with their sex roles. The same thing was true of men, but definitive information is lacking. An example is the song referred to commonly as "enemy songs." Those sung by men were called *wexat,* those by women were called *ʔiswatat* or *ʔiswatily.*

Ownership of property could be transferred to other people by gifting, exchange, or sale. However, there were proscriptions connected with the process. For example, unless an individual bequeathed specific items of property like baskets, manos and metates, to another individual prior to his or her death, it was essential that this property be destroyed after the death of the person. Pottery was smashed, the bottoms of metates were broken and buried so that no other individual could use them. Failure to dispose of property was punished by ghostly visitations and sanctions from the supernatural; failure to destroy the property of the deceased was looked upon as an extraordinarily selfish action. This destruction of the goods and property may have functioned to prevent conflict within the families over the disposition of property, and it may, in some instances, have aided in the control of contagious diseases. Destruction of the property so that the deceased would have property in the after-life served to reinforce in the minds of the living that property rights must always be carefully and judiciously attended to.

Why did the Cahuilla maintain such a great concern for property and ownership? We have seen that a territory belonged to the Cahuilla-speaking people as a whole; other items, such as components of rituals, belonged to moieties; and that each social unit—the sib, lineage, family, and individual—had several property rights which were jealously protected. The Cahuilla ecosystem was also potentially unstable because of various ecological factors. Ownership concepts were structured so that stable and dependable products were protected for the exclusive use of particular groups. For example, some dependable food-producing trees like oak were owned by specific persons or groups. This maximized the protection of that resource and maintained a control over the product without conflict. There were, however, other food-producing trees like pinyon which were not predictable, and therefore a need for regular protection was not so necessary. Strict ownership may have been highly dysfunctional in such instances, because specific ownership may have led to serious conflict between groups. Perhaps the boundaries of several corporate groups, meeting at the borders of the abundant pinyon forest such as Pinyon Flats but open to members of several adjacent sibs, is related to this factor.

Ownership concepts were reinforced in the drama of Creation in which the two creators, *Mukat* and *Temayawut,* originated and owned their parts of the universe, thereby creating a duality in the cosmos represented by the moiety system. Examples of this phenomena will be seen in the chapter concerning world view in which the Cahuilla social universe is shown to include beings other than people. The various spirit beings also owned particular geographic places within the Cahuilla area, such as Taquitz Peak, owned by *Takwiš.* Thus, property concepts in Cahuilla society were developed in such a way that goods and social relationships were carefully articulated. There was little room for conflict over property because rights, privileges, and proscriptions attached to property were closely associated with social categories, and the flow of foods and goods was usually kept in equilibrium.

WARFARE

In comparison to the tribal groups living along the Colorado River and in the plains where institutionalized warfare was well developed, California Indian populations are, as a rule, characterized as having been relatively peaceful in nature. The purpose of the discussion will be to examine the nature of armed conflict as it occurred among the Cahuilla, and to examine whether warfare was ecologically adaptive, and whether the absence of highly developed forms of armed contests can be explained in terms of other adaptive institutions. Data will be given on the sociology of warfare, the methods employed, the stated reasons for the encounters, and a description of the instances of aggression.

Armed conflict was an extreme action and was attempted only when all other efforts failed. Conflicts are recorded between cultural groups, and between Cahuilla sibs, lineages, families, and

individuals. The decision to make war on another group was
formulated within the community, and the final decision was
made by the *net, paxaaꞋ* and the *puvalam,* although in one instance a group of young men of a village are recorded to have
initiated a conflict over the protest of the village leaders. The *net*
usually led the war party, but a person known to be skilled in
fighting was often appointed as a temporary leader. *Puvalam*
usually accompanied the war party, and a community ritual was
performed prior to departure in order to provide supernatural
support. At the conclusion of the conflict, another ritual was conducted to purify the members and protect them from the souls
of those they had killed.

The size of warring units varied from a small party of young
men from one village to large parties of several hundred men
drawn from many villages. Techniques of combat usually involved ambush, attacking at night, or attacking while the enemy
group was gathered in the ceremonial house. War clubs of the
"potato masher" type were used in hand-to-hand combat, and
bows and arrows for distance. Special arrowheads were used for
this purpose and they were sometimes tipped with a poisonous
substance. Another technique used in armed conflict was setting
fire to the structures in which the enemy group was congregated
—particularly the big house. In such events the war party surrounded the structure and threw fire brands onto the roof so
the people would be forced out to where they could be shot with
arrows or clubbed. Hooper (1920:365–366) records that a group
saw a war party coming and hid themselves in a rock shelter which
was "just like a room and had a stone door." The enemy party
surrounded the area, forced the door open, threw fire brands
inside, and closed the door, causing suffocation of the individuals
inside. A persistent feature of these attacks was that close relatives
in other villages could hide or leave the village prior to the impending attack.

The intensity of the conflict varied. At times it was solved with
minimal physical harm. Patencio (MS) recalled that occasionally
a group might submit to minor physical force, such as a beating,
which resolved the affair. In other instances the death or harming of one or several people was sufficient to stop the action.
However, a number of instances are recalled in which entire
villages were destroyed.

Customarily when a village decided to make war on another
village, the leaders requested assistance from other lineage groups.
Sometimes the entire sib was called upon to cooperate, but in

some instances lineages from other sibs joined in the action because of a common grievance against the group to be attacked, or because of obligations due to kinship or ritual reciprocity. Occasionally Cahuilla lineages joined lineages from other tribal groups for conflict. For example, Serrano and Diegueño are said to have joined Cahuilla lineages to attack a common enemy.

The largest warring units recorded are those attempted against the Yuma tribe where some four hundred Cahuillas attempted an attack on the Yuma. This particular expedition, however, did not succeed because of an earthquake which occurred while the party was passing along the Colorado Desert, interpreted by the *puvalam* as a sign that the expedition would fail. Consequently, the action was halted. There is also record of an attempted attack on the Yuma, abandoned because of extreme heat and drought conditions in the Colorado Desert, which even the exceedingly hardy Cahuilla could not bear.

In some instances the target of aggression was a single person, several people, or a family. When these individuals were hurt or killed, the skirmish was over. In more extreme instances, when all-out war was intended, the males of the village were the principal targets. Cahuillas from several lineages report that all the males of their lineage were killed at one time by an enemy group with the exception of a single male child who had been hidden by a female, or disguised as a girl child in order to allow the lineage to survive. In the accounts of this situation—which occur with apocryphal-like frequency—the lone survivor of the lineage was brought to the village of his mother's father where he was raised to adulthood. Upon adulthood he returned with his mother to his rightful area, dispersed the interlopers, acquired a wife, and—by this means—reestablished the lineage.

In severe battles where all males were killed, the heads of victims, particularly of the *net* or leader, were severed and brought back to the village ceremonial house as a symbol of the victory.

There were several reasons for armed aggression. The most frequent one, according to Cahuilla oral literature, was over economic resources, poaching or trespassing into another lineage or sib area being an immediate signal for strife. Usually, however, these were averted by other means unless the poachers were persistent.

A number of instances have been recorded where villages were displaced in order to acquire the food resources of that area; or the area occupied was felt to have belonged to the invading group because of historical precedent. An instance in the oral literature states that a Cahuilla group displaced a Diegueño group from San Jose Valley; another, that a Cahuilla group displaced another from Palm Springs in order to have access to seed-bearing areas (Patencio, 1943:87).

A significant cause for aggression was the failure of a lineage to fulfill responsibilities as part of the reciprocal ritual system which will be discussed later. These rituals were economically significant, so that failure to participate caused great hostility.

Still another frequent cause was witchcraft. If a lineage was suspected of directing sorcery against another lineage, the offended group attacked in order to deter further harm.

Personal insults, kidnapping of women, nonpayment of bride price, and thefts were also cited as reasons for going to war.

Armed aggression had specific, ecologically adaptive functions for the Cahuilla. The primary one being, of course, that a successful war partty commandeered new lands or goods of another group when ecological stress required, or warded off attacks from groups trying to encroach on food resource areas. Armed hostilities further functioned to deter people from attempting to poach or trespass, and the threat of a war party acted as a sanction to coerce groups who were not willing to fulfill their responsibilities concerning ritual reciprocity or affinal obligations.

Yet another function may have been demographic. As there are many recorded instances where entire lineages or large portions of lineages were destroyed through warfare, it may be that in times of real ecological stress when food shortages were critical, armed encounters may have reduced population sizes sufficiently so that the population was once again in equilibrium with its biotic community.

A significant sociological function may have been performed when hostilities within a particular community which were difficult to resolve or unrecognized were averted by the mechanism of selecting particular communities as scapegoats in order to alleviate internal stresses. An example of this is the retaliation over accusations of witchcraft.

GAMES

Competitive games were a form of friendly—but intensely spirited —combat in Cahuilla society and were usually supported by wagers. The types of games that are remembered by Cahuillas will be examined, and their adaptive functions will be discussed.

The games fall naturally into several categories. There were those that involved very strenuous physical activity where endurance and ability to withstand physical punishment were basic to the winning of the game. These were kickball, shinny, races, and tag, which are comparable to football, kickball, and soccer as regards agility, strength, and endurance. Kickball was played by two or more men. Each man kicked a ball made of wood or stone over a rough course of several miles; the individual who reached the end of the course first with his ball won the game. A more strenuous game was a form of shinny or hockey (*kupil*) played by teams of men, approximately ten men on a side (Curtis, 1926:162). Races and tag were usually played with mixed groups of men, women, and children; these games were physically vigorous, requiring endurance and speed.

A second category emphasized games like wrestling, tug-of-war, and mimicry in fighting. These were played primarily by men and boys. Both those categories functioned to prepare individuals for tasks such as hunting, tracking, and warfare because they emphasize skills directly associated with these activities.

A third category of games involved manual and visual dexterity. There were games such as top spinning, jackstones, juggling, and balancing of objects. These were favorite games played by women and girls and had the function of preparing women for the kinetic responses necessary in handcrafts, seed collecting and grinding, basket making, and all other domestic tasks requiring dexterity.

A fourth category of games involved guessing, sometimes together with an interpretation of circumstances based on the reaction of competitors in the games. Such a game was called *peon* (in Spanish).

In addition to preparing individuals for adaptive physical and mental skills, games provided several other important functions for the Cahuilla. They redistributed the wealth because large amounts of goods were wagered on the outcome of various games. They substantiated belief in supernatural power (discussed later) because possession of power was often the principal reason for a person winning a game. Games also emphasized social relationships, enhancing and reinforcing group cohesion and identity because the social unit rallied about and supported its own members whether on the family, lineage, sib, or moiety level.

SUMMARY

Legal machinery was carefully developed in association with ecological conditions. Law was based on traditional literature, and legal authority was vested in particular persons (for example, the *net*) who symbolized and administered the corporate assets of the group. Transgression of property laws was sanctioned by the jural authority of the *net,* by community ridicule, and by supernatural sanction.

Legal support for ownership and use concepts were related especially to productive capacity and dependability of food resources, as demonstrated in the instance of acorn trees in contrast to pine trees. Productive equipment was individually owned, and ritual equipment, which was formed into subsistence goods, was owned by the lineage or sib and held in trust by the *net.*

Ownership of property was recognized at every social level— the Cahuilla cultural group claimed a territory, the moieties each owned ritual knowledge necessary for economic exchange, the sib was a corporate group as was the lineage, and individual families and individuals each owned property. The legal system operated to protect and define the direction in which goods could be distributed.

General and reciprocal exchange systems operated for the regular distribution of goods between groups. Individual exchange allowed goods to flow independently of the kinship and ritual system. Encouragement of special skills in craftmanship facilitated this process.

Mechanisms for solving or creating conflict appear to be ecologically functional. A conquest philosophy has been observed which may have been operationalized during times of great stress. Hostility was immediate concerning poaching and other economically related behavior, such as divorce. The economically dysfunctional aspects of conflict were generally avoided by the ritual system, kin, and value system which usually precluded a need for aggression toward acquiring subsistence goods. This fact likely explains much regarding the role of warfare in and among native California cultures. Gaming was adaptive for developing kinetic skills, providing a means of randomly distributing property not otherwise controlled by the Cahuilla distribution system, and reinforcing the kinship system.

8

Ritual

INTRODUCTION

Ritual was a constant factor in the life of every Cahuilla individual—always directly ahead or immediately finished. Some rituals were scheduled and routine, others were sporadically and situationally performed. Settlement pattern, social organization, law, property, and games were related functionally to the ecological circumstances available to the Cahuilla people. Ritual served comparable functions. The number of people involved in rituals ranged from one to several hundred, and were drawn from several communities. Ritual served as a basic articulating mechanism for all institutions in Cahuilla society. To understand the practical effects of ritual behavior in Cahuilla society I will briefly summarize Cahuilla rituals.

Most Cahuilla rituals have been described by Strong (1929). Consequently, a detailed review here is not necessary except for those aspects required for an understanding of the relationships between ritual and techno-environmental conditions. The rituals will be described in terms of participants, occurrence, where they took place, and their long-range, instrumental functions for Cahuilla society at large. In demonstrating these principles, the organizational concept "ritual congregation" will be discussed, and the functions of taboos and fasting will be reviewed.

THE "NUKIL" AND OTHER
RITUALS FOR THE DEAD

The *nukil,* the most elaborate and extensive Cahuilla ritual, was held annually or biennially during the winter to honor the souls of the dead (*tewlavil*). This week-long ceremony honored all members of a lineage who had died since the previous *nukil* ceremony. It was the last in a series of ceremonies which had as their objective the propitiation and disposition of the souls and property of the dead. It was initiated when there was adequate food and other valuables to provide gifts for the assembled guests, at times involving up to several hundred participants, representing several sibs of both moieties (as well as other tribes).

The *nukil* was the culmination of a long series of rituals associated with the dead. Immediately after the death of a lineage member, a series of rituals began—cremation and funeral activities, followed by a period of mourning when men and women refrained from particular activities, women cut their hair, and the home and possessions of the dead were burned or otherwise destroyed. However, it was not until after the conclusion of the *nukil* that family mourning ended and the souls of the dead achieved release from their earthly environs and entrance into the land of the dead.

The frequency of the *nukil*—annually or biennially—was determined by the number of deaths since the last ceremony, and whether there were sufficient economic resources to provide proper gifts for all invited guests.

Several months before the ceremony, the *net* and other lineage leaders met in council and decided on the timing of the *nukil*. The preparations for the ceremony were exceedingly arduous, and the ritual administrations throughout the observance were highly complex. Once the date was set, every member of a Cahuilla village became active in preparing for the forthcoming event. Everyone was required to contribute food and goods to the *kišʔamnaʔa* and make arrangements for accommodations and entertainment for the expected guests. During the ritual there would be opportunities for trading food and manufactured items for goods brought from other communities. Women would begin to prepare baskets for distribution, trade, or destruction. Men would prepare and string shell beads, manufacture nets and various other material goods for ceremonial use during the ritual or for trade. Families would begin to put away surplus food which the *net* would collect as the ceremonial time approached. Various families would discuss particular aspects of the ceremony: what singers they wanted to perform, favorite songs that the deceased would enjoy hearing, which of the various lineages should be invited, and what living arrangements should be made for the guests. For months the entire community was involved, planning and preparing for this intense Cahuilla ritual.

Relatives in other lineages and lineage leaders of groups with whom the hosts wished to establish ritual reciprocity were invited to attend the *nukil*. The *net* invited other lineages to attend by sending out strings of shell beads to the other lineages' *nets*. Acceptance of the bead string by the other *nets* consummated a contract guaranteeing their presence and support of their lineage at the ceremony. A *net* of a lineage who did not receive an invitation might signify his desire to attend by sending a string of beads or other goods, such as eagle feathers, to the *net* of the lineage planning the ceremony. If the gifts were accepted, it was understood that participation of his lineage would be welcomed at the ceremony. Another means of securing an invitation was the eagle-killing ritual, discussed below.

Strong (1929) has described the seven days and nights of continuous ritual and social activities occurring during the *nukil*. In brief, the observance began with a series of dances performed by the *puvalam* which were designed to "clear the atmosphere" of evil or malevolent spirits or ghosts and to purify the minds of those who might have evil intent. The dances ensured that all rituals would be properly performed. The *paxaa?* also led an extensive rabbit and deer hunt to acquire the surplus food needed for the many guests.

The last four days of the *nukil* were devoted to the cosmologically oriented song cycle performed by ritualists from several lineages. This epiclike series of songs described the Cahuilla universe and established the role of the Cahuilla people in it. The songs recapitulated the saga of the death of *Mukat* and the institution of the first funeral ceremonies of the first *nukil* which was administered by *?isily* (Coyote). On the morning of the last day of the *nukil,* life-size images into which the soul of the dead had entered (during the ceremony) were burned. This last rite, in conjunction with all of the rituals preceding it, provided the soul with sufficient power to follow the arduous path to the land of the dead. The disposition of the soul having been resolved, the somber week ended with a festive distribution of foods and treasure gifts to all guests.

The *nukil* was a time of intense social and economic interaction, therefore significant ecological functions were accomplished by its observance. While the week-long rituals were being conducted, private exchanges of goods took place, marriages were arranged, personal disputes and lineage enmities were expressed and controlled, and competitive games and gambling activities were held.

Whereas the host lineage was responsible for the care and feeding of guests during the week and a final distribution of remaining food and gifts at the end of the ceremonies, both hosts and guests shared the responsibility of ensuring that sufficient food was available to meet everyone's needs. Upon arrival, guests gave and received gifts of food and goods, and when they left they received another sizable gift in appreciation for their help in properly honoring the dead of the host group.

In addition to the gifts of food and manufactured items which guests brought from their own areas for the hosts, they brought along commodities designated for private trade. In addition to these exchanges by trade throughout the week, a significant random factor in the redistribution of goods was gambling.

The redistribution of food and goods at the *nukil* through gifts and private exchange provided some safety factors for a lineage. Any area experiencing a serious food shortage could be partially compensated for that shortage through the *nukil*-related exchange. Areas having extraordinary abundances which might give rise to jealousy or conflict could redistribute their excess with a minimum of embarassment to other less fortunate lineages. At the same time they set up an insurance or savings account for their own future needs in a time of stress because the ritual participation was reciprocal. This function of the *nukil* was manifest in the minds of the Cahuilla. Cahuillas today stress that people who had had a poor economic year brought only a little food to a *nukil* ceremony and were given much by the host. The amount of the gift by the host signified the extent of need of the recipient. A specific request for a disproportionate amount of food at the end of the observance was not necessary because the gossip of guests allowed the *net* to know the different needs of his guests. Figures 5 and 6 indicate the efficiency of the economic flow at the mourning ceremony.

EAGLE RITUAL

This ceremony has been well described by Strong (1929:*passim*) who gave the Cahuilla spelling as *aswitipememiktum* (1929:177).

The eagle was an especially important being to the Cahuilla. He was a *nukatam*—one of the original sacred people created by *Mukat*—who remained in the profane world. Each lineage or sib "owned" an eagle which symbolized the constant life of that lineage. The eagle is said to live forever, and yet, from the "beginning" allowed himself to be "killed" so the people were assured of life after death. As lineage members died each year but the lineage continued in perpetuity, so it is with the eagle. Each year the eagle allowed himself to be "killed," but he lives forever. The eagle flight also represented the magical flight of shamans who conducted souls to the land of the dead. Consequently, veneration of the eagle was reflected in ritual costumes and art work such as baskets and petroglyphs. Eagle feathers were used to make skirts and headdresses for ritual dancers, placed in ceremonial bundles, and used as decorations within the ceremonial house. The use of eagle feathers in these ways emphasized the symbolic importance of the eagle. Therefore, the eagle ritual was primarily one celebrating the perpetuation of the lineage and life after death for its members.

The ritual activities began many weeks before the *nukil* ceremony with the location of an eagle's nest high in a mountain crag. The *net* assigned an individual to watch the nest and report when

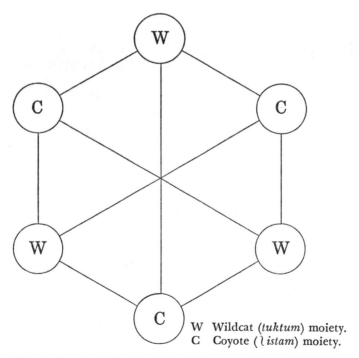

W Wildcat (*tuktum*) moiety.
C Coyote (ʔ*istam*) moiety.

FIGURE 5. Interchange of Food and Goods between Sibs and Moieties.
—— Exchange routes due to kinship and ritual regulations.

eggs were laid, when they hatched, when the down appeared on
the eaglets, and when the eaglets began eating live game. Each of
these events was celebrated by a special ritual in the village,
and guests from other lineages were sometimes invited. Guests
brought gifts of food and goods for the host who reciprocated in
kind.

Upon maturity of the eagle a ritual was scheduled to be held in
the *kišʔamnaʔa* and invitations were issued to a number of lineages.
Ideally the ritual was held every year, but sometimes it was held
less frequently, depending on the availability of an eagle. At each
night of the ritual, which lasted from three days to a week, a different neighboring lineage attended. On the last night all invited
lineages of the previous nights were invited to attend en masse.
The guests brought gifts of treasure items, food, baskets, and the
like when they came and the host lineage distributed similar items
to each lineage when they left.

On the last night of this particularly dramatic event, the eagle
"died." Special songs and dances were performed for this occasion.
Subsequently, the eagle's feathers were plucked for ritual use and
the eagle was buried with great ceremony and mourning with the
feeling on the part of the host lineage that one of their own people
had died. Goods were thrown on the eagle's grave by the women
of the host lineage to be collected by the guests. Each invited
net was presented with gifts of food and goods to be distributed
to his people.

A significant function of the eagle-killing ceremony was the
replacement, by the sponsoring lineage, of dance costume feathers
and ceremonial paraphernalia worn, destroyed, or exchanged in
previous rituals. It thus refurbished its treasure goods, to be used
at later rituals for the exchange of various goods. A second major
function of the ritual was establishing an economically reciprocal
relationship with other lineages. By inviting other lineages to
its eagle-killing ceremony the host lineage was given economic
resources and necessarily invited to rituals performed by the guest
lineages on other occasions. More gifting and exchange would
then occur. Rejecting an invitation meant taking the risk of being excluded on future occasions, thereby weakening lineage participation in the general ritual exchange system.

The ritual also limited witchcraft accusations, frequently responsible for revenge actions such as warfare and counterwitch-
craft, because acceptance gave evidence of friendliness and good
faith. Rejection of an invitation was often interpreted as an open
act of hostility and an affirmation that witchcraft accusations were

true. On a more practical level lineage participation in the ritual had a positive function of protection. Most neighboring lineages were invited, so there was little possibility of a surprise attack by a hostile lineage.

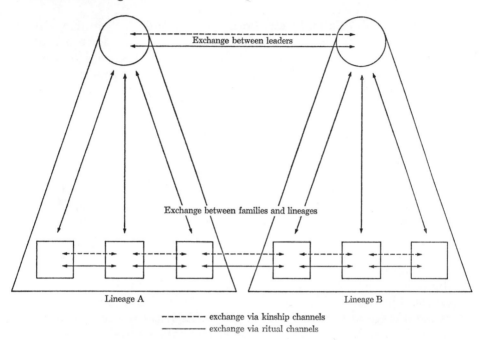

FIGURE 6. Exchange of Food and Goods within and between Lineages.

The lines and arrows indicate the directions of flow of food and goods within a lineage and between lineages. It may be seen that institutional devices directed the flow between lineages on two levels: from one *net* to another via ritual reciprocity, and from one lineage to another lineage via inter-family reciprocity established through marriage. In addition, individuals exchanged food and goods within the lineage and between lineages.

RITES OF PASSAGE

An examination of rituals confirming an individual's new status in Cahuilla society provides examples of ways in which rituals facilitated the adaptation of the individual to his ecosystem. In contrast to the *nukil* and *aswitipememiktum,* where the entire lineage or group was the focus of ritual attention, rites of passage focused on the individual with the immediate family, lineage, and collateral and affinal relatives in other lineages as participants.

As these rituals have been very well described by Strong (1929) and others, detailed descriptions are not needed here. The most significant rituals were: birth; naming ceremonies (*tculuni'l*); boys' initiation rites (*hemwek'luwil*); girls' initiation ceremonies (*ʔewlutni'ily*); marriage; and the public performances announcing changes in adult statuses such as the *net* and *puvalam* when they assumed office.

When a Cahuilla child was born, mother and child underwent a ceremony lasting several days. The mother and child were placed in a pit kept warm by hot stones and sand, and in which were placed various herbs. The child was bathed and both mother and child were given special herbal potions. The mother was forbidden to eat such foods as salt, meat, and the like.

This ritual was sponsored by the husband and his family, and the *net, paxaaʔ,* and *puvalam* who participated, as well as by the relatives of the wife's family, who were usually invited to attend. In addition, the *net* invited all members of the lineage to the *kiṣʔamnaʔa,* together with guests from outside the village. Gifts were brought for the family by the assembled guests, and food and other valuable goods were presented to all guests by the family of the newborn child.

When several children approached the age of four or five years, a naming ceremony was held. The *net* of the lineage announced the time of the ritual, and again the family presented gifts to the guests. The entire village participated in these ceremonies as well as the lineage of the children's mothers. At this time the children were given individual names—sometimes two names, one public and the other secret. The secret name was important, because knowledge of one's family name could aid a malevolent person in performing evil against an individual. Children's names, often the same as some revered ancestry, usually reflected the close association of the Cahuilla with their environment. For example, girls were often given names associated with the floral community; boys with game animals.

Initiation rites for adolescent boys and girls were dramatic rites of passage; the boys' ceremony being held at a time when enough food resources were available to conduct the rite (Strong, 1929: 174). The formal aspect lasted several days, but preparations began much earlier; large amounts of food had to be accumulated for the feast, and the boys instructed for several weeks prior to the public ceremony. The entire lineage was involved in this ritual, administered by the *net, paxaaʔ,* and *puvalam*.

The boys were removed to a private place to be instructed in esoteric matters of lineage history and their obligations toward society. These were dramatized by fasting, food taboos, strenuous physical activities, tests of bravery and resistance to pain, learning dances and songs (particularly enemy songs), observing the drawing of sand paintings (symbolizing Cahuilla cosmology), receiving explanations of the cosmology, as well as undergoing tattooing, ear piercing, and the piercing of the nasal septum. The hallucinatory plant, *Datura meteloides,* was used at some boys' ritual ceremonies, using patterns varying from sib to sib, lineage to lineage. In some lineages all the young boys drank an infusion made from *Datura,* in others only young men who were destined for shamanic roles drank a *Datura* infusion. While under the influence of *Datura,* it was expected that the initiate would indicate any potential he had for contacting the supernatural realm.

The boys' initiation ceremony was also the occasion to establish the future role of the young men. All their special skills and talents concerning subsistence techniques, dancing and singing, and their potential as future *puvalam* were evaluated. Finally, a three-day ceremony was held for the entire lineage and members of the lineages of the mothers. As with all other ceremonies, gifts were exchanged between guests and hosts.

The ritual for girls was associated with their first menstruation. The girls were placed in pits, as in the instance of the parturition rituals for mothers and newborn babies. Here they were given a special diet and elaborate instructions, by lineage ceremonialists and the girls' grandmothers, as to their proper roles as adult women, food producers, and childbearers. Invitations were issued by the village leaders to all lineages of the girls' mothers, and, again, gifts were received and given. Shortly after the ceremony, the girls were eligible for marriage.

FIRST-FRUIT RITES

A major concern of ritual was to ensure plant fertility and control the production and distribution of plant foods. Consequently, a ritual was held celebrating the commencement of the gathering season for most major foods: agave, mesquite, acorn, pinyon, and so on. When these foods were ready for collecting and preparation, the *net* sent a representative to gather a small amount which was brought to the *kiš?amna?a* where the lineage members gathered to eat a ritual portion of food. Each family brought additional food from their winter stores. This ceremony, lasting three days and nights, was held to express appreciation to the supernatural powers for providing the food. The generative powers of Cahuilla cosmology ensured that the plants would continue to produce food in future seasons. The ritual was accompanied by supernaturally and socially sanctioned restrictions to ensure that the people would not collect the food prior to the ritual. Cahuilla supernatural powers would cause anyone collecting food prior to the first-fruit ceremony to sicken or die. Upon completion of the ritual, the *net* declared the gathering season open, and instructed people in the procedural details concerning food collecting.

The first-fruit ritual was ordained from the "beginning" by *Mukat*. Patencio (1945:3) stated that "in the first Creation food was given to the people; but at the same time sickness was put into the food. The function of these rituals was to exorcise the sickness so that the people could eat the food without being harmed."

Beyond the religious overtones, the first-fruit rituals were adaptive to the Cahuilla ecosystem in several ways: they provided a ritual context for reaffirming or reestablishing rights of the lineage to a food-producing area; they protected the group by preventing a premature food harvest which might limit future plant productivity; they controlled potential conflict which might arise due to competition over newly available foods, because at each collecting season collecting procedures were redefined by the economic administrators of the community; they protected the individual and family rights to a specific grove by reaffirming their traditional rights to collect there; they ensured equitable food distribution at times when a valuable crop was smaller than usual; and these adaptive functions further served to reinforce the philosophical assumptions of Cahuilla world view, which explained the positive reciprocity occurring between the sacred and profane dimensions of the universe (explained in greater detail in the next chapter).

"WEYČIYAIL" RITUAL

Frequently in Cahuilla life an individual instigated ritual activity for his own purposes. By donating sufficient economic resources to the *kišʔamnaʔa* the individual could call on *ʔamnaʔa* and lineage administrators to aid him in some personal way. The individual made gifts to ritual leaders and provided the *kišʔamnaʔa* with sufficient food resources to feed a large number of people several meals. The ritual's purpose was left to the individual. For example, if he wanted ritual leaders to interpret a disturbing dream and obtain *ʔamnaʔa's* protection, he could sponsor the *weyčiyail.* If he was going on a hunt, he could sponsor a *weyčiyail* to receive supernatural sanctions for any potential kill.

The ritual provided psychological relief for the sponsor and at the same time he received ideological and community support for his generosity, because prestige was bestowed on the individual for his contribution to the *kišʔamnaʔa.* The action attested to his economic proficiency and generosity, and gave proof of his personal commitment to the community and the moral order. The ritual was expensive, requiring, as it did, the feeding of many people, because relatives and other guests from outside the village were frequently invited. The ritual also included the giving of special gifts to all individuals who participated as ceremonialists.

The adaptive mechanisms here are obvious—the individual with a surplus was encouraged by the system to share it through the ritual of the *weyčiyail,* while at the same time he received community recognition for his magnanimity and respect for tradition and the *kišʔamnaʔa.* This act further encouraged more productive activity on the part of everyone so that they could sponsor other occasions. It also possibly assuaged an individual's feelings of guilt for having a surplus of food, hoarding being a serious breach of the normative order.

RAIN RITUAL

Much of Cahuilla ritual was concerned with manipulating the environment through supernatural means. The control of rain was so important to Cahuilla survival that certain *puvalam,* in addition to their regular powers, exercised control over rain. They acted to stop rain or to cause it to arrive at will because they were the agents of spirit beings associated with rain.

There was a specific set of songs for this purpose, and a rock or charmstone was sometimes rubbed in association with the rite. Calistro Tortes, whose father performed these rituals, recalled that they were performed in especially dry periods and at other appropriate times so the rains would positively affect the future growth of plants. Such songs reflect the keen understanding of the relationship between seasonal patterns of rainfall and the subsequent effect on crops. Calistro Tortes described the psychology of the event as follows: "People talk to it [the rain] if it looked as if it might come. The talker must be a good person, he had to be in the right state, not selfish; he would tell it to go away, we need food, don't destroy it until we pick it; if you are in the right state, he will go away. If you don't mean it, he won't" (personal communication). The ritual was accompanied by a fervent oratory indicating the intense anxiety felt about water conditions in the Cahuilla territory where the precipitation pattern is highly erratic.

CURING RITUALS AND MEDICINE

Curing rituals, important events for the Cahuilla community, were conducted whenever special medical help was needed. They were performed by a *puul* alone, or in conjunction with the *net* and other *puvalam* in the ceremonial house.

To effect a cure, the *puul,* who worked with or without other ritualists, used ritual singing, chanting, dancing, sucking, and smoking, together with practical remedies such as herbs, sweating, prescribed rest, purgatives, massage, and the like.

The very process of attempting to gather and hunt enough food for oneself, the family, and community, in an area where unexpected events such as forest fires, earthquakes, flash floods, torrential rains, drought and other physical and emotional stresses were frequent occurrences, caused a great deal of anxiety. Real and psychosomatic illnesses were frequent results of these stressful conditions which removed people from ordinary activity. Cahuillas have reported numerous cases in which people who were allergic to particular foods were subsequently cured of their symptoms by *puvalam.*

These rituals were significant for the productive system, because a maximum labor force was required for the full exploitation of the environment. The value of the *puvalams'* activity was clear. By effecting cures, they placed people back into the production system, or they legitimized temporary absences from productive activity by explaining the nature of the illness to the community so that suspicions of malingering were reduced.

RITUALS OF SUBSISTENCE

Other rituals which played an impressive part in assuring adequate distribution and supply of food resources were those associated with the killing of deer, mountain sheep, or an antelope. They were performed several times during the year.

The deer ceremony was usually held when a young man had killed his first deer, or when a man had killed a deer and wished to encourage the pleasure of the supernatural beings, or to honor the *kiš²amna²a*. As in the funeral rituals, the rite involved singing over the body of the animal. The purpose was to enlist the aid of the guardian animal spirit so that the animals would cooperate with the hunter. The hunters explained to the spirit of the animal what they were doing and acknowledged their appreciation to the animals for allowing themselves to be killed. The ritual also aided the spirit of the animal to enter into the next world, and ensure that the animal's spirit would carry a good report of the hunter's activities to the animal's spiritual guardian.

When the deer (or one of the other large animals) was presented at the *kiš²amna²a,* food was collected from all families in the village who were then invited to the ceremonial house to take part in the ritual and receive a portion of the deer. During the morning after the ceremony, the butchered deer was distributed to the community at large. Although it is not remembered how frequently this ritual occurred, memory is sufficiently clear to suggest that it was quite frequent and was the mechanism by which sizable amounts of meat were distributed to the villagers. The rituals connected with the capture of large game were also adaptive, providing reward of social prestige and "power verification" to the successful hunter, and acting as mechanisms for encouraging ecological balance between man and the biota.

Another ritual concerned with animal acquisition was connected with the rabbit hunt, a sociologically structured and ritually regulated ceremony. The purpose was to acquire a large number of rabbits and other small rodents for feeding guests at the *nukil* or other ceremonies, which occurred when rabbit populations were very high. The hunt involved a large number of men, women, and children. It usually was organized and led by the *paxaa²a,* who saw that the nets were set up properly, directed the chase, and gave directions concerning the collection and cleaning of the game that was killed. In some instances hundreds of these animals were collected in such an outing.

An ecological function of this ritual was to encourage the regular culling of these and other small animals which might otherwise interfere with the ecological balance of the entire ecosystem. Rabbit hunts were often conducted when fresh greens and seed-producing plants were growing lushly after winter rains. To allow these voracious browsing animals to eat their fill day by day would have reduced the potential food supply of the Cahuilla. The hunt was, therefore, a safety mechanism operating to control overpopulation, thus reducing exploitation of plant life. Certainly the timing appears to be especially advantageous for such an assumption.

This same culling process was used to control overpopulation of a number of other animals, insects, and perhaps birds. One method was to set fire to mesquite groves to flush the animals into the open where they were slaughtered by people surrounding the burning brush.

The appearance of insects in great numbers harnessed the energies of a large number of people for communal gathering; for example, larvae, grasshoppers, etc. These insects also ate greens and destroyed plants that the Cahuilla needed for food. Rituals, such as the first fruit, were held when insect hordes appeared. The gathering was organized by the *net* and, following the ritual eating ceremony held in the *kiš²amna²a,* the proceeds were distributed to the community and to any invited guests.

There were ritual taboos on the killing of most predatory animals. Some ecologists have suggested that the decrease in the number of predators in past years in this area has caused significant and rapid increase of rodents which live on vegetable life. There was apparently more than mythic taboo involved for the Cahuilla—these taboos may have had functional and adaptive values in maintaining ecological balance, because only under particular, ritually dictated circumstances was it admissible to kill predators or scavengers such as coyotes, foxes, wolves, mountain lions, eagles, and owls.

Further, a young hunter was especially beset by ritual restrictions and obligations controlling the distribution of his kill. As has been noted, prior to a marriage he had to give his first large catch to the *kiš²amna²a* and to his future wife's family. In the process he was subject to ritual restrictions of a more personal nature. After his marriage he was allowed to keep game he caught. However, he was still expected to share it with his immediate relatives and other fellow lineage members. Special attention on his part was expected to be given to aged people.

The constant concern the hunter had regarding the reaction of game animals toward him was also reflected in the number and kinds of rites in which the heads of game were treated in special ways. The horns of large game, for instance, were sometimes placed in special piles; rabbit heads were eaten by the hunter and, so the rabbits could not communicate with other game to warn them of the hunter's approach, kept around as trophies.

BIRD DANCE

The bird dance was a festive occasion in Cahuilla life. Although this may not formally belong to the category of ritual, it was occasionally performed at ritual gatherings and was sufficiently wrapped within ideological commitments to include it here for description and analysis. It was an occasion when men and women came together to sing a dramatic song cycle describing various facets of environmental conditions and historic reactions to them by anthropomorphized birds. The songs were performed by men, accompanied by the metered beat of rattles. There were lead singers and followers, some of whom sang while seated with the leader. Others, men and women, participated in the dancing.

The bird dance occurred whenever people felt like joining together for this activity. Considerable food was prepared at the *kiš?amna?a* and made available to all participants and observers. In aboriginal times it is said that the bird dances were usually organized by the *net,* who ritually prepared the big house and the outdoor formal dance ground for the event. If this was inconvenient, the dances could be held at any place the singer chose, thus lessening the ritual requirements of opening the *kiš?amna?a* or "clearing" it for use.

This ceremony was interesting in that it provided a time for considerable social relaxation with a minimum of formal role-playing for men, women, and young people. Women, for instance, were able at this time to invite men to dance, and considerable teasing occurred between sexes and between individuals with whom such behavior was at other times considered improper. Psychologically it was a very festive time.

In more recent times the bird dances have been held for special occasions like birthdays, New Year's Eve, Thanksgiving, and other times which are traditionally festive and joyous in the Anglo ritual pattern.

The ecologically adaptive aspects of these dances appear to have been associated with learning and socialization. The songs recounted stories about risks and difficulties which birds (and people) met in real life. They provided object lessons concerning proper behavior and what happened if the people did not act accordingly. An engaging example concerns birds who kept seeking more pleasant surroundings by ignoring warnings of older and more experienced birds, and consequently found themselves in an

area which was indeed rich in food and comfort for a season. However, it turned out to be a dangerous place: freezing weather came
which killed most of the birds. Those who survived learned their
lesson and returned to their former homeland, content to adjust
to and remain in that land.

"WEXILY" SONGS

Wexily songs were acts of denigration against other specified
lineages. Often they were sung as a subsidiary ritual event conducted during the initiation rituals of young people and the
nukil. They were also sung by individuals in their attempt to
ward off impending disaster, to avert its impact to another group.

The songs varied in their function. They were sung to send
anticipated disaster to a reciprocating group, to sanction behavior
of someone or a group which had "gone against the song," and to
emphasize invidious comparisons with other groups. Each lineage
had another lineage to whom it addressed these songs on a formal
basis. This lineage was usually located at a considerable geographic distance from them, and was one with which no marriage
had been made in recent times. In fact, intermarriage was difficult
between such lineages.

The songs related especially to anxieties occurring at the time
of natural or supernatural disasters: earthquakes, droughts, crop
failures, torrential rainfalls, and the like. When such events were
anticipated or occurred, the disasters were "sent" to the enemy
lineage through the singing of these songs. The songs also had a
socializing function, as they were sung at initiation rituals when
the person's lineage was euphemistically described in comparison
with others. This served to enhance the group identification and
esprit de corps. They were often sung at a time when many lineages were present. Contests were held between lineages to discover
which one could sing the most songs against another group, and
the winning group acquired prestige. Sometimes these contests
led to serious physical conflicts between the competing lineages.
Women usually did the singing and the men stood by to alleviate
or control a serious conflict if it occurred.

The songs performed another socialization function: they were
intended to embarrass the person and his lineage publicly by the
singing. In such instances this appears to have acted as a control on
behavior because of the threat of being denounced publicly. It
also alleviated possible conflict on other social levels between
groups and within groups. The action of the hostile lineage was

sanctioned, thus alleviating possible stress from within the whole system. It also allowed for public, institutionalized, and overt verbal conflict to occur between groups with long-standing enmities—a steam-valve mechanism—which perhaps relieved anxiety at stress periods in a ritualistic and relatively "safe" way which might otherwise have caused intragroup conflict or irrational behavior.

OTHER RITUALS

There were other rituals occurring periodically which will not be discussed in detail. For example, a ritual was held when there was an eclipse of the moon or the sun; this caused group lineage action because of the terrifying and cataclysmic nature of this "supernatural" phenomenon. And there were other special dance ceremonies like the fire dance which were often held either in connection with rituals such as the *nukil* or independently at other times of the year.

RITUAL CONGREGATIONS

Although the lineage as the basic building block for Cahuilla social structure, perhaps the most significant sociological feature of Southern California Indian people (Cahuilla included) were "ritual congregations." The concept "ritual congregations" refers to the joining together, in Southern California, of individual sociopolitical groups (sibs or lineages) in ritual contexts. The groups so joined varied from season to season and year to year so that at any one time there might be many ritual congregations functioning, with memberships possibly overlapping with one another. For example, a given group might belong to several ritual congregations at the same time, but in no single ritual congregation of which it is a member do all the groups' members belong.

I feel that ritual congregations are the most important social units because they allow for otherwise independent and autonomous groups to join together for political, economic, ritual, or military purposes. With its built-in flexibility, economic and political alliances can expand or decrease or change member units in response to changing environmental circumstances. This protects the independency of the basic corporate units which are well adapted to the ecological conditions of Southern California, but allows for redistribution of goods and economic resources in such a way that economic crises rarely reach proportions where severe military tactics are necessary for survival. I suggest that this basic structural device is characteristic throughout most of California, and gives anthropologists a more adequate explanation of why the institution of warfare was weakly developed among California Indians.

Three types or ritual have been described: those usually including only members of one lineage, such as the *weyčiyail,* which acted to redistribute foods within the village and may have included people outside the village; rituals including lineage members and selected individuals outside the village who were related to principles in the ritual (for example, the rites of passage); and rituals such as the *nukil,* which always included several lineages invited by one host lineage. All participating lineages, represented by their leaders, shared in the giving and receiving of foods and goods.

The obligations to invite other moiety and kinship members, together with the obligation to invite lineages that had gifted other lineages, as during the eagle-killing ceremony, meant that several lineages representing both moieties were active participants at each of the *nukil* rituals. However, the specific lineages participating at any one *nukil* varied from one occasion to another. For example, if the *qawiʔsiktem,* or "fox people," lineage gave a *nukil* ceremony one year, they might have had lineages A, B, C, and D as guests. On another occasion a year or two later, A, C, E, and F lineages were invited. Thus, at two points in time, two separate ritual congregations were brought together. Then, within those same years, the *qawiʔsiktem* lineage might attend *nukil* ceremonies hosted by lineages A, C, and F. Thus, a significant structural unit based on ritual participation occurred regularly which cross-cut formal political boundaries of the sib.

In addition to the lineages within a sib which participated in *nukil* ceremonies, lineages from other sibs and tribes were also involved. Some of these relationships tended to be long in duration; that is, the same ritual partners cooperated year after year, and these partnerships were reconfirmed or restated by the exchange of ceremonial beads as has been shown. Therefore, at any one season, all Cahuilla groups were interlocked with several Cahuilla as well as some groups from other cultural units to form such a congregation, Serrano, Diegueño, and Gabrielino being the ones most frequently mentioned. Thus, a complex network of interlocking ritual congregations came together throughout the Southern California area forming an elaborate network of reciprocal exchanges. The figure on page 139 will demonstrate the nature of this system.

These interactions came about because of three rules governing Cahuilla ritual behavior: members of both moieties must be represented in the performance of most rituals; the immediate kin of the personnel celebrated or honored by the ritual must be invited; and gifts must be brought to be given to the host in order for him to provide gifts for the guests at the conclusion of the ritual.

The most frequent form of gifting was in terms of food products, but manufactured goods and "treasures" were also given. The manufactured and treasure goods could be transformed into food directly through exchange, and were substitutes for the gifts of food when these were not available. Thus, a group possessing a surplus of manufactured goods and treasures could transform them into foodstuffs by presenting them as part of the ritual gifting, receiving foodstuffs in return. Consequently, when a lineage had a surplus of foods, it sent these out to other groups and received hard goods in their place. That group, in turn, sent out hard goods when it was short of foodstuffs, receiving food in their stead.

The pattern was most clearly demonstrated in the *nukil* ritual, which was performed by every lineage at regular intervals of at least every two years. Exchange of foods and goods took place at every social level. Each *net* collected foods from his own group and brought them as gifts to the host lineage who had also accumulated surplus from their group; therefore, the surplus of each social unit involved in the *nukil* was, in effect, brought together in one place. The *net* of the host lineage, then, acted as a redistributing agent for all the lineages invited to his *nukil*, because he redistributed the goods and food to all the *nets* attending the *nukil* at the conclusion of the ritual. These *nets* brought the goods back to their individual villages and held another ritual, which distributed the goods to the population at large.

FUNCTIONAL ASPECTS OF
TABOOS AND FASTING

Several rituals were performed by a hunter to ensure maximum power and success during the hunt, and to prevent natural or supernatural forces from interfering with his ability to acquire food needed for himself and his family. A number of these rituals involved behavioral taboos and food restrictions. For example, for some days before the hunt the men ate bland foods; this was necessary for the stalking process because the hunter's body-odor, had he eaten strong flesh, would have been more easily detected by the game animals. For the same reason hunters gathered in the sweathouse to sweat, bathe, rub their bodies with various herbs to "give them the odor of the forest" and to reduce the "human" odor, and to exchange tales of the lore of the hunt. It was also regarded as exceedingly important that the hunter refrain, prior to the hunt, from any activities which would affect the animals adversely (sex, contact with menstruating women). An eighty-year-old Cahuilla woman explained—perhaps facetiously—that, without the taboo prohibiting sexual activity, the hunter might "want to stay at home making babies all the time and not do his hunting."

The negative sanctions that menstrual blood and pregnancy had upon supernatural powers which aided the hunter placed numerous restrictions upon the activities of young, unmarried menstruating women as well as on a man and wife. In such instances a woman was regarded as very "dangerous": she could not touch her husband, step over him while he was lying prone, or touch his hunting equipment. In fact, sometimes a man was even restricted from hunting while his wife was convalescing from a recent childbirth, if it was felt that there was a possibility of some contamination from her afterbirth.

The fasting associated with hunting rituals was adaptive in that it made more food available for the younger and older members of the society, especially in times of food stress. Such activities as sweating, bathing, fasting, and meditating may indicate the psychological preparation of the hunter for the rigors of the hunt. He was often alone in physically dangerous environments for several days. Thus, rituals calling attention to the need for cautious actions on the hunter's part were significant measures for preventing accidents. An additional aspect of ritually enforced rules of hunting was that the hunter carried very little with him, usually only a pouch of chia seed or jerky. He was expected to find water along his trail, and to help himself from food caches in the mountains that were available for his use on such occasions. Because he was not burdened down with equipment he was able to travel more efficiently and carry more game back to the village.

NUTRITIONAL ASPECTS OF RITUAL

An important function of rituals was guaranteeing the distribution of animal foods to large numbers of people at times when nutritional needs were likely to be acute. Rappaport has suggested (1968:22) that: "It is reasonable to assume that misfortune and emergency are likely to induce into the organisms experiencing them a complex of physiological changes known collectively as stress . . . and . . . that disease, rage, fear, or prolonged anxiety can contribute to this condition, in which appreciable amounts of amino acids are essential for growth and tissue repair since . . . an aspect of stress is increased catabolization of protein with a net loss of nitrogen from the tissues." He also observes (1968:85–86) that there is significant improvement with the increased catabolization of protein and a net loss of nitrogen from the tissues during these periods; high protein diets are, therefore, routinely prescribed for surgical patients and those suffering from contagious diseases. The lack of protein under such circumstances delays healing of wounds, encourages anemia, contributes to the failure of gastrointestinal stomas to function, reduces resistance to infection, decreases resistance to shock, increases hypotension, lowers basal metabolism, contributes to lack of appetite, causes general weakness and mental changes including confusion, lethargy, and depression. This is relevant for the Cahuilla because it was in the winter season that ritual activity was most intense, and it was then that nutritional needs were most acute because fresh plant foods were scarce. During these months stored plant foods provided the bulk of the diet. If the food collections were poor the season before, for example, a crop failure of mesquite, acorn, or pinyon, considerable nutritional and psychological stresses were induced within the community. The shortages of food in one area were threatening also because some of the rituals which have been described were cancelled or limited in their performance, thus endangering man's relationship to the entire universe. This caused conflicts between groups which normally maintained long-range, reciprocal ritual obligations because one or more of the groups were not able to meet their responsibilities.

Even without a food shortage this was a difficult time of year as colds and pulmonary infections were common, and many people from diverse areas came together for ritual activity which increased the possibility of spread of contagion.

Warfare and raiding were most frequent at this time, which increased the personal injury and psychological stress.

The belief system itself brought about anxiety because this was the time when the obligations of the living to the dead were very much on their minds, and intense grief because of the loss of loved ones was expressed. Furthermore, fear that the rituals would not be satisfactory to the dead also contributed to the general apprehension. A sociological consequence of death of personnel within the community was the necessity for making new interpersonal relationships among the living.

Even though the rituals served to maintain the equilibrium of the universe which was man's guarantee that he would have sufficient food, they were also a potential source of dread because ritual error could lead to serious consequences for all the people.

Given all the above circumstances it can be seen that stress was indeed high during this time of year. To counterbalance the stress, the need for protein was increased. Vegetable proteins, which were available in the stored food such as acorn meal, lacked the important amino acids needed. Thus the hunts for rabbit, deer, mountain sheep, and antelope, which were held in conjunction with the rituals, provided the high protein diet required to cope with stress.

A major function of ritual was, therefore, the provision of meat protein in such a manner and at such a time that dysfunctional physiological reactions due to stress and shortages of vegetable foods were minimized. Cahuilla rituals were associated with the distribution and consumption of large amounts of meat, as in the instance of the deer ceremony where a large game animal was divided among the participants; and in the instance of the *nukil* rites which lasted several days, where large amounts of rabbit, deer, and other game were dispensed to large numbers of people.

The massive amounts of food (particularly meat protein) and goods which were provided on ritual occasions are indicated by the number of rituals which have been described. Using these as a sample, any given lineage, therefore, hosted and attended several rituals each year. Members of every lineage were guests at several *nukil* ceremonies each winter. Several rites of passage for young children, naming ceremonies and the like, also included guests from several lineages. A single lineage held rituals which included its own members and some invited guests as often as once a week, according to Cahuilla informants. Several rituals required several days to a week to perform, which added to the number of days when rituals were given.

Therefore, an exchange of foods (especially meats) and goods within a given village were ritually induced perhaps fifty times a year, exchanges of foods and goods with other villages were induced perhaps a dozen times a year. In each instance a massive distribution of meat protein was divided among large numbers of people.

FIG. 7 *Annual Round of Ritual and Productive Activities*

January–February	*March–April–May*	*June–July*
Little gathering activity. Agave harvested usually in February. Men went in groups for three or four days, but little other fresh plant food was available. Cahuilla relied on stored supplies; e.g., acorn meal, mashed mesquite and screwbean cakes, dried fruits, berries, etc., to the extent they were left. Much hunting filled out the stored food diet to support intense ritual activities.	Numerous plants came into bloom. Spring blossoms, greens, buds, and grasses grew very near villages in the lower zones. Women gathered; men hunted numerous small game and larger browsing animals.	Fruits, mesquite, and screwbean ripened in the Lower Sonoran zone. Large community efforts were expended to gather yucca, manzanita berries, and fruits of all kinds. Roots were dug. Food was available in all zones.

← – – – – – – – →

August–September	*October–November*	*December*
Grasses and seeds such as chia were harvested; dates and fruits gathered. Pinyon harvests required the efforts of large groups of people who left their villages and camped in the groves for a week or more. Women and children gathered; men helped, and hunted game nearby.	Acorn season. Half to two-thirds of the villagers moved to the groves to collect acorns, grind, and leach the meal to reduce the bulk for easy carrying. Men hunted nearby.	Little gathering; much hunting. Rituals began in earnest and continued through the winter months. Visiting, trading, inter- and intra-group activities heavy. Time for manufacture of goods, teaching the young, recreation, and gambling.

← – – – – – – – →

Legend: ← – – – – → greatest ritual and group activities
         ←————————→ heaviest subsistence activities

157

SUMMARY

Ritual was a significant variable in maintaining ecological equilibrium in Cahuilla society. Some of its functions are summarized below.

Ritual stimulated productive activities at all social levels because the exchange of foods and goods was a necessary feature of the process. The individual was encouraged to provide foods and goods for the support of the rituals, thus enhancing his prestige within the community. Likewise, the family produced foods and goods as a unit in order to sponsor rituals which were enjoyed by all. In each instance the sponsor acquired material benefits in the form of gifts and social prestige as well as supernatural favor.

These same rituals distributed foods and goods throughout the society at large because the surplus of one area was exchanged for surplus of food or treasure goods held in another. This process set up a banking procedure whereby treasure goods could be accumulated for foodstuffs, and subsequently exchanged for food.

The distribution system was arranged so that meat protein was divided among the people at times when it was most needed to relieve physiological and psychological stress. Thus the dispersal had biologically adaptive functions.

The rituals also prevented extreme conflict over economically desirable areas because of the constant exchanges of treasure goods and food between groups. Such occasions brought people together in a market-place atmosphere so that their goods and foods could be exchanged with a minimum of conflict.

Rituals were significant to the economic order in several other ways. They served to verify and support the rules concerning land use and occupancy by reminding the participants of the traditional boundaries held by corporate groups and by clearly defining who had hunting and collecting rights within these boundaries. Automatic retribution was imposed upon all those who violated these rules, for example, first-fruit rites and the use of spirit sticks. The administrative roles of the *net* and *paxaa?* were also reinforced by their participation in the ritual system. Thus, an orderly exploitation of the environment was usually maintained.

Psychologically, the various rituals served to intensify the awareness of hunters and collectors as to the proper conduct of their tasks. This awareness increased their efficiency and relieved anxieties which might otherwise have interfered with their productive activity. Curing rituals placed the infirm back into the productive system or provided acceptable reasons for their inactivity. They also relieved individuals of psychosomatically caused disabilities which interfered with daily tasks.

Finally, the rituals acted as important servomechanisms for the whole ecosystem because the hunts associated with them had the effect of culling herbivorous and omnivorous game so as to maintain a viable balance within the ecosystem. The protection of carnivorous game by taboo and the massive destruction of voracious insects and parasites served similar functions.

9

World View: Existential and Normative Postulates

INTRODUCTION

Cahuilla philosophical assumptions are closely integrated to environmental reality and affect behavior at every level of life. A thorough examination of the philosophical system is not possible at this time, but I will review those existential and normative postulates of Cahuilla philosophy relevant to adaptation to environment. Existential postulates refer to the structure and composition of the universe. Consequently, the nature of supernatural power, some assumptions about the nature of the system, and the beings within it, will be outlined. Normative postulates provide guidelines for behavior for the participants of a culture. Some of these will be outlined, reviewed, and the effect they have on day-to-day behavior explored in relation to the making of a living in Cahuilla society.

Several existential postulates are: the existence of ʔivaʔa, a power or energy source; the Cahuilla universe was systemic; all phenomena were potentially unstable and unpredictable; the Cahuilla universe was divided between phenomena containing ʔivaʔa which had "will" and the potential for action, and phenomena which did not contain ʔivaʔa and did not have "will" or the power to act; and the social universe was divided into named beings ranging in all times and dimensions in Cahuilla history.

The various tasks, demonstrated in the discussions of status and role, kinship, law, social structure, ritual, and subsistence activities, were supported by normative postulates maintaining, channeling, and stimulating behavior consistent with the long-range adaptive consequences for the society. Consequently, some idealized criteria for decision making (values) were emphasized as being more important than others in day-to-day decision-making situations. These will be discussed below. They are: tradition, age, maleness, industriousness, reciprocity, order and precision, moderation and personal control, secrecy and caution.

ʔIVAʔA (POWER)

According to Cahuilla philosophy, *ʔivaʔa* was the basic generative force from which all things were created; *ʔivaʔa* formed the corporeal world through cataclysmic interaction of two masses of force identified with maleness and femaleness. From these forces came the creator beings *Mukat* and *Temayawet,* who demonstrated the proper and improper uses of power. *Mukat* was the older of the two. He used *ʔivaʔa* correctly, and, thus, became the grand designer of the universe. *ʔivaʔa* was very intense in the beginning, but it has constantly and elusively diminished through time. Its presence and availability to men throughout history, however, have testified to its earlier potency, and it has continued to account for phenomena in the present.

The theory of *ʔivaʔa* explaining the Cahuilla universe carried with it certain assumptions. A principal assumption was that all things were composed of *ʔivaʔa*—or were created through or by it —and nothing existed independent of it. It was demonstrated through all things which happened. In everyday life it was manifest in the actions of spirit beings, in the activities of fellow Cahuillas who had unusual talents or power, such as the *net* and *puvalam,* the *maiswat,* and life itself. Unusual events and differences in cultural attainment were also explained by the presence of *ʔivaʔa*. Some groups had greater amounts of power than others. Thus the cultural dominance of the Pacific Coast cultures (Gabrielino and Chumash) was due to their greater access to *ʔivaʔa*. *ʔivaʔa* was greater in the west and diminished as it moved to the east. Curiously, the Colorado people were not mentioned in this context.

Power was independent. Unusual amounts of it could be acquired at birth, through placation, manipulation, gift, or ritual. Power operated for the benefit of man. But occasionally it was harmful. In fact, it was neither good nor bad. If one treated power properly, the result was usually beneficial; if improperly, serious harm. Thus, it was something people wanted, but something which they feared—its presence was gratifying but demanding; it was necessary, but it was also an awesome responsibility. Ideally the individual receiving the power used it for the good of his people. But often he did not. *ʔivaʔa* was used in practical affairs to manipulate and control the environment. Thus, a man who was able to cope successfully with the environment demonstrated the possession of power, whether it was for the capture of game, or in performing rituals which caused abundant foods, curing disease, or whatever.

Belief that *ʔivaʔa* was dangerous was intensified because some people used it malevolently. Many unusual events such as the desiccation of food plants, the disappearance of game, earthquakes and flash floods, as well as personal misfortunes, were attributed to such persons. *Puvalam* and *nenaŋiniš* often were held responsible for these dire events, but others were sometimes implicated. Several women are remembered as having used secret magical formulae for harming people.

Special precautions were taken at ritual occasions to prevent the harmful use of power. The "witches' dance," for example, was held to clear the "big house" and grounds of harmful forces placed there by persons or other beings who wanted to harm participants. Many people from diverse areas came together at this time, so there were opportunities for "witching" an enemy. The "witches' dance" served as a constructive notice that such action was not welcome, and to warn that the perpetrator would be punished by the combined power of the *puvalam* performing the dance. If other beings (*nukatem*) wished to harm the participants, the *puvalam* could intercede or at least tell the ceremonialists to postpone the ritual until the danger was resolved.

The harmful uses of *ʔivaʔa* were also guarded against by carefully destroying or hiding such things as the umbilical cords of the newborn, hair cuttings, nail parings, and feces so they could not be used for magical purposes. Suspicion of witchcraft as a causative agent for disaster was a typical Cahuilla reaction to environmental stress such as crop failures, flash floods, faulting, epidemics, or mass invasion by grasshoppers. Frequently villages were relocated as a result of these events. Thus, resettlement was often caused by the good or evil uses of *ʔivaʔa*, its absence or presence determining the well-being of the people in a particular locality.

ASSUMPTION OF INSTABILITY
AND UNPREDICTABILITY

A corollary to the postulate of *ʔivaʔa* was that all matter was subject to unpredictable change. Since *ʔivaʔa* itself was quixotic, it might leave unexpectedly, causing any number of disasters. For example, dramatic changes in topography are vividly and frequently recalled, and social relations were seen as unpredictable because this year's ally in ritual exchange might be next year's enemy. In political life there was always the apprehension that a *net* or *puul* would suddenly use power against his own people. Thus, the possibility of such an alteration in the system was always present.

This instability was true from the beginning. Creation of the earth and life itself was fraught with indecision, mistakes, and conflicts of power between the creator brothers. There was conflict between *Mukat* and his creations in the "beginning." The Creator himself was unpredictable and unstable because he tricked people into performing acts which were harmful to them. He also violated basic moral principles by molesting *Menily*, "moon maiden" who was a mother symbol, and caused her to leave the people. The *nukatem*, also the first beings created by *Mukat* and *Temayawet*, treated *Mukat* in devious ways—they spied on him, talked against him, and finally caused his death through witchcraft. This cosmological precedent justified replacing unstable or unpredictable political leaders when they behaved as *Mukat* did.

The nature of groups (lineages) was seen as flexible, because segmentation of lineages into independent corporate groups was justified by precedent in the oral literature. Thus, stress factors (whether sociological, psychological, or ecological) which created severe conflict within a lineage could be relieved by one part of the lineage breaking away to form a new unit.

Linguistic evidence also indicates this assumption. Seilor has said:

For not only may existential predication be qualified as uncertain; there are other indications in our texts that the Cahuillas, in contradistinction to speakers of West-European languages, express factual and observable things as if they were uncertain. One such indication is the frequence of such particles or phrases of indecision or doubt as

(16) (i) ʔesan   'I guess'
     (ii) wam   'maybe'
     (iii) ha·kiʔi 'or not'

in description of things or situations that can be seen both by the informant and by the linguist (1969:15).

The all-pervasive and intense feeling of apprehension toward the present as well as the future was a realistic orientation to the environment which was indeed full of real and continual changes. When living in an area where great effort must be exerted daily to acquire sufficient food, and where disasters could—and did— occur to upset the balance of nature, the rituals and constant vigil to keep their world in balance were adaptive; they encouraged certain institutional mechanisms which precluded, averted, or alleviated distress from various sources. They encouraged the caching of food, assiduous efforts in collecting and hunting, and careful attention to the principles of reciprocity and ritual which spread economic risk throughout a ritual congregation.

To reinforce this orientation, each member of Cahuilla society was carefully socialized to anticipate stress and to act appropriately to emergencies or disasters. This preparation for life was adaptive in that it encouraged the development of a psychological expectation to stress, with the effect of inuring the individual to all but catastrophic changes.

ASSUMPTION OF
NEGATIVE-POSITIVE INTEGRATION

$?iva?a$ could be useful for harmful or beneficial purposes, so all phenomena containing $?iva?a$ were capable of negative and positive actions. Whether the Cahuilla was thinking of human behavior, the habitat, or other beings, either negative or positive actions were assumed to be possible. This assumption, logical and consistent with the nature of the environment, provided both sustenance and stress. Power benefited and harmed men. *Mukat* gave life and creative genius to the Cahuilla, but he also gave death, sickness, and frustration. He made and broke rules.

This integration of negative and positive aspects of the universe had adaptive functions. It prepared the individual to deal with contrasting qualities in all phenomena. While encouraging the Cahuilla to anticipate positive results from their universe, it prepared the individual for negative results as well. The ritual system and the regulations regarding kinship reciprocity were mechanisms for coping with these expectations. Moreover, expectations of negative phenomena further stimulated economic activity.

On a day-to-day level, accepting the reality of negative-positive aspects of the universe made it possible for each Cahuilla to see that every individual was both beneficent and malevolent, and categorized as neither one nor the other unless his actions approached intolerable levels. As a sociological consequence of this it allowed for maximum use of the individual without disrupting the system as a whole. For example, a good ceremonialist was allowed to function as a ritualist—a significant and necessary cultural action in terms of survival itself—although he might otherwise be deviant. The same was true of skilled hunters or collectors.

Many negative actions, then, were tolerated by the system in order to maximize the useful talents of all people. Only in very extreme instances were productive members of the community eliminated from the system.

ASSUMPTION THAT MAN IS
PART OF A SYSTEM

Another assumption and a corollary of the postulate of *ʔivaʔa* was that man was an integral part of nature, and that most of the universe was an interacting system. Man was seen as one of a number of cooperating beings, who, together with his fellow Cahuilla, shared in the workings of the universe. Thus, an ecologic ethic existed which assumed that any action affected other parts of the system. It was a reciprocal process, therefore man had an obligation to the rest of the universe. For instance, permission had to be granted from *pemtexweva,* whose role it was to provide the Cahuilla with game, to exploit the food resources such as deer, mountain sheep, and antelope. The reciprocal obligations were that the deer allowed themselves to be caught, while man was careful not to overkill or waste the products provided by the deer. Man also was obligated to give ritual support to the system, thereby aiding in the regeneration of all life on earth. Various restrictions functioned to prevent man from unnecessarily destroying food crops. A collector never picked all the edible part of a plant; all the seeds were not gathered—something was always left over. A protectiveness toward other forms of life was represented by this action. Furthermore, Cahuilla hunting actions and rituals helped maintain equilibrium in various animal populations. It was man's integral part of a cooperating system.

THE SOCIAL UNIVERSE

The Cahuilla universe was composed of a number of beings, all falling within a category which was separated into types: *nukatem,* those who *Mukat* and *Temayawet* created in the "beginning" such as *teyawa,* an agent of a *nukatem; tewlavil,* soul spirits; *taxliswiten,* living men; and others, for example, *suqtam.*

NUKATEM

Most of the *nukatem* were no longer active, but were visible in transformed states such as *Menily* (moon maiden) and others who became various stars and other natural phenomena. Most of these functioned as symbols reminding the Cahuilla of the "early times." However, there were some *nukatem* who remained active in worldly affairs. These and other various beings were associated with the control of *ʔivaʔa* and often manifested themselves as natural phenomena.

The history and their continued presence is well illustrated in the following remarks taken from Patencio by Margaret Boynton. (Patencio was a Cahuilla *net* of the *qawiʔsiktem* lineage.)

The spirits are seen in the morning in the desert in the form of mirages; people, bodies of water, and villages. Thus the people know the spirits still live and show their power to the people. We know that we are not forgotten. . . . Spirits were in the valley before the first people arrived. Spirits of rainbows—spirits of the colors—came and stayed here. When the rainbows went away, they hid behind clouds to live there. They came out to visit the dawn in the morning and played games with the sunsets at night. The spirits of color, they come with the sun, the wind and the rain. They come with the light and the water and the mist. These colors shine with the moon and the stars at night—(they never leave us). . . . The Indians always they know that the salt water fights the fresh water. Always it tries to push, to hold it back. Even a small stream of fresh water, the salt water fights it back (MS).

The most active and vividly remembered *nukatem* were:

1) *Taqwuš*. He was the most dramatic member of the *nukatem*. He was frequently seen in the form of a meteor or an anthropomorphic form emitting blue-colored sparks. *Taqwuš* lived on San Jacinto Peak, his base of operations, from which he traveled about capturing souls, *tewlavil*. *Mukat* created him and appointed him as the first *puul*, but he transgressed *Mukat's* ways. *Puvalam* were often sponsored and instructed by *Taqwuš*. In addition to stealing souls, *Taqwuš* was held responsible for other misfortunes to man, for example, the presence of tannin in acorns, and, more recently, the disappearance of antelope in the Cahuilla area. He was most active at night and in the early morning hours.

2) *Kutyaʔi* (firewind). *Kutyaʔi*, often seen in the form of a whirlwind, was most active at night capturing souls. Like *Taqwuš*, he sponsored and instructed some *puvalam*. The late Salvador Lopez, one of the last practicing *puvalam*, was sponsored by *Kutyaʔi*. Any form of contact with *Kutyaʔi* was dangerous. For example, Alice

Lopez said, "If whirlwind comes and knocks your clothing from the line, you can't pick it up or wear them or *Kutya?i* will take your *tewlavil.*"

3) *Tenauka* was seen in the form of wind action. Like *Kutya?i*, he traveled about capturing souls, but in daytime hours.

4) *Pemtexweva*, master of the hooved animals, was the being given thanks when deer, antelope, or mountain sheep were obtained. He was especially associated with the *pa?vu?ul* who had the ability to transform themselves into other beings (for example, deer, antelope). *Pemtexweva* was often seen in the form of a white deer.

5) *Pa?akniwat* lived in springs. He was frequently heard crying out and is described as taking various forms, such as a water serpent or a young baby. He owns the water places, and the Cahuilla requested permission and indulgence from *Pa?akniwat* to use water sources. *Puvalam* were sometimes sponsored by him.

6) *Palpukawil* was referred to as the "water demon" in Strong's recounting of the Cahuilla creation story (1929:132). In that version *Palpukawil* came out of the water and lived in the sky. Sometimes he took on the form of a water spout and was associated with thunderclouds which preceded a rain storm.

7) *Tematsuwet* took the form of a star. He was like *Taqwuš* but traveled in the daylight hours. He, too, captured souls and was seen in the form of a flash or streak of silver in the air.

8) *Muut* was the messenger of death. He was assigned the role by *Mukat,* who argued that death was a necessary factor in the Cahuilla universe lest overcrowding would result. *Muut* frequently took the form of an owl—or, even though not seen—the hooting of owls.

9) *Yavi* was the northwind according to Hooper's report. She says this being was one who made things dry up (Hooper, 1920:320). The term recorded is probably *ya?i* (wind).

10) *Aswut* was the name for eagle. A representative of *Mukat*, *Aswut* furnished the Cahuilla with feathers for ceremonial purposes.

11) *Tukut* or wildcat represented the moiety of the *tuktum* moiety.

12) *?isily* or coyote represented the *?istam* moiety. He often assumed the form of a white coyote.

13) Another being was associated with rain. He was created in the "beginning" and was sent to the sky to make things grow.

These are some of the primal beings which connected the distant past with the present. The energies of creation were demonstrated by the presence of these *nukatem* who were active in mundane affairs. For example, *Taqwuš* and *Tanauka* stole souls and thus caused death and disease, but they also gave power to the *puvalam,* thus benefiting their people.

TEYAWA

Teyawa was an agent which existed within the body of the *puul;* it was responsible for maintaining the link between the *puul* and his guardian spirit (for example, *Taqwuš* and *Kutyaʔi*). It took on some physical form—sometimes as an animal such as a lizard or snake, or as a substance which looked like a rock or a feather. Salvador Lopez had a piece of ice which served the purpose.

"TEWLAVIL" (THE SOUL SPIRIT)

The *tewlavil* (a soul or spirit) existed in the body of the living and had a separate existence after the death of an individual. It was able to leave the body and return at will. Empirical indicators of *tewlavil's* departure from the body were dreams, trance states, and death. The *tewlavil,* therefore, had a constant life—even when it left the body it did not die. Until the proper funeral ceremonies (*nukil* ritual) were finished the *tewlavil* remained near its corporeal existence. After the *nukil* the *tewlavil* entered *telmikiš,* the land of the *tewlavilem.*

The *tewlavil* left the body frequently during the life of an individual, especially if one was a *puul.* It left when a person was dreaming, and at such times the body was vulnerable. Because the *tewlavil* sometimes left the body during sleep, special care was necessary when awakening a sleeping person because death or serious illness could result if the soul was not able to return immediately. A *puul* was especially vulnerable while he was asleep because his *tewlavil* was likely to be away on a special mission. Prior to the death of an individual, a *tewlavil* could leave the body and travel about while the corporeal form might not show symptoms of death. At such times the *tewlavil* appeared in dreams, in the form of a coyote, an owl, or a falling star. These appearances signalled that death was approaching, and at such times a ritual was performed in the *kišʔamnaʔa* in order to encourage the soul to return to the body and avert death. The *puvalam* were responsible for these accomplishments.

When the *tewlavil* left the body, the body was cremated. At this time the *tewlavil* was in a state of freedom or limbo until the *nukil* ceremony was completed. Prior to the *nukil* ritual, however, the *tewlavil* appeared frequently to the living in various forms. Sometimes it was seen as a visual image; more often it appeared in dreams or manifested its presence in some other way—such as a cold draft of air, an odor, or in the thoughts of the living. The purpose of these appearances was to communicate with the living. The *tewlavil* often asked the living to join it so it would not be so lonely. It sometimes expressed displeasure that the rituals at the time of death had not been properly carried out. They were particularly concerned whether their personal property had been disposed of properly. The living were often accused of keeping property which was not theirs, instead of burning or destroying it so that it would become available to the *tewlavil* when it reached *telmikiš*.

"TELMIKIŠ" (AFTERLIFE)

The land of *tewlavilem, telmikiš,* which lay to the east of the Cahuilla territory, was the home of all *tewlavilem* and those *nukatem* who were no longer on earth. The *tewlavil* of *Mukat* was there too. Entrance to this land was not automatic—or easy. Some *tewlavilem* never reached *telmikiš* because of antisocial behavior prior to their death. These *tewlavilem* sometimes took other forms, remaining forever in a homeless and anxious state. Most *tewlavilem,* though, were able to reach *telmikiš* after arduous ritual on the part of the living, together with great effort on the part of the *tewlavilem*. The approach was extremely difficult and required considerable ritual aid from the living for successful entry; hence the extensive rituals concerned with the dead. Attendance at funerals was not just to honor and show respect for the dead; each individual brought power which added to the power resources necessary for entrance into *telmikiš*. Therefore, the larger the number of participants at a funeral, the greater the ease with which the soul could enter *telmikiš*.

From *telmikiš* messages were passed on to the living. One example is a great-aunt whose *tewlavil* spoke to a niece, giving her messages from other members of the family. The *tewlavil* also carried out important sanctioning powers for the community. They watched the behavior of people and would cause illness and misfortune to those who had "gone against the song." Thus the *tewlavilem* were directly involved in Cahuilla social life—advising, sanctioning, and aiding those still on earth.

"TAXLISWETEM" AND OTHER BEINGS

The term *taxliswetem* refers to all Cahuilla since the "early" times, that is, the people created after the time of *Mukat*. Translated literally the term means man or human being. Like *nu-*

katem, some *taxliswetem* demonstrated extraordinary powers, for example, a *paʔvuʔul* who could transform his body into another form; a *puul* who could cause natural things to change their form; the *tetewiš* could see what was not immediately visible to ordinary men and could see into the future.

Many plants, animals, and birds were anthropomorphized, and were, therefore, part of the social universe. They had intelligence, wishes, feelings, and as part of the social universe in which they interacted could not be taken for granted. Many natural phenomena (wind, rain, stars, rocks, "unsafe places") also contained *ʔivaʔa* and were a part of the social universe. They had intelligence and could act in relationship to other beings. This phenomena is empirically demonstrated by accidents or misfortunes a person may have in a strange place. For example, "rocks that walk," where a rock moves from one place to another unaccountably.

As pointed out, the Cahuilla world contained things which had *ʔivaʔa* and those which did not. *ʔivaʔa* could be anywhere, any time, and in any form, though not everywhere, in all forms, at all times. And men—*taxliswetem*—were at the center of the *ʔivaʔa* orientation, having greater power than some beings, but less than others.

TRADITION WAS AUTHORITY

The past was the reference point for the present and future. The "proper" cultural system was created by *Mukat,* and it was at that time that *ʔivaʔa* was manifestly present in great quantity. However, through time *Mukat's* children disobeyed his instructions. They made their own "songs," and their access to *ʔivaʔa* lessened. In accounts of the world's creation it is affirmed that correct behavior and access to power were correlates of one another; thus, innovative actions might cause a loss of *ʔivaʔa.* In the social world, the roles of *net, paxaaʔ,* and *haunik* were modeled after actions of the past, for example, *Mukat,* and *nukatem,* and various culture heros. *Mukat* assigned to these men obligations to maintain tradition. This mandate supported their political power and functioned to maintain stable decision making within each lineage. In turn, this had direct economic consequences because they controlled the subsistence process and managed the system of exchanging food and goods between groups.

Precedents for most actions were established in the oral literature. It was used to assess the value or appropriateness for taking action in most situations: for example, whether it was wise to go to war, whether it was prudent to segment a lineage under stress conditions. Consequently, pressures to act in ways that might be dangerous or innovative were temporized by referring to the immediate past or examples in the oral literature. Thus, a concern for traditional ways of problem solving ensured the maintenance of a social and political system highly efficient for human survival in a particular environment. Tradition also provided day-to-day guidelines for behavior and techniques for slowing down decision making during times of crisis, preventing precipitous decisions from being operationalized. The function of this is symbolized in the creation myth where the slow, gradual, and careful creation procedures of *Mukat,* resulting in man as he is today, are contrasted with the creations of *Temayawet* who worked rapidly and injudiciously.

AGE

A value closely related to the idea that tradition was the baseline for authority was that age was a criterion for privilege, power, and honor. The subject of age was a primary primeval conflict because *Temayawet* and *Mukat* struggled to establish who was the older, and *Mukat* was successful. He demonstrated that older people were more cautious, precise, orderly, and had more creative power than did the younger people. His activities set the stage for all beings to defer to their elders. This had adaptive significance for the Cahuilla in several ways. Deference for elderly people was protected by tradition, therefore their decision-making power was supported. Deference allowed the elders to function as repositories of knowledge and lore. This fostered adaptation to a diverse and sometimes harsh environment. Having lived through more emergency situations, the aged were better prepared than the young to resolve emergency situations. As we have seen, some ecologically induced stress situations occurred only every two or three generations. By having old people on hand, solutions proved in the past could be applied to the present stress situation. Such orientations limited the development of overt patricidal institutions found among some hunting and gathering societies.

There were other immediate reasons why the aged were revered. They taught the values and skills necessary for day-to-day successful survival to the young. The older women made baskets, rabbit-skin blankets and nets, ground the seeds, and performed other time-consuming tasks; they taught the young girls the techniques and values of womanhood. The older men manufactured arrowheads, bows, rabbit sticks, and hunting nets, and taught the young boys traditional values of the society, as well as the intricacies of hunting techniques which fostered the maximum learning for successful and productive adulthood. Thus, they contributed directly to the economic well-being of the group, releasing the middle-aged adult population for immediate subsistence activities such as hunting game and gathering plant foods. Because the old were the young's teachers, traditional means of coping with problems were always being passed on. This no doubt acted to impede social innovation so that significant cultural differences did not develop within the culture at such a pace that sociological equilibrium would be disrupted.

In effect, aged Cahuilla men acted as a legislative body, making decisions about the community. Deference to these authorities provided an automatic decision-making channel resolving or relieving community conflicts through fairly automatic means, thus limiting internal conflict in the community and assuaging anxiety.

Age correlated with power and knowledge because the elders' decision-making functions, based on their knowledge and adherence to traditions, effectively settled disputes—as well as making recommendations for action in particular instances requiring wisdom and judgment.

MALENESS

Maleness was valued as were tradition and age. Throughout Cahuilla cosmology the male is dominant in leadership, creativity, and political power. The creator gods *Mukat* and *Temayawet,* as well as all *nukatem* involved in Cahuilla everyday life, were males. Only a few female *nukatem* are mentioned in the oral literature. Maleness reinforced corporate group membership because patrilineality was the rule by which inheritance was reckoned. All political and religious roles were held by men in contrast to the subsidiary role of women in Cahuilla society, who, although always members of their fathers' lineages, had no formal decisional power within the lineage. What was the adaptive nature of this value?

Steward (1955:43–63) has argued that emphasis on the male line of descent is functionally related to the hunting of large game animals. Although the Cahuilla did not depend on large game to the same extent as some hunting societies, the acquisition of large game provided a significant addition to their diet; and there was sufficient dependence on game for a functional relationship to exist between the hunting process and an emphasis on their patrilocality which is causatively related to patrilineality. Game patterns in each area were related in a complex fashion to the specific ecological circumstances within the area; game roamed from place to place and from season to season, as has been shown. Consequently, men needed their boyhood years to learn the subtleties of animal behavior within the territory. Thus, patrilocality, supported by the belief in male supremacy, was functionally related to the effective exploitation of faunal resources.

Another facet to the value of maleness in Cahuilla society may be suggested from a point made by Sahlins (1968:50–51). He contended that segmentary lineage systems were adaptive to conquest and defense situations, allowing for an interlocking cooperation between groups of segmented lineages. This provided more manpower to carry out effective offense or defense. A need for this type of organizational ability in the past is suggested in statements by Kroeber (1925:574–580) and Aschmann (1966:231–264) that considerable displacement of tribal groups occurred in the recent past because of intrusions of foreign peoples into Southern California and the changes in the ecology of the Colorado Desert which required considerable shifting of local populations. The occasional conflict between sibs among the Cahuilla and between Cahuillas and other tribes also support this thesis. Thus, a social-structural mechanism, such as a patrilineage, allowing for rapid, easily-called-upon and readily identifiable groups of men acting in concert, would have significant long-range adaptive value in the Cahuilla system.

INDUSTRIOUSNESS

An arduous and persistent worker was a virtuous person; a lazy person, a disgrace. The former were the qualities *Mukat* demonstrated when creating the world. This value orientation is mentioned frequently in all forms of Cahuilla oral literature. Children were told stories which served as examples of the virtue of hard work, and the value was reinforced again and again at ritual occasions, especially during initiation ceremonies. Industriousness was the most important attribute sought in a spouse.

The primary adaptive function of industriousness was that it increased the effort of the individual to acquire more food, produce more goods, and learn complex ritual knowledge. The industrious woman prepared food efficiently and tastefully, collected in excess of immediate needs, was creative in her production of baskets, pottery and the like, and was attentive to the needs of those near to her with respect to cleanliness and orderliness. The industriousness of men was seen in their attention to the hunt, which was especially important when game was scarce. Constant and energetic attention to the various other food-producing activities and ritual further demonstrated their personal worth.

The desire and ability to produce and a man's attention to the reciprocity-sharing syndrome marked a man worthy. The Cahuilla who produced for the *kiš'amna'a* which—in effect—was for the community, was a man who provided sustenance to his immediate lineal relatives, his affinals, especially to the aged and infirm. He was then a man of great worth. His rewards were immediate because of the positive responses which he received from his family and friends. These psychological rewards were reinforced and formalized because supernatural powers were attributed to him for his success. If he were continually successful—and followed the rules of etiquette regarding his success—he was brought into the formal religious system as a ceremonialist or as a *puul;* it was certain then that he had access to *'iva'a*. Thus, the economic, psychological system, value, and religious system all operated together to encourage the individual to be productive.

RECIPROCITY

Anthropologists discussing values in hunting and gathering societies frequently mention that generosity is of paramount importance. I do not agree. Rather, I feel that generosity is merely a euphemism for a situation which could be more correctly labeled reciprocity. A well-balanced and rigidly enforced system of reciprocal relations operated at every level of Cahuilla society as well as throughout the universe. The reciprocity theme was established from the beginning of Cahuilla life, when two generative forces associated with maleness and femaleness joined together to create the twin creator gods. The creators reciprocated by designing and constructing the universe and, thus, a pattern of reciprocal dyadic relationships began. It was ordained that man should reciprocate with the supernatural powers to maintain the world order. The performance of ritual was man's reciprocal responsibility to the *nukatem* and *Mukat,* who supported man's existence by their usage of *'iva'a*.

Moieties were instructed by *Menily* (moon maiden) to reciprocate by carrying out the necessary rituals to dispose of the dead as she ordered the *'istam* and *tuktum* peoples to exchange their women in marriage. Reciprocity was also manifested in the neatly balanced kinship system. Each Cahuilla was taught and encouraged to share possessions, food was shared, and capital equipment frequently loaned and borrowed. It was proper to give, and it was proper to accept what was offered, neither action requiring much formal recognition. The concept of "thank you," for example, which is so typical of the American culture, was absent. Stinginess or failure to reciprocate were serious breaches of behavioral norms, and were punished frequently by public ridicule. Few things could shame a Cahuilla or his family more than the accusation that he or his family were unable or unwilling to reciprocate.

Criteria accompanying reciprocity were fairness and equality. Lineages and sibs reciprocated in collecting privileges by inviting one another to collect and hunt in each other's areas when surpluses were apparent. The system then was characterized by dyadic transactions which occurred at all social and cosmological levels.

The adaptive functions of these values are clear. They provided a compensatory mechanism to cope with real or felt imbalances which might be present in the economic and social system, whether this was between individuals and groups, between lineages and sibs, or sibs and neighboring tribal peoples. Psychologically it acted to relieve the anxiety which was often expressed about the future, because anticipation of mutual aid was always present, although in practice it was not always carried out in ideal terms.

ORDER, PRECISION, AND DEPENDABILITY

Each Cahuilla man, woman, or child was expected to be orderly, precise, explicit, and dependable. The values of order and precision were reinforced by the retelling of the Creation myth. When the twin creators made mankind, *Mukat,* who was the older and who was to become the real Creator, made his people slowly and carefully; whereas *Temayawet* was careless and rapid in his work. *Mukat's* people, however, were perfect!

The lesson of the myth carried with it long-range demands for perfection, for doing things slowly, well, and deliberately, and for the value of thinking about all the ramifications of one's actions in the process of creating something—no matter what it was. *Temayawet's* creations were rejected because they were not good in spite of his humane intentions. His haste and misplaced sympathy resulted in inappropriate actions in the realities of the world and were a poor product, practically and aesthetically.

Failure to acknowledge these characteristics was dangerous because the universe was filled with many unknowns. Thus, considerable rituals were required in the attempt to control and eliminate error. Rituals were conducted cautiously and precisely because proper performance of rituals assured the Cahuilla of a well-balanced world where sufficient food would be available. A primary criteria for evaluating a ritualist's performance was order and precision, although stylistic factors such as voice quality and rhythm were also important. For example, a ritualist was required to memorize vast amounts of material to perform the numerous rituals correctly. Such care was rewarded by *mukatem,* who could give power to ordinary men and the community, rewarding the ritualist with prestige and wealth. Failure to perform these rituals in an exact manner meant that they must be repeated until perfection was attained or the ritualist was disgraced. This disgrace was not only personal but extended to his family and lineage, jeopardizing his potential ability for reaching *telmikiš.* Other indications of this value were the finite placement of persons into correct kin categories, so that precise role play would be maintained. Proper recognition of these values evoked praise from the community to this day, while the failure to do so invited ridicule.

What was the adaptiveness of this orientation to orderliness and precision? On the surface it would appear to be ritualistic—a psychological compulsion to force order on a tumultuous world—and this would be a reasonable interpretation. There is, however, a more direct value that can be suggested. In the day-to-day efforts to acquire food, collecting and hunting had to proceed with great caution and precision. The Cahuilla man was vigilant in pursuing his economic goals. It was his duty to be alert—to observe carefully the habits of animals, their tracks, their whereabouts—in minute detail to adjust his own behavior so that the success of the hunt would be assured. Sensitivity to detail was involved in his interpersonal relationships, so that his etiquette and his actions concerning reciprocal kin obligations would not—in some infinitesimal and yet critical way—lead to interference with his activities and success. Ritual taboos, such as the scrupulous avoidance of menstrual blood and sexual abstinence especially before the hunt, were exceedingly numerous, as has been shown. This set of behavior patterns further emphasized the need for delicate attention to detail for a successful life.

The Cahuilla woman was also involved in these commitments. If she were a "proper" woman, she was careful in her conduct with her husband—particularly with respect to the menstrual and pregnancy restrictions. A woman was granted high praise for her womanliness when she met the criteria of neatness, cleanliness, and efficiency when observing taboos and conducting domestic duties. A woman who was careless in food processing, for example, could ruin a large food resource which had required the energy of many to collect; a hunter could easily lose his prey by not keeping his bows, nets, and other hunting equipment in good working order; a man could destroy a social relationship by not remembering precisely who his relatives were, thereby offending many.

Integrity and dependability, sought constantly in personal relations, were evident in the manner in which Cahuilla presented information to one another. As we have seen, one's actions were expected to be as explicit and direct as possible to reduce misunderstandings. In the annals of Cahuilla etiquette, therefore, it was proper to state the purpose of a visit immediately upon arrival: "I have come to tell you about such and such," or "I have come to visit [or to say hello]." Such statements made manifestly clear the purpose of the visit and set the stage for the proper responses.

An example from a linguistic analysis demonstrates the Cahuilla attention to exactness which differs from Western languages. Seilor has noted:

In Cahuilla, we find a class of local adverbs which show the following contrastive semantic components:
        1. direction vs. non-direction (or place),
        2. proximal vs. medial vs. distal deixis
Informants will unhesitatingly give the following translation equivalents for proximal: ʔipa 'here', ʔika 'in this direction', ʔpax 'from (correlative). For distal: peŋa 'there, far away', pika 'to a far away place' (one cannot see), peŋax 'from far' (1969:12).

The same concern for explicitness and integrity in memorizing exact details was necessary for keeping account of numerous kin and ritual obligations, and for complex economic exchanges continually, and usually, charged with emotion. On the ritual level, the concern was symbolic; ritual error, no matter how small or whether committed by an individual or group, could bring harm not only to the individual but to one's relatives and kin group, as well as bringing shame upon the lineage.

These values were adaptive to Cahuilla subsistence. If the interchange of information concerned the location of food sources, the individual who had the correct information was encouraged to give it explicitly. If a hunter met a group of women on the trail, he told the women the exact location of the trees they sought and whether or not they were ready for picking. This precise and factual information saved many precious hours for the Cahuilla whose livelihood depended upon being on the scene at the right time and the right place to make maximum use of food resources.

The effective exploitation of the environment, achieved by

means of orderly and precise coordination of mind and body, led to a better, larger, and more varied nutritional base, and smoother interpersonal relationships. These, taken together, facilitated the complex exchange system on the personal, family, lineage, and intersib levels, all of which were necessary for the maximum use of subsistence materials and avoidance of accidents and difficulties for all. The striving for equilibrium through integrity and dependability was high on the list of moral values. And, concomitantly, there was little abstraction of data into generalizations.

MODERATION AND PERSONAL CONTROL

The Cahuilla individual was not expected to display excessive zeal in most activities. His work was to be done quietly without calling special attention to himself. Rewards for good behavior were given with little ceremony. It was anticipated that grief, affection, and gratitude would be handled quietly and with subtlety. The excessive release of emotion was considered proper only at rituals such as funerals, or while performing particular ritual or social functions. The expression of emotion seems to have been as structured and controlled as other aspects of the society.

This control over behavior had considerable advantage to the stress-laden society which foresaw danger and change. The adaptiveness of this was connected with subsistence. Control of emotion and moderation was a necessary part of the hunter's activity. Precipitous action due to an excess of anxiety and excitement could frighten game or lead to traumatic injury. Likewise, loss of food or equipment were possible while collecting or processing plant foods.

The psychological stress accompanying the departure or prolonged absence of parents from their children—or, for that matter, any person from the community—was also controlled. However, when these departures were lengthy or took the person into an unsafe area for traveling, as in hunting and mourning were allowed because it was feared they might never return. Then, on the safe return of the person, intense weeping and wailing were admissible as an expression of relief for their safe return.

Moderation and personal control of emotion were also particularly emphasized in rituals. Undue emotional reactions were considered dangerous because of the disruption of the delicate balance maintained by the ritualists with their sources of power. For example, a child allowed to attend such an occasion was carefully instructed to be absolutely quiet so as not to interfere with the activities. Moreover, the excessive show of emotion was considered bad taste.

Control of emotions was also critical in social affairs. If personal feelings were expressed with too great an intensity, social equilibrium of the group could be disturbed. A sudden burst of anger could lead to conflict involving many people, and the flow of economic goods could be radically impaired. The *wexily* songs operated as a safety valve in such situations where group anger was intense, because anger and hostility were expressed in a controlled situation. Control of sexual behavior was also adaptive because it acted as a mechanism for limiting the growth of population.

SECRECY AND CAUTION

Secrecy and caution in dealing with knowledge were repeatedly reflected in Cahuilla oral literature and everyday life. The judicious use of this knowledge brought praise and reward; failure to do so generated severe punishment. Precedent for this is abundant in the oral literature which contains many tales of persons who had been given secrets only to reveal them indiscretely to the wrong people. The usual reason given for this transgression was lack of self-control, or a misunderstanding as to the importance of the information and the need for caution. Ignorance, however, was no excuse, and such individuals were castigated. This obviously implied the risk of allowing gossip to disrupt the relationships of people, and to provide undue advantage to individuals who could maliciously misuse the information.

Certain kinds of information were related to subsistence. The location of a cache of food hidden in the mountains was kept secret, to be used in times of food shortage only by those who had secreted it. Knowledge of the location of a pocket of particularly fine clay for pottery making was useful to the craftsman. The location of hidden ceremonial paraphernalia and other treasures which had both power and value was closely guarded. The places where fingernail clippings, hair cuttings, or fecal material were buried was kept secret so the individual could keep himself protected from witchcraft. The knowledge of the locale of especially attractive game-hunting areas and personal secret names were heavily guarded.

The adaptiveness of these values was psychological, sociological, and economic. They protected the individual from witchcraft, they maintained a balanced relationship between individuals by curtailing gossip, and they allowed the individual to keep some assets to himself, rather than distributing them throughout the system.

SUMMARY

The existential postulates of Cahuilla world view, their corollaries, and the normative postulates (value) were in adjustment to the environmental and economic needs. A basic postulate—the existence of *ʔivaʔa*—explained the existence of a social universe peopled with several types of beings distributed in space and time who served to integrate and influence worldly affairs. These beings were correlated directly with environmental factors such as wind, rain, water, animals, and foods—and they acted as the transmitters of *ʔivaʔa*.

ʔivaʔa was the source of all things—and yet it was erratic and unpredictable—at one and the same time it was the cause and explanation of all phenomena. Varying expressions of power accounted for economic good fortune or misfortune—hunting skill or lack of skill. Thus, there was an internal consistency with ecological reality in that the environment—which provided food for survival—could be unpredictable in the same way that power —which was necessary for survival—could be unpredictable.

Magical uses of power further explained economic reality. It accounted for ecological change, changes in settlement pattern, and disease.

Three other significant assumptions the Cahuilla carried with them in dealing with life were:

1) The assumption of unpredictability and constant change was adaptive because it induced functional stress. The stress stimulated economic productivity and reciprocity by predicting that hard times were to be expected. This further encouraged the spreading of economic risk, justified political segmentation, and changes in leadership when this was necessary.

2) The assumption that man was an integral part of an interlocking system was consistent with the close relationship of the Cahuilla with his environment. This assumption socialized the Cahuilla to a reciprocal system—a mutually interacting network. It reminded the Cahuilla that he must interact with his environment in a responsible manner, and this was reflected in behavior promoting conservation of natural resources.

3) Another philosophical assumption was that of negative-positive integration. Each person and being was potentially benevo-

lent and malevolent; the environment was at times benign, at other times malevolent; power was sometimes benevolent and sometimes malevolent; and yet people, environment, and power were integral parts of the whole. This condition prepared the Cahuilla individual to anticipate stress and to produce at a maximum level in order to minimize the possibility of shortage of food and goods during times when the environment was harsh. Careful attention was paid to the behavior of kin and in dealing with individuals felt to have covert or overt malevolent qualities, without risking the loss of their productive talent or loss to the labor force.

These existential postulates were reinforced by a system of normative postulates which stimulated behavior in ways that were economically productive for the given environmental exigencies shared by members of the Cahuilla community. Although they appear to be internally conflictive, they are not. Rather, they provided a system of checks and balances for the individual and for groups to face, realistically, the problems of their existence.

In summary these postulates are:

1) *Tradition* was relied on as the basis for most decisions. This allowed the use of historic precedent to solve problems arising from stress and change within the environment. Tradition was one of the basic motifs of the oral literature. The value of holding to tradition tended to prevent precipitous dysfunctional decisions regarding land use, war, and settlement pattern. It also reinforced the status and authority system which was economically significant.

2) The value placed upon *age* meant the elders in a community were deferred to for decisions affecting the community as a whole. The care and protection of the aged was enhanced, and, consequently, the knowledge and lore which had been accumulated by the elders was passed on to the younger members; this again countered tendencies toward erratic or dysfunctional innovation. Age deference operated to guarantee or foster judicious decision-making concerning the most effective methods for meeting crisis situations, limiting total war, lineage segmentation, and extreme solutions to crisis. At the same time the status positions of *puvalam* and *tetewiš* provided flexibility for the system because they, the *puul* together with the *paxaaʔ*, had certain ritual license for innovations, allowing for modifications as needed. However, all activities were under the control of the elders and the ceremonial leaders.

3) *Maleness* was an adaptive value because of the unique con-

tribution of men to the economic order—particularly their hunting skills and talents. The concept of the supremacy of males supported the corporate patrilineage by emphasizing the significance of maleness through inheritance and decision making.

4) *Industriousness* was an adaptive value in an environment where constant attention to the food acquisition and storage was essential. Social prestige, economic, and psychological reward and supernatural favors were associated with those who were especially productive and skillful in meeting present and future subsistence needs.

5) Reciprocity, cooperation, and sharing were adaptive values clearly developed in economic, ritual, and kinship activities. They assured that food and goods would continue to flow throughout the system. Work production was stimulated; consequently, selfishness or acquisitive behavior which might have approached dysfunctional proportions was discouraged.

6) *Order and precision* were adaptive values which helped to eliminate errors, and to foster efficient efforts in the manufacture of goods and treasures and subsistence activities, to promote the smooth operations of social and ritual ceremonies. These values acted to counterbalance a turbulent world.

7) *Moderation and personal control* functioned to increase the yield from hunting and collecting because a skillful hunter tended to be in command of himself and his physical actions; thus he was more able to stalk and capture game successfully. The careful food collector was less likely to waste or lose valuable foods by careless behavior. Moderation and personal control also enhanced amicable relations between reciprocating social groups—families, lineages, sibs, moieties, or between tribes. Furthermore, outbursts of anger and violence were kept to a minimum, which otherwise would have disrupted the carefully constructed and economically significant interaction system. Self- and ritually imposed sexual abstinence controlled the population.

8) *Secrecy and caution* were valued because gossip could be especially disruptive in a small-scale society, causing intragroup disputes which could interfere with the smooth operation of the community. Secret food caches, water supplies, and individual exploitation of resources were admissible by this value. Knowledge was like "treasure goods," therefore its possession was a means of acquiring prestige, honor, and economic well-being. Thus secrecy and caution were important. The values operated to protect the individual from excessive demands placed upon him by other values such as reciprocity.

10

Conclusions

INTRODUCTION

In this chapter I review the original discussion, and point out that the apparent conflict in anthropology concerning the role of ritual and religion may be more apparent than real. Perhaps more complex problems in anthropological explanation are at the heart of the matter. There may be no real conflict as to whether ritual and world view are economically functional or dysfunctional in cultural systems. Rather, under given circumstances, anticipation of functionality or dysfunctionality depends upon historic circumstances of the society under study. Finally, I suggest probable epistemological factors relevant to the conflict.

A REVIEW OF THE HYPOTHESES
AND THEIR RESOLUTION

The reader will recall that I examined anthropological literature and found that there were two contrasting assumptions regarding the role of ritual and religion in articulating society and its relationship to the environment. They were: ritual and world view were more ecologically nonadaptive than adaptive; and ritual and world view were more ecologically adaptive than nonadaptive. Using the Cahuilla as a test case, I then developed hypotheses for examination, based upon the above assumptions. From the first assumptions I hypothesized: the economic needs of society were impeded by ritual action which was not only wasteful of productive goods but decreased the production of goods by taking people away from productive activities because of ritual obligations; and the economic needs of society were impeded by normative and existential postulates, which suggest that certain valuable resources were outside the realm of the economic order and disrupted the production of goods by encouraging people to behave in such a way that they were taken away from productive activity. The second assumption allowed the hypotheses: the economic needs of society were facilitated by ritual action which conserved and increased the production of goods and fostered productive activity by directing personnel toward producing activities; and the economic needs of society were facilitated by normative and existential postulates which fostered the use of valuable economic resources and increased the productive process by directing people to productive activities.

A series of questions related to the hypotheses demonstrated the validity of one set of hypotheses or the other. All these questions have been answered in the text of this study. They overwhelmingly support the hypotheses that ritual and world view were more ecologically adaptive than they were nonadaptive. A review of these questions and the answers derived will demonstrate the point.

The question was posed as to whether goods were wasted because of ritual action, and whether ritual took people away from productive tasks. The findings indicate that although a large amount of food and goods were utilized in the conduct of ritual, these goods were used in an economically advantageous manner. They were not destroyed or wasted but were redistributed in new ways and directions so the produce of an area was shared by people in other areas.

The second question asked whether ritual action took people away from productive activities or directed people to produce more goods. This question was answered by indicating that ritual was most intense in Cahuilla society when time-consuming subsistence tasks were at a minimum (for example, winter months), thus productive labor time was not lost. In fact, the contrary situation existed; that is, rituals brought together many people into subsistence activities as in the rabbit hunts and by the creation of a marketlike situation at ritual occasions. Goods and services were exchanged at a time of year which was minimally disruptive to other productive efforts.

The third question asked whether valuable resources were placed outside the realm of the economic order by existential postulates. The data do not indicate any such condition. Those food resources which people were expressly discouraged from eat-

ing were carnivores; their undue destruction would have inter-
ferred with the balance of the biotic system. Furthermore, these
animals could be eaten under certain circumstances when they
were needed for food, so that even when they were killed they
were not wasted. Moreover, the tabooed game was not particularly
attractive as a food source; for example, coyote.

On the contrary, the postulate ?iva?a and the other existential
postulates efficiently supported full but controlled use of the environment by placing the Cahuilla person into the ecosystem as
an integral part of it, and commanding that plant and animal life
support man.

The fourth question posed was whether the normative postulates disputed the production of goods by rewarding behavior
which took people away from productive efforts, or if they rewarded behavior which fostered the production of goods. In our
review of normative postulates in the previous chapter values stimulated productive behavior. Each of the values was in some way
functional to the productive process. There was no indication of
significant dysfunctional action due to the value system in the
Cahuilla's case.

Along with these questions which directly relate to the hypotheses, several others were posed so that particular points quoted in
the introduction could be brought into perspective. The first was
whether ritual and world view encouraged the full and rational
use of the environment. In both cases the answer is yes. Ritual
was instrumental in distributing goods from one region to another, and the corollary that man was a part of a system both justified and explained how man utilized the environment of which
he was a part. It was also asked if ritual and world view aided in
adjusting man-land ratios. This question is also answered affirma-
tively. The redistributive nature of the ritual system is most significant in this regard because surpluses of one area were sent to
other areas where there was a shortage. However, the development
of philosophical justification for the movements of people and
conquest, in particular, supported actions which were ecologically
necessary.

Another question was whether ritual and world view supported
a social structure and organization which was environmentally
adaptive. Partilocality and patrilineality were shown as devices
which were functional to the environmental potential of the area.
In addition, the social organizational principles were shown to be
set forth in the Creation stories and were supported by supernatural authority. Each of the organizational components of

family, lineage, sib, and moiety was represented and supported by the traditional literature. At the same time, the larger ritual system (ritual congregation) integrated all the groups into one economic-social system. Each of these rituals in turn had definite subsistence advantages for each group and sometimes for the groups as a whole.

It was also asked whether ritual and world view supported institutions that were adaptive such as law, property, concepts, warfare, and games. All these institutions, as demonstrated, aided in meeting ecological needs and were defined and justified in the oral literature. Furthermore, they were supported by ritual activity and the use of *ʔivaʔa*. The principles of each were taught through the ritual system.

Other questions which were asked were:

1) Did ritual and world view stimulate or facilitate the distribution of economic goods from one part of the system to another? This question has already been answered above.

2) Did ritual and world view have regulatory functions, and did they limit the frequency and extent of conflict over valuable resources? The answer to both of these is yes. Rituals had regulating functions in the culling of certain animal populations in the area such as rabbits and other herbivorous animals. Similar functions of ritual activity occurred with insects and parasites. Warfare was limited and controlled through ritual and world view. The rituals themselves, by redistributing goods which might be a source of conflict, limited the need for active conflict. Furthermore, the advantages of remaining within a ritual congregation unit were usually greater than the possible advantages of warfare. The philosophy of the Cahuilla, as expressed through the value of reciprocity, also aided in this regard.

The question of whether regulatory mechanisms were efficiently developed in Cahuilla culture can be seen even more clearly in conjunction with the statement by Dice (1955:109): "they must be automatic in their responses; uniformly dependable in their application, and not easily subject to change according to whims of persons who have authority and power, smooth and effective in operation by increasing or decreasing their control in proportion to the need for it and economical in that the mechanism should consume as little as possible of the resources of the ecosystem." In the Cahuilla instance all these services are provided. Regulatory mechanisms were present and uniformly dependable; ritual regularity was required of all groups by forces external to the subsistence functions which they provided. For example, the *nukil* was required because of a mandate from *Mukat* and the need for transferring the *tewlavil* of dead persons to *telmikiš*. The regulatory mechanisms were not subject to change according to the whims of persons who had authority and power because the existential and normative postulates required that action be based on traditional precedents; persons who misused power could be legitimately replaced as was *Mukat* himself when he harmed his people. A smooth and effective regulatory mechanism was accomplished by increasing or decreasing the control of authority figures in proportion to need, for authority was facilitated by the segmentary lineage system which could expand or contract as different needs arose, and various members of the authority system were in competition among themselves for controlling power. This precluded a rigid power élite from developing. Finally, regulatory mechanisms were economical, consuming as little as possible of the resources of the ecosystem: rituals were not wasteful. Consequently, the hypotheses derived from the assumption that ritual and world view were more ecologically adaptive than not is supported by the Cahuilla case.

The various institutions in Cahuilla society meshed together very neatly and were closely related to the needs imposed upon the culture by their environmental conditions. Although this society was stable and the institutions generally adaptive, this is not to say that there were not dysfunctional aspects or quirks in the system. Obviously all societies change. Thus, no society is perfect in its adaptive structure in meeting all problems efficiently all the time. The near perfect appearance of Cahuilla culture, as described in this work, results from many generations of experiments in adjustment, and because an ideal model for problem solving was developed which worked—most of the time.

In the Cahuilla case, in spite of the efficient distribution system which it had developed in reaction to temporary food shortages and other stresses, there were times when extreme conditions caused actions which the normal regulatory mechanisms had difficulty in handling. For example, economic circumstances occasionally necessitated severe warfare and malnutrition, and psychological stress sometimes proved to be a serious problem. Although these were dysfunctional aspects in the culture for the individual and for the society as a whole, over a long period the institutions functioned together so that viability was generally enhanced.

The integrated institutional framework provided a set of rules which allowed most of the Cahuillas most of the time to predict what they should do. As a result, successful adaptive patterns were logically extended throughout the culture, for example, reciprocal relations. This came about over hundreds of years of striving for answers to problems which occurred over and over again. Nor does the demonstration that ritual and world view were more adaptive than nonadaptive in the Cahuilla case imply that all systems worked equally well. Obviously they did not, and this matter will be discussed later.

Another question arises: why was the meshing of cultural parts and the adaptive responses listed here not noticed by earlier observers? The reason is because these observers did not use a systems approach when studying the Cahuilla. They studied the culture as an entity by itself, not as part of an ecosystem, seeing Cahuilla culture as a product of influences from other cultural traditions. On the other hand, I have presented the Cahuilla as a product of historical processes *in situ*.

In all societies technological and sociological institutions are not in themselves sufficient to direct behavior necessary for survival. Thus, ritual and philosophical systems are imperative for maintaining technological and sociological patterns if they are to be successful adaptive mechanisms. The meshing of these into an integrated system takes time. Thus, when a significant variable such as an economic base of a society changes, we would anticipate a dysfunctional association between various parts of a culture. Thus, certain institutions and beliefs may be maintained and exist in apparent contradiction to one another or without clear meaning to their original purpose or cause.

This condition, I feel, is at the heart of the conflict in modern anthropological theory regarding the adaptiveness or nonadaptiveness of ritual and world view. In light of this, as one looks at the Cahuilla during the period described in this paper, ritual and world view were adaptive. If, however, one looks at the Cahuilla culture today—or even thirty or forty years ago—it might be demonstrated that ritual and world view were not as adaptive as they once were in the sense demonstrated in this book. In recent years Cahuilla rituals have been very expensive but do not support a subsistence system as they once did. One of the common causes given by the Cahuilla for the decrease in ritual participation is that it is so costly. The continuance of these rituals today could be attributed to the factors which Homans (1940) and others attribute to ritual. For instance, ritual provides psychological support for its participants in times of personal stress. In the Cahuilla case the self-image has been attacked by a foreign culture threatening the validity of their belief system, and new needs for social cohesion and identity have arisen because of pressures placed upon them by the outside culture.

The problem in theoretical development in anthropology regarding these hypotheses may be dependent, then, on the point in time at which an anthropologist looks at a culture. The culture may be at a stage of "culture lag," or as Phillips puts it, "in a nodal stage of culture change." (Phillips, n.d.). This is not to suggest, however, that ecological factors may not be operative in a situation when a society is in a state of change, but merely that in this situation the original adaptive functions of the institution—developed under other circumstances—are not likely to be serving the previous ecological goals. As a result, when societies are seen in a state of transition, an ecological function may be more difficult to discern. The institutions may take upon themselves more implicit and subtle forms of ecological adaptiveness; this may explain the "sacred cow" argument which Harris so aptly raised as a central issue in his writings. The institution may take on new forms of ecological adaptiveness, which will require very extensive and deep analyses to discover.

Still another factor may be complicating the issues with which this book has been concerned. I wonder if the main factor in the argument regarding the adaptiveness or nonadaptiveness of ritual and world view lies in the assumptions of a social science formulated in the context of European history. For several hundred years rapid social change has been characteristic of Western cultural development. A major characteristic of this period has been the increasing separation of religious institutions from economic ones. Nonadaptiveness or conflict between ritual and world views and other institutions (for example, economic and political) have been pronounced within the experiential field of social philosophers. Philosophies develop from the conditions under which they are formed: does the tendency to see nonadaptiveness of religious matters arise from a philosophical bias developed in this way because of trends in Western European history? Have Western social scientists lived so closely to their rapidly changing culture that they find it difficult to understand one which changes slowly? Are equilibrium models more meaningful to scientists who live in highly stable cultures? Are there antireligious assumptions present in western social science which preclude scientists from seeing religion through unjaundiced eyes? I expect the answers to these questions are all yes. I further expect that our present era of "new religion" is indicative of affirmative answers. As our culture becomes less afraid of the nonordinary (or nonrational) perhaps we can see more deeply into the subtle and practical relations of religious belief and ritual.

Bibliography

ABRAMS, LEROY
  1910.   A phytogeographic and taxonomic study of the Southern California trees and shrubs. Bulletin of the New York Botanical Garden, September 27, 6(21):300–485.

AMOS, AJATO
  1968.   The use of oral tradition for reconstructing the past. 8th International Congress of Anthropological and Ethnological Sciences. Tokyo: Science Council of Japan, 3:368–370.

ASCHMANN, HOMER
  1959a.   The central desert of Baja California: its demography and ecology. Berkeley and Los Angeles: Ibero-Americana, 42, 282 pp.
  1959b.   The evolution of a wild landscape and its persistence in Southern California. Annals of the Association of American Geographers, 49(3)2:34–57.
  1966.   The head of the Colorado Delta. *In* Geography as human ecology. S. R. and G. R. J. Jones, eds. New York: St. Martins Press, pp. 231–264.

BALLS, EDWARD K.
  1965.   Early uses of California plants. California Natural History Guide No. 10. Berkeley: University of California Press, 103 pp.

BARROWS, DAVID PRESCOTT
  1900.   The ethnobotany of the Cahuilla Indians of Southern California. Chicago: University of Chicago Press, 82 pp.
  n.d.   Unpublished papers. Berkeley: University of California Bancroft Library.

BARTHOLOMEW, GEORGE A., and JOSEPH B. BIRDSELL
  1953.   Ecology and the protohominids. American Anthropologist, 55:481–489.

BAUMHOFF, MARTIN A.
  1963.   Ecological determinants of aboriginal California populations.

Berkeley and Los Angeles: University of California Publications in American Archaeology and Ethnology, 49(2):155–236.

BEALS, RALPH L.
1956.   An ecological interpretation of the Southwestern culture area. *In* Estudios antropologicos, publicados en homenaje al Doctor Manuel Gamio. Mexico, D. F., pp. 256–260.

BEALS, RALPH L., and JAMES HESTER
1956.   A new ecological typology of the California Indians. Selected papers of the Fifth International Congress of Anthropological and Ethnological Sciences. Philadelphia: University of Pennsylvania Press, pp. 411–419.

BEAN, LOWELL JOHN
1960.   The Wanakik Cahuilla. The Masterkey, 34(3):111–119.
1961.   The ethnobotanical report sheet. Los Angeles, Archaeological Survey, Annual Report. Los Angeles: University of California, pp. 233–236.
1964.   Cultural change in Cahuilla religious and political leadership patterns. *In* Cultural change and stability. Essays in memory of Olive Ruth Barker and George C. Barker, R. L. Beals, ed. Department of Anthropology, Los Angeles: University of California, pp. 1–10.
1967.   David Prescott Barrows: an ethnographic perspective. *In* The ethnobotany of the Cahuilla Indians of Southern California. Banning, California: Malki Museum Press, pp. xi–xx.

BEAN, LOWELL, and HARRY LAWTON
1967.   A bibliography of the Cahuilla Indians of California. Morongo Indian Reservation, Banning, California: Malki Museum Press, 24 pp.

BEAN, LOWELL, and WILLIAM H. MASON
1962.   Diaries and accounts of the Romero expeditions in Arizona and California in 1823–1826. Palm Springs: Palm Springs Desert Museum, 117 pp.

BEAN, LOWELL, and KATHERINE SAUBEL
1961.   Cahuilla ethnobotanical notes: the aboriginal uses of oak. Los Angeles, Archaeological Survey Annual Report. Los Angeles: University of California, pp. 237–245.
1963.   Cahuilla ethnobotanical notes: aboriginal uses of mesquite and screwbean. Los Angeles, Archeological Survey Annual Report. Los Angeles: University of California, 1962–1963:51–78.

BEARDSLEY, RICHARD K.
1955.   Functional and evolutionary implications of community patterning. Memoirs of the Society for American Anthropology, 11, 22(2): 131–157.

BEATTIE, GEORGE W.
1933.   San Bernardino Valley before the Americans came. Los Angeles, California Historical Society Quarterly, 12:111–124.

BEATTIE, GEORGE W. and HELEN PRUITT BEATTIE
1939.   Heritage of the valley. San Bernardino's first century. Pasadena: San Pasqual Press, 459 pp.

BENNETT, JOHN
1967.   Discussion of weather modification as an uncertain innovation by Fred L. Strodtbeck. *In* Social sciences and environment, Morris

Garnsey and James R. Hibbs, eds. Boulder: University of Colorado Press, pp. 114–120.

BIRDSELL, JOSEPH
1958.   On population structure in generalized hunting and collecting populations. Evolution, 12:189–205.

BOHANNAN, PAUL
1963.   Social anthropology. New York: Holt, Rinehart & Winston, 375 pp.

BOLTON, HERBERT E., ed.
1930.   Anza's California expeditions. Berkeley: University of California Press, 5 vols.

BOOTH, ERNEST SHELDON
1968.   Mammals of Southern California. Berkeley and Los Angeles: California Natural History Guides, University of California Press, 99 pp.

BRIGHT, WILLIAM
1965.   A field guide to Southern California Indian languages. Los Angeles, Archaeological Survey Annual Report. Los Angeles: University of California, 1964–1965:389–408.

BURTON, H. S.
1856.   Report respecting the Indians of San Diego County and vicinity, January 27, 1956. U.S. National Archives, R.G. 98. War Records, Department of the Pacific, B-8 MS.
1857.   Captain Burton's report, June 15, 1856, on a visit to Chief Juan Antonio and his subcaptains at San Timeteo. *In* 34th Congress, 3rd session, House Executive Document 76, Serial No. 906. Washington, D.C.: Government Printing Office, pp. 125–127.

CABALLERIA, JUAN
1902.   History of San Bernardino Valley from the padres to the pioneers, 1810–1851. San Bernardino, California: Times-Index Press, 130 pp.

CARNEIRO, ROBERT
1968.   Cultural adaptation. *In* International encyclopedia of the social sciences, 3:551–554. David L. Sills, ed. New York: Macmillan and the Free Press.

CAUGHEY, JOHN WALTON, ed.
1952.   The Indians of Southern California in 1852. The B. D. Wilson Report. The selection of contemporary comment. San Marino, California: Huntington Library, 154 pp.

CLELAND, ROBERT GLASS
1929.   Pathfinders. Los Angeles: Powell, 452 pp.

COLLINS, PAUL
1965.   Functional analyses in the symposium "Man, Culture, and Animals." *In* Man, culture, and animals. A. Leeds and A. P. Vayda, eds. Washington, D.C.: American Association for the Advancement of Science, 78:271–282.

COOK, S. F.
1955.   The aboriginal population of the San Joaquin Valley, California: Anthropological Records, 16(2):1–78.

COUNTY OF LOS ANGELES
n.d.   Census of 1860, Los Angeles County.

CURTIS, EDWARD S.
1926.   The North American Indians, 15:508–543. Cambridge, Massachusetts: Norwood Press.

DICE, LEE R.
  1955.   Man's nature and nature's man: the ecology of human communi-
           ties. Ann Arbor: University of Michigan Press, 547 pp.
DOBYNS, HENRY F.
  1966.   An appraisal of techniques with a new hemispheric estimate. Cur-
           rent Anthropology, October, 7(4):395–416.
DRIVER, HAROLD E., and WILLIAM C. MASSEY
  1957.   Comparative studies of North American Indians. Transactions,
           American Philosophical Society, 47(2):209–251.
DRUCKER, PHILIP
  1937.   Culture element distributions: Southern California. Berkeley and
           Los Angeles: Anthropological Records, University of California
           Publications. 1:1–52.
DUNCAN, OTIS DUDLEY
  1961.   From social system to ecosystem. Sociological Inquiry, 31:140–149.
DUNN, FREDERICK L.
  1968.   Epidemiological factors: health and disease in hunter-gatherers.
           In Man the hunter, R. B. Lee and I. DeVore, eds. Chicago: Aldine,
           pp. 221–228.
EARLE, R. R., and QUENTIN JONES
  1962.   Analysis of seed samples from 113 plant families. Economic Botany,
           16(4):221–250.
EDMUNDSON, MUNRO S.
  1958.   Status terminology and the social structure of North American
           Indians. Seattle: University of Washington Press, 84 pp.
EGGAN, FRED, ed.
  1955.   Social anthropology of North American tribes. Chicago: University
           of Chicago Press, 574 pp.
EMERSON, ALFRED E.
  1954.   Dynamic homeostasis: a unifying principle in organic and ethical
           evolution. Scientific Monthly, 78:67–85.
EVANS, Col. ALBERT S.
  1889.   Alta California, sketches of life in the Golden State. San Fran-
           cisco: Bancroft, 404 pp.
FORBES, JACK
  1965.   Warriors of the Colorado. Norman, Oklahoma: University of Okla-
           homa Press, 378 pp.
GARCES, FRANCISCO
  1965.   A record of travels in Arizona and California in 1775–1776. A new
           translation by John Galvin. San Francisco: John Howell Books,
           45 pp.
GARNSEY, MORRIS E., and JAMES R. HIBBS, eds.
  1967.   Social sciences and the environment. Boulder: University of Col-
           orado Press, 249 pp.
GAYTON, A. H.
  1946.   Culture-environment integration: references in Yokuts life. South-
           western Journal of Anthropology, 2:252–268.
GIFFORD, EDWARD W.
  1918.   Clans and moieties in Southern California. Berkeley and Los
           Angeles: University of California Publications in American Ar-
           chaeology and Ethnology, 14:155–219.

1922.   California kinship terminologies. Berkeley and Los Angeles: University of California Publications in American Archaeology and Ethnology, 18:1–285.

1928.   Miwok lineages and the political unit in aboriginal California. American Anthropologist, 28:389–401.

GLUCKMAN, MAX

1953.   Rituals of rebellion in Southeast Africa. The Frazer Lecture, 1954. Manchester: Manchester University Press, 26 pp.

GOLDSCHMIDT, WALTER

1959.   Man's way: a preface to the understanding of human society. New York: Henry Holt, 253 pp.

GOODE, WILLIAM

1951.   Religion among the primitives. The Free Press of Glencoe, Collier-Macmillan, 321 pp.

GOULDNER, ALVIN

1960.   The norm of reciprocity: a preliminary statement. American Sociological Review, 25:161–178.

GRANT, CAMPBELL

1966.   The rock paintings of the Chumash. Berkeley and Los Angeles: University of California Press, 162 pp.

GRINNELL, J., and H. S. SWARTZ

1908.   Birds and mammals of the San Jacinto Mountains. Berkeley: University of California Publications in Zoology, 10:178–397.

HALL, H. M.

1902.   A botanical survey of the San Jacinto Mountains. Berkeley: University of California Publications in Botany, 1:1–140.

HALL, H. M. and J. GRINNELL

1919.   Lifezone indicators in California. San Francisco: Proceedings of the California Academy of Science. 4th series, 9(2)37–67.

HARDIN, GARRETT

1970.   To trouble a star: the cost of intervention in nature. Bulletin of the Atomic Scientists. Science and Public Affairs, January 26, (1):17–20.

HARRIS, MARVIN

1965.   The myth of the sacred cow. *In* Man, culture, and animals, A. Leeds and A. P. Vayda, eds. Washington, D.C.: American Association for the Advancement of Science, pp. 217–228.

1966.   The cultural ecology of India's sacred cattle. Current Anthropology, 7(1):51–64.

1968.   The rise of anthropological theory. New York: Thomas Crowell, 806 pp.

HARVEY, H. R.

1967.   Population of the Cahuilla Indians: decline and its causes. Eugenics Quarterly, 14(3):185–198.

HAYES, BENJAMIN

1929.   Pioneer notes from the diaries of Judge Benjamin Hayes. Los Angeles: privately printed, 307 pp.

HEINTZELMAN, S. P.

1857.   Report on Southern California Indians. *In* 34th Congress, 3rd Session, House Executive Document 76, Serial No. 906. Washington, D.C.: Government Printing Office, pp. 34–58.

HEIZER, ROBERT F.
1941. California earthquakes of the Mission period of 1769–1838. California Journal of Mines and Geology, Report No. 37 of the State Mineralogist, pp. 219–224.
1968. The Indians of Los Angeles County. Hugo Reid's letters of 1852 edited and annotated by Robert F. Heizer. Los Angeles: Southwest Museum, Highland Park, Southwest Museum Papers, 21, 142 pp.

HICKS, FREDERICK
1959. Archaeological investigations in the Yucaipa Valley. Quarterly of the San Bernardino County Museum Association, 6(1):1–43.
1961. Ecological aspects of aboriginal culture in the western Yuman area. Doctoral dissertation. Los Angeles: University of California.

HOMANS, GEORGE C.
1940. The human group. New York: Harcourt, Brace & Company.
1941. Anxiety and ritual: the theories of Malinowski and Radcliffe-Brown. American Anthropologist, 43:164–172.

HOOPER, LUCILLE
1920. The Cahuilla Indians. Berkeley and Los Angeles: University of California Publications in American Archaeology and Ethnology, 16:316–379.

HUGHES, TOM
1938. History of Banning and the San Gorgonio Pass. Banning, California: Banning Record, 213 pp.

IACOPI, ROBERT
1964. Earthquake country. Menlo Park, California: Lane Book Company, 192 pp.

JAMES, HARRY C.
1960. The Cahuilla Indians. Los Angeles: Westernlore Press. Banning, California: reprinted 1969 by Malki Museum Press, 185 pp.

JENSEN, LLOYD B.
1953. Man's foods. New York: Garrard Press, 278 pp.

KOWTA, M., J. A. APPLETON, JR., D. V. HARRIS, D. A. M. LANE, and C. A. SINGER
1965. Excavations of the Christensen Webb site, Menifee Valley, 1963–1964. San Bernardino: San Bernardino County Museum Association, 8(13):1–73.

KROEBER, A. L.
1907. Shoshonean dialects of California. Berkeley: University of California Publications in American Archaeology and Ethnology, 4:65–165.
1908. Ethnography of the Cahuilla Indians. Berkeley: University of California Publications in American Archaeology and Ethnology, 8:29–68.
1909a. Classificatory kinship systems. Journal of the Anthropological Institute, 39:77–84.
1909b. Notes on Shoshonoean dialects of Southern California. Berkeley: University of California Publications in American Archaeology and Ethnology, 8:235–269.
1922. Basket designs of the Mission Indians. Anthropological Papers of the American Museum of Natural History, 20:149–183.

1925. Handbook of the Indians of California. Washington, D.C.: Smithsonian Institute, Bureau of American Ethnology Bulletin, 78:1–995.

1962. The nature of land-holding groups in California. Berkeley: University of California Archaeological Survey, Department of Anthropology, pp. 19–58.

KUNKEL, PETER H.

1962. Yokuts and Pomo political institutions: a comparative analysis. Doctoral dissertation. Los Angeles: University of California, 492 pp.

LAUGHLIN, WILLIAM S.

1968. Hunting: integrating biobehavior system and its evolutionary importance. *In* Man the hunter, R. B. Lee and I. DeVore, eds. Chicago: Aldine, pp. 304–320.

LAWTON, HARRY W., and LOWELL BEAN

1968. A preliminary reconstruction of aboriginal agricultural technology among the Cahuilla. The Indian Historian, 1(5):18–24, 29.

LEE, RICHARD B., and IRVEN DeVORE

1968a. Problems in the study of hunters and gatherers. *In* Man the hunter, R. B. Lee and I. DeVore, eds. Chicago: Aldine, pp. 3–12.

LEE, RICHARD B., and IRVEN DeVORE, ed.

1968b. Man the hunter. Chicago: Aldine, 415 pp.

LEEDS, ANTHONY, and ANDREW P. VAYDA, eds.

1965. Man, culture, and animals. The role of animals in human ecological adjustments. Washington, D.C.: Publication No. 78 of the American Association for the Advancement of Science, 304 pp.

LEWIS, I. M.

1971. Ecstatic religion. An anthropological study of spirit possession and shamanism. Middlesex, England: Penguin Books, 221 pp.

LINTON, RALPH

1936. The study of man. New York: Appleton-Century-Crofts, 504 pp.

LOVETT, W. E.

1865. Report to the Superintendent of Indian Affairs, Annual Report. Washington, D.C. United States Commission of Indian Affairs.

LOWIE, ROBERT

1920. Primitive society. New York: Boni and Liveright, 463 pp.

1938. Subsistence. *In* General anthropology, F. Boas, ed. New York: Heath, pp. 282–326.

MATHIAS, MILDRED E., *et al.*

1961. Ornamentals for low-elevation desert areas of Southern California. California Agricultural Experiment Station Extension Service Circular 496, Division of Agricultural Sciences, University of California. February, 35 pp.

MILLER, ROBERT J.

1964. Cultures as religious structures. *In* Symposium on new approaches to the study of religion. Proceedings of the 1964 annual spring meeting of the American Ethnological Society. June Helm, ed. Seattle: University of Washington Press, pp. 91–101.

MOORE, O. K.

1957. Divination—a new perspective. American Anthropologist, 59:69–74.

MUNZ, PHILIP A., and DAVID D. KECK
  1959.   A California flora. Berkeley and Los Angeles: University of California Press. 1681 pp.
NORDLAND, OLE J., ed.
  1968.   Coachella Valley golden years. Indio, California: Little Grant Printers, 88 pp.
ODUM, EUGENE, P.
  1959.   Fundamentals of ecology, 2nd ed. Philadelphia: Saunders, 546 pp.
O'NEAL, LULU RASMUSSEN
  1957.   A peculiar piece of the desert. The story of California's Morongo Basin. Los Angeles: Westernlore Press, 208 pp.
ORR, ROBERT, and DORING B. ORR
  1968.   Mushrooms and other common fungi of Southern California. Berkeley and Los Angeles: University of California Press, 91 pp.
OSWALT, WENDELL H.
  1966.   The Cahuilla gatherers in the desert. *In* This land was theirs— —a study of the North American Indian. New York: John W. Wiley, pp. 141–184.
PARK, WILLARD Z.
  1938.   Shamanism in Western North America: a study in cultural relationships. Evanston and Chicago: Northwestern University Press, 166 pp.
PATENCIO, FRANCISCO
  1943.   Stories and legends of the Palm Springs Indians as told to Margaret Boynton. Los Angeles: Times-Mirror Press, 132 pp.
  n.d.   Unpublished notes collected by Margaret Boynton. Palm Springs, California: Archives of the Desert Museum.
PHILLIPS, ANDREW
  n.d.   Introduction to theories of social change. Unpublished MS.
RAPPAPORT, ROY
  1964.   Ritual regulation of environmental relations among a New Guinea people. Ethnology, 6:17–40.
  1968.   Pigs for the ancestors. New Haven: Yale University Press. 311 pp.
REDFIELD, ROBERT
  1965.   The little community and peasant society and culture. Chicago: University of Chicago Press. 93 pp.
RUSSELL, RICHARD JOEL
  1932.   Land forms of San Gorgonio Pass, Southern California. Los Angeles: University of California Publications in Geography, 6(2): 23–121.
RYAN, R. MARK
  1968.   Mammals of Deep Canyon. Palm Springs, California: Palm Springs Desert Museum. 137 pp.
SAHLINS, MARSHALL D.
  1961.   The segmentary lineage: an organization of predatory expansion. American Anthropologist, 63:332–345.
  1968.   Tribesmen. Englewood Cliffs, New Jersey: Prentice Hall. 188 pp.
SALISBURY, RICHARD F.
  1962.   Ceremonial economics and political equilibrium. Actes du VIᵉ Congres International des Science Anthropologiques et Ethnologiques, I. Paris.

SANDERS, WILLIAM T., and BARBARA J. PRICE
 1968.   Mesoamerica. New York: Random House, 264 pp.
SAUER, CARL
 1929.   Land forms in the Peninsular Range of California as developed
          about Warner's Hot Springs and Mesa Grande. Los Angeles: Uni-
          versity of California Publications in Geography, 3(4):199–229.
SEILOR, HANSJACOB
 1969.   On the interrelation between text, translation and grammar of an
          American Indian language. *In* Fortdruck aus Linguistische be-
          richte. pp. 1–17.
SERVICE, ELMAN R.
 1966.   The hunters. Englewood Cliffs, New Jersey: Prentice Hall, 118 pp.
SHEPARD, EUGENE
 1965.   Southern California weather cycles. Pacific Coast Archeological
          Society Quarterly, 1(1):9–10.
SIMOONS, FREDERICK J.
 1961.   Eat not this flesh: food avoidances in the Old World. Madison:
          University of Wisconsin Press, 241 pp.
 1968.   A ceremonial ox of India. Madison: University of Wisconsin Press,
          323 pp.
SPIER, LESLIE
 1933.   Yuman tribes of the Colorado River. Chicago: University of Chi-
          cago Press, 431 pp.
STAKEMAN, E. C.
 1947.   Plant diseases are shifty enemies. American Scientist, 35:321–350.
STEWARD, JULIAN H.
 1926.   Petroglyphs of California and adjoining states. Berkeley: Uni-
          versity of California Publications in Archaeology and Ethnology,
          24:47–238.
 1937.   Ecological aspects of Southwestern society. Anthropos, 32:87–104.
 1955.   Theory of culture change, the methodology of multilinear evolu-
          tion. Urbana: University of Illinois Press, 244 pp.
 1968.   Causal factors and processes in the evolution of prefarming socie-
          ties. *In* Man the hunter. R. B. Lee and I. DeVore, eds. Chicago:
          Aldine, pp. 321–334.
STRODTBECK, FRED L.
 1967.   Weather modification as an uncertain innovation. *In* Social science
          and environment. Morris Garnsey and James R. Hibbs, eds.
          Boulder: University of Colorado Press, 124 pp.
STRONG, WILLIAM DUNCAN
 1927.   An analysis of Southwestern society. American Anthropologist,
          29:1–60.
 1929.   Aboriginal society in Southern California. Berkeley: University of
          California Publications in American Archaeology. Ethnology, 26:
          1–349.
SUTTLES, WAYNE
 1960.   Affinal ties, subsistence and prestige among the coast Salish. Amer-
          ican Anthropologist, 62:296–305.
 1962.   Variation in habitat and culture on the Northwest Coast. Proceed-
          ings of the 34th International Congress of Americanists, 1960.
          Horn-Vienna: Verlag Ferdinand Berger.

1968.   Coping with abundance: subsistence on the Northwest Coast. *In* Man the hunter. R. B. Lee and I. DeVore, eds. Chicago: Aldine, pp. 56–68.

SUTTON, IMRE
1964.   Land tenure and changing occupations on Indian reservations in Southern California. Los Angeles: Doctoral dissertation in geography on file at the University of California, 338 pp.

TAX, SOL
1955.   Some problems of social organization. *In* Social anthropology of North American tribes. F. Eggan, ed. Chicago: University of Chicago Press, pp. 3–34.

TAYLOR, ALEXANDER
1860–   The Indianology of California. California Farmer and Journal of
1863.   Useful Science. Vols. 12–20.

THOMAS, RICHARD M.
1964.   The Mission Indians: a study of leadership and cultural change. Los Angeles: Doctoral dissertation in anthropology on file at the University of California, 254 pp.

THOMPSON, LAURA
1949.   The relations of men, animals and plants in an island community (Fiji). American Anthropologist, 51:253–267.
1961.   Toward a science of mankind. New York: McGraw-Hill, 276 pp.

TREGANZA, ADAN E.
1945.   The "ancient stone fish traps" of the Coachella Valley, Southern California. American Antiquity, 10(3):285–294.

UNITED STATES OFFICE OF INDIAN AFFAIRS
1849–   Reports of the Commissioner of Indian Affairs to the Secretary of
1917.   the Interior. Washington, D.C.: Government Printing Office.

VAYDA, ANDREW P.
1961.   A re-examination of Northwest Coast economic systems. Transactions of the New York Academy of Science, Section 11, 23(7): 618–624.
1966.   Pomo trade feasts. Humanité, Cahiers de l'Institut de Science Économique Appliqué, pp. 1–6.
1969.   Review of "social sciences and the environment." American Anthropologist, 71:70–71.

VAYDA, ANDREW P., and ROY A. RAPPAPORT
1968.   Ecology, cultural and non-cultural. *In* Introduction to cultural anthropology: essays in the scope and methods of the science of man, J. A. Clifton, ed. Boston: Houghton Mifflin.

VAYDA, ANDREW P. and D. B. SMITH
1961.   The place of pigs in Melanesian subsistence. Proceedings of the 1961 Annual Spring Meeting of the American Ethnological Society, V. E. Garfield, ed. Seattle: University of Washington Press, pp. 69–77.

VOGEL, VIRGIL
1970.   American Indian medicine. Norman: University of Oklahoma Press, 583 pp.

VOGT, EVON Z.
1969.   Zincantan: a Maya community in the highlands of Chiapas. Cambridge, Massachusetts: Belknap Press of Harvard University Press, 733 pp.

WALLACE, ANTHONY F. C.
  1966.   Religion: an anthropological view. New York: Random House, 300 pp.
WATERMAN, THOMAS T.
  1909.   Analysis of the Mission Indian creation. American Anthropologist, 11(1):41–45.
WEBSTER'S NEW INTERNATIONAL DICTIONARY OF THE ENGLISH LANGUAGE
  1942.   2nd ed. Springfield, Massachusetts: G. C. Merriam.
WEINLAND, JOHN
  n.d.   Unpublished correspondence to and from Rev. John Weinland, Moravian missionary to the Morongo Reservation. San Marino, California: on file at the Huntington Library.
WHITE, RAYMOND C.
  1963.   Luiseño social organization. Berkeley: University of California Publications in American Archaeology and Ethnology, 48(2), 194 pp.
WILLEY, GORDON R., and PHILIP PHILLIPS
  1958.   Method and theory in American archaeology. Chicago: University of Chicago Press, 270 pp.
WILLIAMSON, Lt. R. S.
  1856.   Report of explorations in California for railroad routes to connect with routes near the 35th and 32nd parallels of north latitude. Vol. 5. Washington, D.C.: Beverly Tucker Printer, 370 pp.
WILLOUGHBY, NONA CHRISTENSEN
  1963.   Division of labor among the Indians of California. Report of the University of California Archaeological Survey 60:9–79.
WYNNE-EDWARDS, V. C.
  1962.   Animal dispersion in relation to social behavior. Edinburgh and London: Oliver & Boyd, 652 pp.
YANOVSKY, ELIAS
  1936.   Food plants of the North American Indians. Washington, D.C., U. S. Department of Agriculture, Miscellaneous Publication, 237: 1–83.
YANOVSKY, ELIAS, and R. M. KINGSBURY
  1938.   Analysis of some Indian food plants. Journal of the Association of Official Agricultural Chemists, 21(4):648–465.
ZIGMUND, MAURICE
  1941.   Ethnobotanical studies among California and Great Basin Shoshonean. Doctoral dissertation, Yale University, 296 pp.